IDIOT'S GUIDES.
AS EASY AS IT GETS!

Beginning Investing

by Danielle L. Schultz, CFP®, CDFA™

ALPHA
A member of Penguin Random House LLC

Publisher: Mike Sanders
Associate Publisher: Billy Fields
Senior Acquisitions Editor: Brook Farling
Development Editor: Mike Thomas
Cover Designer: Lindsay Dobbs
Book Designer: William Thomas
Compositor: Ayanna Lacey
Proofreader: Monica Stone
Indexer: Brad Herriman

First American Edition, 2016
Published in the United States by DK Publishing
6081 E. 82nd Street, Indianapolis, Indiana 46250

Copyright © 2016 Dorling Kindersley Limited
A Penguin Random House Company
16 17 18 19   10 9 8 7 6 5 4 3 2 1
001-289042-NOVEMBER2016

ISBN: 9781615648832
Library of Congress Catalog Card Number: 2015941381

Note: This publication contains the opinions and ideas of its author(s). It is intended to provide helpful and informative material on the subject matter covered. It is sold with the understanding that the author(s) and publisher are not engaged in rendering professional services in the book. If the reader requires personal assistance or advice, a competent professional should be consulted. The author(s) and publisher specifically disclaim any responsibility for any liability, loss, or risk, personal or otherwise, which is incurred as a consequence, directly or indirectly, of the use and application of any of the contents of this book.

DK books are available at special discounts when purchased in bulk for sales promotions, premiums, fund-raising, or educational use. For details, contact: DK Publishing Special Markets, 345 Hudson Street, New York, New York 10014 or SpecialSales@dk.com.

Printed and bound in the United States of America

idiotsguides.com

Contents

Appendixes

Introduction

Whether you think you can, or think you can't, either way you're right.

—Henry Ford

Most likely, you're given the opportunity to select investments for your 401(k) every year at work. And every year, if you're like most people, you have no idea what to choose or whether the options you do select are the best for you. In this book, I help you make informed decisions.

But maybe you've realized you're never going to get rich through your 401(k) (or 403[b], or IRA, or—wait, you do have savings, right?). We also look at how you can accumulate money to invest and how to make that money work for you.

Maybe you've never invested in anything before and aren't really clear about the difference between a stock and a bond. What about mutual funds versus ETFs (exchange-traded funds, by the way), active versus passive, index versus managed? After you read this book, you'll know what's right for you, how to invest in these options, and when to cash out and go home.

Do you suspect other people are in on secrets or hot tips that make them a ton of money, while you toil along with a measly return? After reading this book, you'll know how they do it (or if they really do!).

I'm a financial planner and investment adviser, always in that order. I believe you cannot choose investments that are right for you unless you have a plan for all the aspects of your life. No, I don't think life is all about money, but money does touch most aspects of life. How we choose our careers, where we can live, what we can or are willing to do for our children, what we can afford to enjoy, and even our health and well-being into old age are all somewhat dependent on whether we have at least adequate funds to support our lifestyle, goals, and dreams.

How you approach this book, and what you hope to get out of it, might depend on your age.

If you're 20 to 40 years old, time is on your side. Sure, you've seen something of the world. You're current on the latest and greatest. Not only can you spot trends, you *make* them. This book teaches you when to act on those hunches and how to put some sober analysis to work on your initial ideas. You have time to make mistakes and recover from them as well as time to make, change, and achieve your goals.

If you're 40 to 60 years old, you probably wish you had saved more when you were younger. Even if you did invest in the stock market or contributed regularly to your workplace retirement account, you probably wish you had done a better job of understanding and monitoring your money. Maybe you're trying to make up for lost time and wonder if you should take more or less risk with what you already have. This book helps you make good judgments to improve your financial situation.

If you're 60 years old or older, maybe you just want to be a good steward of what you already have. Maybe you had a significant life change—divorce, illness, a late layoff, or early retirement—and need to adjust to the changed circumstances. Or maybe you've just received "sudden money"—an inheritance, pension lump-sum payout, business buyout—and you have no idea how to invest your windfall. If you're retired, you might decide you finally have time to really understand investments and can take the time to analyze and follow your choices in a way you never could before. This book helps you sort through the alternatives to decide what's the right type of investment mix for your situation.

If you've never put your money into anything more than a piggy bank, this book walks you through the decisions you need to make and shares the basic information you need to begin a lifelong investing program.

If you've made a few investments and they've gone south, you'll learn how to do it more prudently and expertly this time with the information in the following pages.

And if you've made some investments that turned out well, you'll be able to analyze why and improve upon your success after reading these chapters.

When I give financial advice, I tell my clients I've already made all the mistakes so they don't have to. It is my fond hope that I can help you steer clear of the worst mistakes, productively learn from any others, and cruise smoothly to a secure financial future in which your investments support your dreams.

How This Book Is Organized

This book is divided into five parts:

Part 1, Laying Your Investing Foundation, shows you how to build a solid foundation for constructing your investments. We consider setting goals, look at what's possible, and learn to prevent disasters. We explore the advantages you have and drawbacks you face, no matter what your age, and discover ways to use them productively. You'll begin to understand how adventurous you are: whether you can afford to be aggressive in your investments on the chance of greater gain, or whether you'd prefer more stable investments that make you feel confident in your decisions. We also consider the trade-offs for your choices.

Part 1 also helps you find the money to get started. We review whether you already have money to invest; how you can improve your spending plan to generate money for investing; and how to handle self-employment, windfalls, and other intermittent sources of funds. In addition, we look at where to stash your money for the short term while you take time to think through your investment goals and learn about the possibilities.

In **Part 2, Planning Your Investment Strategy,** we begin to develop an investment strategy. You learn what the right mix is for you—all your eggs in one basket (carefully watched, as Mark Twain said) or distributed among a number of baskets in case any one tips over. How many baskets depends on your timeline for your goals, what you already know or are prepared to learn, and how comfortable you find you are with risk. We also look at all the ways financial and investment advice is pitched to you, who's worth listening to, and how to use your own good judgment to sort through all the noise.

In **Part 3, Where to Invest,** we drill down on the types of investments you should consider. We consider the more conventional investments like stocks, bonds, and mutual funds, but we also consider whether alternatives might be right for you, such as collectibles and real estate. I also warn you off some investments I've seen clients founder on.

By the time you reach **Part 4, Investing for Specific Goals,** you have a pretty solid grounding in the options available to you. In this part, we consider the specifics of investing to achieve four of the most common financial goals: retirement, home purchases, college financing, and luxury purchases. If you've had a sudden change in financial circumstances or a major life change, we'll discuss ways to change your investment and spending plans to meet the new reality.

Although Warren Buffett has said his preferred holding time for an investment is forever, he doesn't, always, and neither should you. In **Part 5, When to Buy and Sell Investments,** we look at when you should buy or sell and how to know the difference.

At the back of the book, I've included a glossary to help you understand investing lingo and a list of resources you can use to further your investing education.

Extras

Throughout the book, I include small asides to augment the text. Here's what to look for:

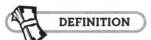

DEFINITION

These sidebars offer easy-to-understand explanations of investing-related terms.

TIP

Check out these sidebars for helpful tips that steer you in the right direction.

WARNING

Investing comes with many pitfalls. These sidebars alert you to be careful.

Acknowledgments

I would like to thank my daughter, Nicole C.S. Barker, who provides an unfailing source of feedback, advice, and attitude adjustment. Thank you, dear, for keeping me in touch with a constant stream of new ideas and for your steadfast support of every project I take on.

Thanks also to my fellow members of the Garrett Planning Network and the National Association of Personal Financial Advisors, who provide great input and resources no matter how complex or unusual the financial planning issue that occurs.

My clients have provided me with so many interesting challenges that they've been the best education. Thank you for your faith and trust in me.

Finally, thank you to Jeff Kostis, who has so often helped to set me straight. Your reading of this book has been invaluable.

Special Thanks to the Technical Reviewer

Idiot's Guides: Beginning Investing was reviewed by an expert who double-checked the accuracy of what's presented here to help us ensure learning about getting started investing is as easy as it gets. Special thanks are extended to Jeff Kostis.

Jeff Kostis is an independent financial planner and the president of JK Financial Planning, Inc., with offices in Vernon Hills and Chicago, Illinois, where he provides expert, objective advice free from conflicts of interest. Jeff earned his Master's in accounting from The University of Texas at Arlington and his Bachelor's in accounting from Bradley University in Peoria, Illinois. In addition to earning the Certified Financial Planner designation, Jeff is a Certified Public Accountant and received certification as a Personal Financial Specialist (PFS) by the AICPA. Jeff also earned the Certified Divorce Financial Analyst designation to provide specialized services to people going through a divorce. Jeff has written several articles for the *American Journal of Family Law* and has been quoted in *The Wall Street Journal, USA Today, The New York Times, Reader's Digest, Newsweek, Consumer Reports Money Adviser, Investment News,* and the *Chicago Tribune,* among others.

Laying Your Investing Foundation

In Part 1 you'll learn to make choices based on assessing your current financial situation. You'll determine exactly how much you can invest, what dreams you want to achieve, and how long it will take you to achieve your goals.

We'll think about how much risk you're willing to take (if any) and how that will determine what investments you should choose. While no investment is completely safe, we'll sort through the types of risk so you can weigh how to balance taking risks with maximizing your investment growth.

Because you're reading this book, you're probably eager to get started investing. Whoa, there! Take a little time to plan your strategy and learn the basics. We'll look at how to build up the money to invest, and where to put it temporarily while you're learning and accumulating. Let's get started!

How Much Can You Invest?

You don't need to be wealthy to begin investing. In fact, you probably won't ever *become* wealthy unless you invest. And contrary to what you might think, your current income doesn't matter. In my practice, I see people with very modest incomes who sometimes have more money to invest than those earning in the mid-six figures. Get the basics in place, and you can begin your investing journey.

In this chapter, we'll consider how much money you can afford to invest. We'll also discuss how to analyze your spending, cut costs, and increase your savings so you have the proper foundation in place to invest. When you've analyzed your lifestyle and spending needs, you'll be able to know how to have more available to grow in investments.

In This Chapter

- Creating a spending plan
- Establishing an emergency fund
- Paying off high-interest debt
- Tips for cutting costs
- Smart strategies for increasing your savings

What Can You Invest?

You shouldn't begin an investing program until you're meeting your basic living expenses, have established an emergency fund, and have your debts under control. Before you invest in anything beyond a savings or *money market* account, you need to be able to wait out the daily ups and downs of the stock market without needing to cash in your investments to pay the rent.

> **DEFINITION**
>
> A **money market** account is a fund offered by investment companies that pays the same or more interest than a bank savings account. You can usually write checks to withdraw from the account or pay bills.

Establishing Your Emergency Fund

An emergency fund is your backstop to make sure you have enough money to cover unforeseen expenses: repairs, job loss, vet bills, dental work, or whatever you haven't directly budgeted for.

Your very first goal of saving should be to build an emergency fund. You might think you should pay off credit card debt before building an emergency fund. But unless you have an emergency fund, you will never get out of debt because every new emergency will be paid by credit card.

What's an adequate emergency fund? How much you need depends on a variety of factors: what is your income? Are you the sole support, or do other family members have earnings or investments they could draw on? How much debt repayment are you obligated for? How secure is your job? How many dependents do you have? Do you have investments that you could draw on if necessary?

At a bare minimum, you should have 3 months' worth of *necessary expenses* if two people in the family are working or have significant investments, and 6 months' worth of expenses if you are single or one partner does not earn money.

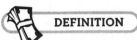

> **DEFINITION**
>
> **Necessary expenses** are the bills you'd have to pay even if you were unemployed or disabled. You can estimate what the rock-bottom figure is by looking at your fixed expenses, then adding a minimum of discretionary expenses.

Let's say you're single and make $50,000 a year and your fixed expenses (see "Assessing Your Spending Needs" later in this chapter) are about $48,000 a year or $2,500 a month. Suddenly, you get fired. You're not going to be saving into a 401(k) during this time, and you're going to have to cut back on clothing, vacations, and eating out. The ideal emergency fund in this situation is about $15,000, and you could probably squeak by on $10,000 to $12,000 if you also collect unemployment. If you have a spouse who continues to be employed, you won't be kicked out of your house, and with some belt tightening, you probably could get through the crisis with $7,500.

 TIP

You may have fewer emergencies if you're young and healthy, single, and don't own a home, but you're still going to have them (fire in the next apartment, job loss, car crash, sick dog or cat).

If you own a home, you need to be on the higher end of that range to cover unexpected expenses. A new roof or furnace: $5,000 and up. A large tree rooted on your property falls across the sidewalk on a Saturday (happened to me): emergency removal is $2,500. And if the roof leaks or the tree falls when you're unemployed, that emergency fund can go to $0 very, very quickly.

That might seem like a lot to build up, and you're going to hate seeing it sitting in a savings account when you're itching to invest it, but this is money you simply can't afford to risk on investing. Think of it as an insurance policy.

 **WARNING**

If you *do not* have an emergency fund, you can't afford to invest. Instead, devote your energies to learning about investments, and work on establishing some emergency funds.

Your emergency fund won't just magically appear, of course. You have to work on establishing it, and adding to it. If you devote 10 percent of your gross income (see "Assessing Your Spending Needs") to your emergency fund first, it will take about 2 to 5 years to accumulate the fully funded amount.

You should do this when you're just starting out and keep augmenting it as your salary rises. Devote bonuses, raises, cash gifts, rebates, and extra income to it—or at least half of those monies—and you'll achieve it sooner and get to the more fun goals faster.

Paying Off Debt

The second goal should be to pay off high-interest debt (and not accrue any more, at least on credit cards). If you have low-interest debt (mortgage, some student loans), you may choose to continue paying them over time, but credit card debt or time payment plans are generally worth getting rid of because of high finance charges. (See Chapter 21 for further discussion on handling debt.)

In a low-interest-rate environment, should you save or pay off debt? There are two answers: the numbers answer and the emotional answer.

Numbers answer   Take a look at the interest rate you're paying for the debt. If it's less than you could make on a conservative investment, you're probably better off investing any surplus and making the payments that will pay off your debt in a reasonable time. Currently, I'd say that includes any debt for which the charges are less than about 5 percent annually. At the moment, this would be mostly home mortgages, some homeowners' lines of credit (be careful here because some are interest-only with a big principal payment due at the end of term), and some student loans.

Any debt that charges more than that rate—i.e., just about every credit card—is better paid off before you start an investment program. You can't guarantee you'll make more than the debt is already costing you.

Emotional answer   Pay off the debt. You're going to feel better being debt free (including the mortgage if you're near retirement), you'll be able to control your cost of living better, and your peace of mind and confidence to take considered risks in investing will be vastly improved.

A Word on Mortgages

Should you pay off your home? This is probably the most common question I get from near-retirees. My comments about deciding what debt to pay off here apply: if your mortgage interest rate is less than about 5 percent, the financial answer is that you're better off investing the money you would use to pay off the mortgage, at least over the long haul. A quality, prudent mix of investments will probably earn more than you're paying in a low-interest mortgage.

On the other hand, people who retire with a paid-off house generally feel more secure. You always can cut back on the cost of the car you drive, how much you eat out, and whether you have a lawn service, but your mortgage has to be paid. A paid-off mortgage will reduce the obligatory outflow, even if you still have some housing costs like property taxes, maintenance, and utilities.

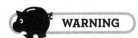 **WARNING**

If the value of your house represents more than a third of your total assets, think carefully before devoting cash to the payoff. A house won't generate retirement income for you; in fact, it's a use asset, something that has value but costs money to hold. It's also more difficult to sell compared to other assets, and it pays no dividends. You don't want all your wealth tied up in your house, leaving you rich on paper but with inadequate income to live on.

Methods for Paying Off Debt

Maybe you've considered that a really successful strike in an investment would take care of all your debt. That's a possibility. But you're still going to need an actual, realistic plan.

You need to face up to all your debts and list the interest rate, the amount owed, and the minimum payments necessary for each. Then you should begin either the snowball or the avalanche method of paying off your debt.

Snowball method With this method, you devote all the extra payments you can muster to the debt with the lowest balance, paying the minimum on all the other debts. When you pay off your lowest-balance debt, you devote the amount you were paying on that debt to your next-smallest debt.

I like this method the best because it's great to see your debts being paid off and eliminated one at a time. Seeing the progress is a terrific psychological boost.

Avalanche method With this method, you use the same technique, but you pay off your debts from the highest interest rate down to the lowest. This saves you some interest (although not as much as you might think), but it has less psychological satisfaction than the snowball method because you usually see each account disappear more slowly.

The most important method of all is to organize your finances so you aren't incurring any further high-interest debt ever again. If you can only pay for something with your credit card, you can't afford it, and you most certainly can't afford any of the risks of investing.

 TIP

What's too much debt? One rule of thumb is when you owe more than 25 percent of your gross income in nonmortgage debt. Another is when the payments on your debt (including your mortgage debt) exceed about 35 percent of your income. This may be flexible if your other living expenses are low (for example, if you're living with your parents), but you should still make a powerful effort to pay off what you owe.

Assessing Your Spending Needs

Do you know what you spend in a month? It can be enlightening—shocking even—to record every cent you spend, and it can be helpful for uncovering any leaking holes you're experiencing. But if you're like most people, you won't keep up the monitoring. So let's make this easy: take your total (gross) monthly earnings and subtract what you save, including what you put into your 401(k). What's left is what you spend in a month. Whether that's what you really *need* to spend is what we're going to look at next.

Looking at the Percentages

Start by looking at your earnings and expenses by percentages. I'm happy to share this terrific idea from Ramit Sethi's website (iwillteachyoutoberich.com). Divide your income into four groups:

- 60 percent is fixed expenses—the bills you have to pay no matter what, such as taxes, insurance, food and clothing costs, and so on.

- 10 percent goes toward retirement savings, such as your 401(k), IRA, and similar investments.

- 10 percent is earmarked for goal savings. Goal savings include short-term goals such as buying a car or house; mid-term goals such as starting your own business; and long-term goals such as retiring by age 50. (Building up your emergency fund is your first goal.)

- 20 percent is for *discretionary* spending—eating out, going to movies, the fun stuff.

DEFINITION

Discretionary means those expenses for which you have some choice as to how much you spend.

Identifying Your Fixed Expenses

Your fixed expenses include all the stuff you *have* to pay. This should be no more than 60 percent of your gross income.

Your gross income is the total you earn before any federal, state, local, or Social Security taxes are deducted. You may also have deductions for health insurance, 401(k) contributions (which is investment money), flexible spending accounts, and so on. Your net income is probably what you think of as your take-home pay—what you actually have available to spend after paying for fixed expenses like insurance and income tax deductions.

TIP

If you're self-employed, remember that your gross income is not your take-home pay. Taxes and the cost of normal benefits still need to be considered.

Here's what goes into that 60 percent:

Federal, state, and local income taxes   These are deducted from your pay before you ever see it, unless you're self-employed.

Housing costs   Rent and renter's insurance, or, if you own a home, mortgage payments, home-owner's insurance, property taxes, and any association or condo fees.

Basic utilities   Gas, water, electric, heat, and internet. Cable, cell phones, and landlines might also be considered basic utilities.

Basic food and clothing costs   I'm not talking about your wine collection or farm-to-bar chocolates. Think about what you'd eat if you were suddenly unemployed. That's your basic food cost. Clothing costs would be the basics you need to get through a day.

Debt service   Student loan payments, credit card payments, and any personal loans you are repaying. Car lease and car loan payments are fixed, once you commit to them. However, you do have a choice as to what level of expense you incur.

Insurance   No one should be without health insurance and insurance on their dwelling and possessions. If you have a car, car insurance is a fixed expense. Depending on your personal situation, stage of life, and how many people are depending on you, life insurance, disability insurance, and long-term-care insurance also may be essential fixed expenses.

Alimony and child support payments   If you have court-ordered payments, these are definitely fixed and obligatory—even bankruptcy won't erase them. They must be paid, and if there's not enough room in the fixed expense category, you must reduce your discretionary spending to supply them.

Ways to Cut Fixed Expenses

Fixed expenses offer plenty of potential for saving money. Lowering your fixed expenses can have a lasting impact on your ability to accumulate wealth and free up more money for saving and investing.

Reduce Your Housing Costs

Housing should cost no more than 28 percent of your gross income (if you have other debts) or up to 33 percent of your gross if you have no other debts. The sum total of all debt payments should not exceed 33 percent of your gross. This is a prudent standard. Some mortgage lenders allow you to borrow at higher ratios of debt to income, but just because you *can* doesn't mean you *should*. If you borrow a higher proportion of your income, you will feel very burdened by housing costs, and it will pinch all other parts of your spending and saving plan. (See Chapter 16 for a discussion of mortgage lending and how you qualify.)

Housing costs include rent and renter's insurance, or mortgage, homeowner's insurance, property taxes, and homeowner's association or condo fees.

If part of those fees includes utilities, you can be picky and count them as fixed expenses but not include them in the 28 percent. The basic message is: keep it low.

Look for ways to reduce your housing costs. For example, don't automatically upgrade your housing every time you get a significant raise.

And consider what you need versus what you want. Most people would do well to buy a starter home and, later, a moderately nicer home, and stop there.

> **TIP**
>
> People who live in homes that are less than they can afford generally smile all the way to the bank.

When you significantly upgrade your neighborhood, you upgrade property taxes, landscape services, and all your other costs, too.

Request New Insurance Quotes

The insurance marketplace is competitive, and getting new auto and renter's or homeowner's insurance quotes at least every 2 years can save you money.

You might feel loyal to your insurance agent, but you'll be dropped like a hot potato if you have a few claims. I know.

Other Money-Saving Tips

Always question whether you can keep things a little longer and stretch them a little farther. Also think about what you really need versus what you want if it'll give you money for investing. I've seen clients who could afford a Bentley drive 25-year-old cars—and have money to invest.

Also, turn out the lights when you leave the room, don't run the washer with half a load, and compare prices when you shop. Sure, these are small things and can take time to add up, but these habits will do you, and your investing income, well and help you make other prudent investment decisions.

Many books and websites are devoted to frugal living, and I urge you to browse them to pick up tips. However, it's the frugal mindset that I'm urging you to adopt.

TIP

What's the difference between frugal and cheap? *Frugal* means seeking the best value, prioritizing durable, well made, and well priced. *Cheap* means seeking the lowest price in all cases.

Planning for Irregular Expenses

Expenses you pay every month can be easy to plan for, but what about those that come once or twice a year, like property taxes? You don't want to be caught by surprise.

Tally your intermittent or one-time-only bills from last year and divide the total by 12. That amount needs to go into a savings account each month; you can draw from the account when those bills come in. Have that amount deducted automatically from your checking account, or, if you can, automatically deposit it from your paycheck to your savings account.

TIP

Freelancers, who don't get a regular paycheck, often have trouble paying quarterly estimated income taxes. Ask your accountant to project how much you'll need for all four quarters and then figure out what percent this was of *last year's income*. Then deposit that percentage of each check into a savings account designated for taxes. If you have no idea what you'll make this year, save 10 to 15 percent of each check. That'll give you a start. If it turns out to be too much, you'll have extra money to invest!

Building Your Savings

Your savings is the basis of your investments. Too often this category is considered expendable, and the money is redistributed to discretionary spending. Don't do it! The only way to begin building wealth is to spend less than you earn and save the difference. You should earmark 10 percent of your income to retirement savings.

Your Workplace Retirement Plan

We'll discuss long-term retirement savings more thoroughly in Chapters 6 and 15, but let's begin thinking about it now. You should earmark at least 10 percent of your income for your workplace retirement plan. Your workplace retirement plan is the place to begin your investments because it offers several advantages:

- Your employer is likely to match it, giving you a great guaranteed return right out of the gate.

- You can't easily access the money, so it's likely to stay invested longer.

- If your plan permits, you may be able to borrow from it for real emergencies or to pay for college.

- Depending on the type of plan, it may reduce your taxable income.

IRAs and SEP-IRAs

Even if you manage to stash the legal maximum in your retirement plan, you should strive to save money on your own, in a Roth or traditional individual retirement account (IRA) if you're eligible, or a simplified employee pension individual retirement arrangement (SEP-IRA) if you're self-employed. A regular brokerage or mutual fund account is a good idea as well.

The trouble with 401(k)s is that the investment range they offer is often quite limited. If you want to invest in stocks or many asset classes, the opportunities just aren't going to be there. Plus, even if you make the maximum contribution, it may get you to retirement with a sufficient total to provide your basic income needs, but it's not going to make you rich. You're going to need to accumulate more.

Goal-Based Savings Accounts

Your savings for retirement is a long-range savings goal. General goal savings usually have a shorter time frame in which they may be spent. I recommend you devote 10 percent of your income to saving for nonretirement goals.

Want to buy a home? This 10 percent goal savings goes to the fund. Need a kitchen remodel or a down payment for a new car? You know where that money is going to come from.

College savings come from this category, as well as any goals you have for luxury purchases (for example, a second home, a boat, or a dream vacation).

Identifying Your Discretionary Expenses

Here's where you pay the restaurant bill, shop at Nordstrom's instead of Target, or buy anything else you wouldn't buy if you were suddenly unemployed. If you don't have anything left for building wealth each month, what you spend in this category may be the reason why.

TIP

How much money do you spend on clothes? Now, how much money do you spend on *clothes you don't wear?* The difference might surprise you. Try turning all your clothes hangers around, returning them to the forward position after you wear the piece. You'll soon see what you really wear, which will offer some revelations on what you actually want to spend money on.

The difference between what you spend and what you earn is critical to your ability to build an investment plan. If you don't have excess—or are spending even more than you earn—you can't put anything aside for investing.

Saving sometimes sounds punitive, whereas spending is fun. Think of your saving as deferred spending, and start realigning your current spending to make those important goals possible.

The Least You Need to Know

- No matter what age you are, you can improve your future by learning how to invest wisely.
- Establishing an emergency fund and paying off high-interest debt should be your first two goals.
- Plan your spending by using percentages to categorize where you spend your money.
- Consider savings a need, not a want. Put a priority on savings before you start spending in areas where you have a choice.
- Find money for investing by managing your costs and making frugal choices.

Defining Your Investment Goals

Many investment decisions will be rooted in your personal goals and timetable, so in this chapter, we're going to define what they are and build a timeline for achieving them. Before setting off on any adventure, you need to have some idea of where you want to go, how long it will take, and how you'll know when you've arrived.

In This Chapter

- Is investing right for you now?
- What types of investments might work for you?
- Defining your short- and medium-term goals
- Setting longer-term goals

Getting by Versus Getting Ahead

If you've worked through the percentage-of-income exercise I suggested in Chapter 1, you know what your spending and saving goals should be. If you really have no idea what you're spending, consider employing the assistance of some type of budget software or app. You may find that you spend more on certain categories than you think. Set up two categories, fixed and discretionary expenses, or whatever works best for you and your situation. Commit to using the software or app for at least 3 months to capture your expenses, including any irregular ones.

 TIP

If saving money sounds somehow punitive, try thinking of savings as your stash for increased spending in the future. You could also change the way you think about your accounts. Instead of your "emergency fund," think of it as your "peace of mind fund." Rather than "investment savings," consider it your "wealth builder war chest." Instead of your "401(k)," it could be your "job freedom account." Whatever works for you.

If you're just getting by—or not even getting by—you don't have enough money to invest just yet. What you should be investing in at this point is yourself: learn to create and manage a budget and read all you can to improve your investing knowledge. You can also start to ask yourself some important questions. We'll explore these questions in the rest of this chapter.

What Types of Investments Interest You?

As you read through this book, think about the investments that appeal to you. Are stocks or mutual funds an appealing investment for you? Do your research, pick out a few stocks you'd buy if you could, and start following them. This is called *paper trading,* and it can prepare you for the ups and downs of what happens to your money when it's invested.

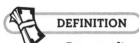 **DEFINITION**

Paper trading is the process of choosing a stock or even a whole portfolio and tracking its performance on a regular basis. Keep records of what you buy, what it costs to purchase, and its variations in price. You can set this up in your Quicken software or at Morningstar.com or other financial sites. You don't actually *buy* the investment, but you observe it as if you had. This offers you a good way to understand performance and your reactions to changes in value (your risk tolerance—see Chapter 4).

Do you want to invest in real estate? Start scanning the for-sale listings and driving by properties that would interest you. You'll learn all about neighborhoods, curb appeal, and property size.

Create a watch list of specific properties to see what they sell for versus what the asking price was, how long they were on the market before they sold, and so on. Attend open houses—any real estate agent will tell you they get plenty of nosey neighbors, so you won't offend them. Ask the Realtor plenty of questions at an open house—you'll figure out which Realtors are knowledgeable and maybe find one to work with in the future.

We're all eager to jump into investing so we can make money. However, doing some research and working through a simulation can help you prevent some of the real-life losses that go hand in hand with lack of experience.

What Are Your Short- and Medium-Term Goals?

It's good to have dreams, but when it comes to investing, think of dreams as goals. Goals encourage you to think in specifics. When you know exactly what you want, you can rank your goals based on how much money you have now and how much time you'll need to work your investment strategy, as different time frames require different strategies. How fast do you need your money to grow? How long can you wait out market downturns?

Determining What You Need

Why do you want more money? Do you want to buy a house? Cover the expenses involved in adopting a baby? These and other short-term (fewer than 5 years) goals require you to think about specific costs. How much money do you need, by when?

You may choose to accept more risk with your investments in the hope of achieving a goal sooner—but only if *not* achieving the goal in your desired time frame is acceptable. For example, if you want to buy a house within 5 years, you could invest in stocks, knowing that stocks fluctuate more than a safer investment such as bonds. Because of a stock's fluctuations, you might achieve the goal sooner—say, in 3 years—but if the market turns against you, you might need to wait longer than you'd planned—perhaps 6 or 7 years.

If, on the other hand, a goal is particularly important to you, such as covering the expenses of adopting a baby, you might need to stick to a more rigid time frame. In this case, you will want to choose steady investments that can build a reasonable, more predictable (but lower) return with less chance of loss and easy ability to cash out in a specific period (for example, diversified or balanced mutual funds or even bond funds or cashlike investments).

Changing Careers or Starting a Business

Changing careers or starting a business can be a short- or medium-term goal (5 to 10 years). These goals also require some calculations in order to assign a precise goal amount. It's true that no one would ever start a business if they waited until they had "enough" money, but if you're contemplating a major employment change, you must put some numbers to this. How much would you need to replace 2 years' worth of salary? That's a good place to start.

If you have a spouse or can move into your parents' basement, you may need far less than someone who depends on a single salary for support. (Steve Jobs built the first Apple computer in his parents' garage.) If your business will require capital for producing a product, renting office or warehouse space, and so on, it's essential that you work through the production of a business plan to know how much you'll need.

 TIP

The U.S. Small Business Administration (sba.gov) offers many courses available online and in person to help you develop a business plan and budget, plan for specific types of businesses, and learn to apply for loans. Invest your time in learning how to give your business idea the best chance of success.

Where to Put Your Money

Money earmarked for short- and sometimes medium-term goals should be held in safe investments like savings accounts; certificates of deposit (with a term consistent with when the money will be needed); money market funds; possible short-term, high-quality bond mutual funds; or (for those with longer or more flexible time horizons) possibly balanced mutual funds or a small selection of diversified mutual funds. The latter two types of investments may carry more possibility of both loss and gain. (See Chapter 10 on mutual funds.)

 **WARNING**

Money you will need in fewer than 5 years should not be considered available for investing. A serious economic downturn during the period you need to liquidate the funds can cause you to come up short on business capital as well as lose money on the investment itself. If you rack up some serious debt on a credit card trying to stay afloat, you'll be searching the internet for bankruptcy advice, not investment advice.

Different short- and medium-term goals require different investment strategies and different mixes of investments and levels of risk tolerance. The loftier the goal you have for net worth, the more you should look to a combination of strategies to build it and the earlier you should start.

TIP

In 2013, *Forbes* analyzed how 400 billionaires made their money. Of the 400, 127 inherited it. Of the rest, here are the top 10 ways they made their money: investments, technology, real estate, fashion and retail, media, food and beverage, energy, health care (inventions and patents), sports, and manufacturing. Unless you're really good at sports, you'd better start investing, buying real estate, inventing something, or starting a business.

What Are Your Long-Term Goals?

Short- and medium-term goals differ from person to person, but for most people, one long-term goal is the same: have enough investments (plus guaranteed income like Social Security and pensions or income annuities) to allow you to comfortably retire. (See Chapter 15 for a discussion of retirement strategies.)

You might have other longer-term goals as well, such as achieving a specific net worth or leaving an inheritance to your loved ones.

Amassing Enough to Retire

What's enough money to enable you to retire? How do you know how much you'll need? There are numerous answers to this question—and more questions. What do you earn now? Is it enough to make you feel comfortable? Would you like to live better in retirement than you do now?

Are you saving anything now, or are you in debt? Also, how old are you? If you're at the beginning of your career, you may be expecting to earn a much higher salary by the time you retire. On the other hand, by retirement age, you probably won't be raising children or paying for college tuition. And in retirement, you won't be paying Social Security taxes, and perhaps your income taxes will be lower. (But don't bank on it.)

To determine how much you need to retire, take your current earnings, subtract what you're currently saving, and add any credit card expenses you don't pay off every month (that's what's beyond your current means). Now divide that figure by .04 (a rough estimate of what you can safely withdraw from a portfolio and expect it to last through 30 years of retirement). If you want a higher spending level in retirement, substitute your desired income level and divide by .04 to get the amount of the investment portfolio you would need to generate that income.

Let's say you're 35 years old, making $85,000 a year, and saving nothing. To replace that income in retirement, you're probably going to need 100 percent of that amount to live the same lifestyle. (If you anticipate that your expenses might go down a bit—say, less in taxes, lower commuting expenses, or a smaller clothes budget—you might reduce that percentage a bit.) Let's say you'll get $2,000 a month ($24,000 a year) in Social Security. So your portfolio (workplace retirement, outside investments, IRAs) needs to be large enough to withdraw $61,000 a year, or at least $1,525,000. Is that a terrifying amount? But wait—that's all in *today's* dollars. We're not factoring in inflation over the 30 or so years you will continue to work. The good news is, we're also not factoring in the return you're going to achieve on your investments. You won't have to save it all.

> **TIP**
>
> How long will it take to double your money? How long will it take inflation to erode your money's spending power? The formula for estimating this is 72 divided by rate of investment return (or inflation). For example, if you have $1,000 and are paid a 3 percent dividend: 72 ÷ 3 = 24 years to double your money. If your $1,000 earns 8 percent: 72 ÷ 8 = 9 years to double your money. How long before inflation erodes your buying power? With 3 percent inflation, in 24 years, your $1,000 will buy what $500 buys today. This isn't precisely the way to calculate inflation-adjusted returns, but it gives you an idea of how investments need to out-earn inflation.

Achieving a Specific Net Worth

Is your goal to achieve a specific net worth by a certain age? Do you want to be a millionaire by 35? Retire at 55 with an income equal to what you're earning now? Do you want to continue to work as long as you choose, but have a portfolio that could support you if needed?

Accumulating significant wealth generally requires saving a high proportion of your salary to generate enough excess to invest. This may entail being very frugal or focusing on continually improving your salary while living below the increases. You also might need to be much more willing to make risky investments that might have a big payoff (individual stocks) or ones that require personal investment of your time and effort, like direct real estate investment or starting a business.

As with all wealth building, you somehow must generate more than you spend. If you're in a hurry, you don't have time on your side to slowly build so you must figure out ways to generate investment money more quickly. (For more information, see Chapters 11 and 14, on stocks and investment real estate, respectively.)

Having Enough to Leave an Inheritance

People vary widely in their desire to leave an inheritance to their family. Whatever your feelings on the subject, I can practically guarantee your children will be hoping for something to remember you by.

Some people feel that after raising their children, and possibly putting them through college, they've done enough and intend to spend it all. Or as one person told me, "We want enough money to last us for one year past our lifespan." Other people want to leave as much as possible to their children or other relatives (and usually as little as possible to the tax man), or would like to make a significant bequest to charity.

If you achieve significant wealth (more than about $5 million under current federal tax policy), you'll need the help of a financial planner and an estate attorney to structure your estate for tax efficacy. Less than $5 million and your ability to leave a legacy may be about how you insure yourself against the risks of old age and disaster. Also, check your state's estate limits. Some states tax smaller estates than the federal threshold.

 TIP

In a study conducted by the Institute on Assets and Social Policy, among households with positive wealth growth during the 25-year study period, the number of years of homeownership accounts for 27 percent of the difference in relative wealth growth between white and African American families, the largest portion of the growing wealth gap. The second-largest share of the increase, accounting for 20 percent, is average family income. Highly educated households correlate strongly with larger wealth portfolios, but similar college degrees produce more wealth for whites, contributing 5 percent of the proportional increase in the racial wealth gap. Inheritance and financial support from family combine for another 5 percent of the increasing gap.

What Is Your Definition of Wealthy?

Another way to determine your investing goals is by defining wealth for yourself. When would you consider yourself wealthy? Consider the possible levels:

- **Secure**   When your inflow reliably meets or exceeds your outflow

- **Wealthy**   When your inflow always exceeds your outflow, and you can choose luxury (at least sometimes) over practicality

- **Filthy rich**   When your inflow (especially from assets) is more than you can spend in your lifetime

Many of us, at least by retirement, would be very happy to reach the first level. But note that there are two components to every level of wealth. Not only do we strive to improve what's coming in, by improving our income and investment return, we also can improve our wealth by managing our outflow.

At the point of retirement, my parents lived in a modest, paid-off home, drove their cars for about 8 to 10 years (always well maintained), and ate out 3 nights a week—nearly always at the senior special. They took a 2-week vacation every year, and they lived on Social Security and the income generated by a $300,000 portfolio. Mom made it to age 90, and Dad to 96. They left a substantial chunk of their portfolio intact, did anything they wanted (which was modest), and had enough to handle their health care in their last years. They were, most certainly, wealthy. And as children of the depression, they felt very well off, if not wealthy.

On the other hand, I see people who make more than $250,000 a year, have home-equity loans in addition to their mortgage, carry significant credit card debt, and have to cash out their IRAs to pay for their kid's college. By my definition, they're not wealthy—in fact, they're on their way to being broke.

If you have any aspirations to build wealth, it's not so much about what you earn as about what you can hold on to and then grow through well-chosen investments.

People are more likely to achieve, if not their actual goals, then at least some progress toward them, if they have a *measurable* goal. "Saving as much as possible and making as much as possible on my investments" is *not* a measurable or satisfying goal because you will never know when you achieve it. So right now, think about how much you would need to have as income to achieve each of these levels of wealth. If you estimate that you can safely withdraw 4 percent of the value of your investments each year, how much would you need to have invested to achieve each level? (You can include your work earnings if it makes you feel better, but I don't think you'll feel wealthy until you really don't need to work.)

For any and all goals, write down a goal you can measure and an aspirational goal for achieving them. Gather the best advice you can, and think through what tools (investments) are appropriate to use. Of course, you might need to revise your goals periodically as you change or if you achieve the goal. Some may be tweaked, and some may even be discarded. Then, you'll begin again to set new goals.

The Least You Need to Know

- Start thinking about what types of investments interest you, and consider starting a paper-trading account.
- Define your short- and medium-term financial goals as specifically as possible, and define the period of time you will need to achieve them.
- Keep your eye on your long-term goals. They'll take longer, but you should monitor that you're making progress over time.

- Your goals can be mundane or lofty, but to achieve them, you need a plan and a measureable way to know if you have met them.
- Know what your own personal definition of wealth is.

Assessing Your Timeline

When I was studying for my CFP® certification, one of my much younger classmates reported on a call she'd received that left her aghast. A professional couple in their 50s had called seeking financial planning help and had total savings of $40,000. She kept saying, "How can you get to be that age with no savings?"

Let me tell you how: in your 20s, you're trying to pay off school loans while having some semblance of a social life. In your 30s, you're trying to buy a house, furnish the place, pay taxes, and have kids. By your 40s, you're trying to pay for the kids' college and a more expensive house. And suddenly you're in your 50s and haven't saved a dime.

In This Chapter

- How your investment goals depend on your age
- Improving your long-term financial success
- Creating a schedule to meet your goals
- Devising strategies for unique goals

In this chapter, we're going to look at how to go from where you are to where you want to be. I discuss what advantages and challenges you have, wherever you are in life, and the steps you can take to make the most of your situation. Based on when you want or need to achieve your goals, we look at how to put time on your side.

Investing in Your 20s

The younger you are, the more risk you can afford to take. When you're in your 20s, you have plenty of time to learn and recover from bad mistakes—and worse markets. Even if you were to lose everything, you still have time to recover. However, you also may have obligations (school loans, family, furnishing a first home) and job uncertainties that make it difficult to accumulate much extra money to invest. Perhaps you've seen your parents make poor spending or investment decisions, and you're terrified of what the market can do.

The younger you are, the more you can improve your chances of reaching your investment goals by taking four steps:

- Investing in yourself
- Making it a habit to delay consumption
- Investing in your employer's retirement plan
- Investing elsewhere in addition to your retirement plan.

Let's take a look at each.

Invest in Yourself

It's essential to learn as much as you can about investing strategies. Subscribe to a reputable personal finance magazine, and make it a goal to read at least a few investing books per year. Many blogs and websites are dedicated to building your financial savvy, and it's worth subscribing or visiting a few on a regular basis. (I offer suggestions in Appendix B.) You may not understand everything you read, but it's a start.

In addition to upgrading your knowledge, try to take advantage of your employee benefits. Many employers offer talks on retirement planning and investments in conjunction with your 401(k). Sometimes private consultations with a planner are also available. It's free, so why not take the time to do it?

TIP

Many workplace retirement plans offer a brochure explaining the investments available. If you're investing your money, spend some time reading and trying to understand your program.

When you're young, you may not have much financial capital yet, but you have a lot of human capital: room to grow and develop in your career, your capabilities, and your contacts. Any opportunity you are offered for career development should be seized to build your résumé and earning potential.

If there's a professional organization appropriate to your field, don't ignore their emails and newsletter. In addition to professional development, many of these organizations will offer talks and seminars on financial planning specific to your career interests. Besides developing networking contacts, professional organizations can offer you a lot of education.

If your salary is not growing as fast as you would like, consider consulting a career counselor. With a targeted program of résumé development and targeted job hunting, some people are able to change jobs and improve their salary far more than by waiting around for a raise.

Grow your earnings and you should be able to grow the amount you have available for investing.

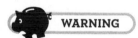 **WARNING**

Don't believe everything you read. As with all investing advice, know what they're selling. For blogs, websites, and publications, it's especially important to determine whether sponsors get favorable mention in editorial content. (Hint: if it comes with a "free lunch," you should be extremely careful about investing until you know more.)

Delay Consumption

If you're a college student, or just out of college, you're probably like nearly every other American college student who has nightmares about having to move back into their childhood room.

But you know what? The people who do, and who can find a job, can save far more than their classmates who are living in studio apartments in urban high-rises with "amenities."

Don't rush out to buy a car. In fact, don't rush out to buy anything. After exorbitant housing, the biggest drains on a spender's budget are usually eating out, entertainment, and clothes. Drink the beer instead of the fancy cocktail. I don't expect you to watch Netflix with your parents every Saturday night, but do try to ratchet it down while you save money.

If you're older, you still need to control spending so that you end up with money to invest. It's all too common to upgrade your lifestyle every time you get a raise. If you do, you'll always be living on the edge. Consumer products companies will love you, since you'll be helping to grow their profits, but you won't be reaping the benefits.

You especially want to avoid over-upgrading things that add to your fixed costs. Adding a much higher housing or car payment locks you into required outgo that could go into investments that would work for you instead. Taking luxury vacations on a regular basis, or eating most of your meals in restaurants, is a common way to find yourself without funds to invest while wondering why you're so strung out financially.

> It's better to own the stock of a company producing great products than to own the products themselves. Which is likely to be worth more in 5 years?

Invest in Your Employer's Retirement Plan

You *must* invest at least enough in your employer's retirement plan to get whatever the employer match is—after all, it's free money! But don't stop there. Keep increasing your contribution every time you get a raise, or when you can, until you're contributing the maximum allowed. A raise should be a way to improve your wealth, before you improve your lifestyle. (See Chapter 15 to learn how to navigate and maximize workplace retirement plans.)

While I'm recommending you save at least 10 percent of earnings for retirement, that's a floor, not a ceiling. Upgrade your lifestyle less than you upgrade your salary and you'll have more and more money to invest and build real wealth.

> If you contribute to a 401(k), 403(b), or another type of workplace retirement plan, many employers match some part of your contribution. Some contribute a flat amount—3 percent of your salary, for example. Some contribute a percentage of what you contribute—they'll match 50 percent of what you contribute, maybe. Find out what your employer match is. Your employer isn't being kind and generous to you; these plans enabled companies to stop providing pensions. Don't pass up this benefit!

Invest in Addition to Your Retirement Plan

In addition to contributing money to your retirement plan, you also should begin investing on your own. If you consistently invest 10 percent of your earnings from the time you're in your 20s until retirement, you'll probably have saved enough to retire at the secure level.

But what if you're unemployed for a while, or you started at 35 or 40, or skipped a few years somewhere down the line? In this case, you need to save more whenever you can. At the very least, you should invest any bonus, windfall, rebate, or gift.

No one ever became wealthy by simply contributing to a 401(k), so if you have dreams beyond "secure," think about opening other tax-sheltered accounts, such as Roth or traditional IRAs, health savings accounts (HSAs), and maybe even a mutual fund or brokerage account. (See Chapter 6 and the discussion of individual investment types in Part 3.)

Investing in Your 30s and 40s

If you're in your 30s or 40s, especially if you haven't begun saving much just yet, you need to pick up the pace. Everything I said for the twenty-somethings applies to you, only more so. If you haven't begun saving for retirement by age 40, you need to do everything you can to make the maximum contribution to your workplace retirement plan. If you're still within the limit for IRAs, you should strive to open and fund those, too. In fact, IRAs are a great option for a wide range of investments; your choices won't be limited in the way they are in the workplace plan.

In addition, you should strive to begin and build a college fund if you have children. If I had a dollar for every parent who's told me they weren't worried about paying for college because "My kid is so smart they'll get a scholarship," well, I wouldn't have worried while writing those five-figure checks to Bryn Mawr for my daughter.

The truth is, your child probably isn't going to get an all-expenses-paid merit scholarship and will need some type of financial aid to pay for college if you haven't saved enough. Too often, that "financial aid" is going to be loans, subsidized if you're lucky, and very little else. Saving for college is going to be something you will be very pleased to have done, right after your child gets the acceptance email.

Even if you can't save and invest your way to the full amount your child will need, it's worth saving *something*. See Chapter 17 on the realities of financial aid and advice as to how to invest your college savings.

Investing in Your 50s and 60s

If you're in your 50s or 60s, you finally may have the time to pay attention to your investments. If you haven't saved by now, or if your savings aren't enough for retirement, you'll have to think through what lifestyle changes you can make to cut your expenses and really start seriously saving.

If all your money has been parked in your house and your workplace funds, you may be confronted for the first time with rolling them out and having them, and the investment choices, completely up to you. Bearing in mind that this money needs to last you through what can be more than 30 years of retirement, you don't want to get exceptionally risky or desperate—that's a gambler's strategy, not an investor's. You should think through your investment options, your tolerance for risk, and your level of experience.

You may want to meet with a financial planner to explore possibilities and options—to ensure your investments are in line with your goals and are neither too risky nor too conservative. That portfolio needs to last you!

Plotting a Time Schedule for Your Unique Goals

Whatever your goals, you need a target completion date—and a plan B. Why a target completion date? Because investing is often one of those things that are important but not urgent. Knowing how long you have to complete this (or any) project drives action. Having a plan B is important because both opportunities and challenges arise as you take action and gain experience. It's a lot less nerve-racking if you try to envision possible variations and roadblocks and think through how you might cope with them.

Let's review what you need to think through in order to drive your investment selection for your specific goal and timeline:

- What is my target date for achieving my goal?

- How much risk am I willing to take to achieve this goal?

- How much have I saved already for this goal?

- How much am I willing to contribute, or what will be the source of funding?

- How much time am I willing to spend monitoring and adjusting my investments?

- What will I invest in, and why?

- How will I measure my progress? Will I review this quarterly, yearly, or at some other interval?

- What is my standard for having achieved this goal? How will I know when I've arrived?

Your answers may vary, depending on your situation. Here are a few possible scenarios:

Planning for College Costs

First goal: Sally Northshore wants to fund half of the costs of her daughter Sallyette's college education. She wants to have $120,000 available by the time her daughter, now an infant, is 18. She's received $1,000 in gifts from Sallyette's grandparents, and she wants to add to that on a monthly basis. Sally wants it all to be simple, so she selects a *529 plan*, sets up an automatic withdrawal from her checking account, and chooses an age-based index fund mix, which will rebalance to more conservative investments as Sallyette gets closer to college age. Sally checks in with the fund at least yearly to ensure she's making some progress toward her goal.

When Sallyette is 5 years old, Sally gets a much better job that reliably pays a big bonus. Sally decides maybe she can put a little more toward college in the hope that even more than half can be covered. She decides to open a *Coverdell Savings Plan* to invest in some speculative stock picks. If they do well, great. If not, she'll still have her savings in the 529 plan. She's willing to roll the dice in hopes of adding a little extra to the college fund. She contributes $2,000 a year to the Coverdell and buys some stocks using the methods of evaluation she learned at her investment club. She monitors these stocks quarterly. Not only are they a possible source of college funding, but they also are teaching her about stock selection and portfolio management without risking huge amounts of her possible investment capital. (See Chapter 17 for a discussion of these types of accounts and further information on college planning.)

DEFINITION

529 plans are state-sponsored savings plans designed specifically for college savings. The earnings grow tax-free, and withdrawals are tax-free if used for qualified educational expenses. There is no minimum investment, and anyone can contribute, regardless of income. **Coverdell Savings Plans** are individual accounts in which earnings grow tax-free and withdrawals for qualified educational expenses are tax-free. You can contribute a maximum of $2,000 per child, and must have an income under certain limits to contribute.

Retirement Planning with a Sudden Windfall

Another scenario: Dick and Jane have built up a healthy balance in their 401(k)s. They're retiring, and they want to transfer their accounts to a self-managed IRA so they have a better selection of investments. They choose an array of mutual funds for most of their retirement investments, keeping a conservative mix and checking in once a year to rebalance back to that target mix, withdrawing a yearly predetermined amount of retirement income.

However, Jane inherits $25,000 from a long-lost aunt, and Dick finds he can still do a bit of consulting for 2 days a week after he retires (which will maybe last until he is 72). Dick and Jane decide they will segregate this money in a separate brokerage account (for the inheritance) and open a *Roth IRA* for contributions from Dick's consulting. They devote these sums to a somewhat more risky investment selection, planning to supplement their vacation budget with whatever this special-purpose portfolio can generate. They let the dividends and *capital gains* build up, and every few years, they have enough to take a little better vacation than they otherwise would. If it does poorly, they spend their time at local museums.

DEFINITION

Capital gains are the increase in the value of an investment over the original purchase price (not including dividends or interest). If you buy a stock for $10 and sell it for $15 (and the stock pays no dividends), your capital gain is $5. Mutual funds may pay capital gains even if you haven't sold them because the manager will have bought and sold investments during the year.

Retirement Planning with a Guaranteed Income Supplement

A third set of circumstances: Jack and Jill have Social Security and a small investment portfolio. They have no children and not much experience in investing. They select a conservative Target Retirement Income fund for most of their money, or a balanced fund, and put one third of the money into a *single premium fixed annuity*, effectively buying themselves a pension.

DEFINITION

A **Roth IRA** is an individually owned and managed retirement account. Earnings grow tax-free, and withdrawals are tax-free if you are over 59½ and have owned the account for 5 years. A **single premium fixed annuity** is an insurance investment product designed to provide lifetime income. You purchase the annuity in a single lump-sum payment. The insurance annuity provider guarantees you will receive a specific monthly check as long as you live (see Chapter 15).

Long-Term Investing for a Young Worker

A different age group: Nicole has started her first job after college. She has some student debt, but she has chosen to live with her mom so she can save money and pay off her debt. She pays her mom some rent and expenses and knows her mom won't kick her out if she loses her job. Since Nicole can afford some risk (with the basics of living taken care of) she contributes the maximum to her retirement plan, choosing the appropriate year target date fund for now (which will be almost entirely in stock funds). However, she can fund a Roth IRA, so she parks a Roth contribution in a balanced fund until she's accumulated enough to buy a few shares in four or five carefully selected stocks. If she makes money, she'll roll it into more stocks or more shares of what she already owns. If she loses it, she has plenty of time to save some more, and in the meantime, she's gotten experience and education in the market.

Setting Goals, Meeting Deadlines, Adapting a Plan

In the above scenarios, each person has a solid goal in mind, a deadline, and an adaptable plan for achieving it.

Sally's goal is funding her daughter's education. She begins with a reasonable contribution to a tax-sheltered college savings plan. When circumstances improve, she adjusts her saving with a plan B of improving the funding possibilities due to improvement in her salary. She can afford to take more risk with the Coverdell account because she already has a solid baseline savings program in place. She has a medium timeline.

Dick and Jane have a baseline program to pay their retirement expenses, but it's perhaps a little stretched. When Jane inherits money, they see the possibility of investing it to provide a little more luxury. Dick has also realized that he can work longer than he originally planned to improve their overall financial picture and improve the security of their retirement plans. While Dick and Jane have immediate goals (to fund retirement), they also have a long-term goal of maintaining retirement for many years.

Jack and Jill have decided they're not comfortable with depending entirely on their investments, and need a supplementary income that's a sure thing. They're more worried about outliving their money than they are about eking out the maximum return, so they've chosen to back up their investing plan with a guaranteed income annuity designed to last for a long time horizon.

Nicole has time on her side and can make the riskiest investing choices because she has her basic living needs taken care of. Her goals are to maximize her very long-term returns while learning about investing by doing. She has organized her spending so that she can make progress on debt repayment while still having enough to save. She can afford to chance the greatest loss because her timeline is so long until retirement.

No matter what your age, you'll have advantages and challenges in your financial management. Depending on your age and goals, you may choose safer or higher-return investments. But at any age, having money to invest means managing your spending so you can have excess above living expenses.

The Least You Need to Know

- Depending on your age and goals, you may be able to choose riskier or more conservative investments.

- In your 20s and 30s, time is on your side, so once you've gotten control of spending and any debt, and have an adequate emergency fund, you can consider being very aggressive in investments.

- In your 40s and 50s, retirement is closer and you may have other obligations (mortgage and college costs, for example) so you need to keep saving as well as making prudent investment choices based on your goals.

- In your 60s, you're at retirement or getting close so you need to be sure your investments, pension, and Social Security will provide enough income to fund your retirement for the rest of your life.

How Much Risk Can You Take?

We'd all like to make as much money as possible, as quickly as possible. On the other hand, we want to hold on to every penny of our savings, with no loss. Is it possible to do both? Is there a way to balance taking risks with maximizing gain?

In this chapter, we'll look at the different types of investment risk, ways to measure your risk tolerance, and how to invest accordingly.

In This Chapter

- How risky you're willing to be—or should be
- Understanding the different kinds of risk
- Comparing stocks, bonds, and mutual funds and assessing their risk levels
- Choosing the right investment mix for your level of risk

Types of Risk

All investments carry risk, but some are more risky than others. Even if you stash your savings in your mattress, you still run the risk of burglary, fire, or other disaster.

The main types of risk include investment-related risk, lost opportunity risk, inflation risk, market risk, business risk, political risk, and interest rate risk.

Investment-Related Risk

Following is a list of investment types, ranked in approximate order from safest to riskiest:

Relatively safe   Cash, U.S. bonds, corporate bonds rated BBB or better, and international bonds.

Moderate risk   Balanced or equity/income funds (stock/bond), large-cap mutual funds, mid-cap mutual funds, and international developed market (Europe, Australia, New Zealand, Japan) funds.

Higher risk   Small-cap mutual funds, large-cap individual stocks, mid-cap individual stocks, small-cap individual stocks, junk bond funds, individual junk bonds, and international emerging market funds.

WARNING

Some alternatives to traditional investments include publicly traded real estate investment trusts (REITS), natural resources, commodities, and specific sectors (health care, biotech, energy, gold, and so on). Carefully study these investments for market risk as well as the risk of the individual investment. Some also have unique taxation rules that might affect your actual return. If you're wondering about crazy-risky investments, here are a few: nontraded REITS, Master Limited Partnerships, hedge funds, and venture capital businesses.

I just threw several new terms at you, so let's pause to take a look at some quick definitions:

Stock   A share in a company. Generally, you will only be able to buy shares in a publicly traded company (one where shares are sold on a stock exchange). Owning a share is owning part of a company, and sharing in the ups and downs of that company. The price of shares will depend on whether other investors think the company is doing well or poorly.

Bond   An IOU for a loan you've given the company or government. In return, the company or government usually promises to pay you interest, and to return your initial investment by a specific date in the future.

Mutual fund   A fund that pools the money of many investors to buy a collection of stocks, bonds, and other investments. Some mutual funds are funds of funds, meaning they buy shares in other mutual funds. Mutual funds generally pay dividends based on the payouts of their underlying investments, and may pay out capital gains because of sales of the investments in the mutual fund.

Capital gain or loss   The difference between what you paid for an investment (your capital) and what you sell it for (your gain or loss). Currently, capital gains are taxed at a lower rate than interest payments.

Market capitalization (cap)   The dollar-amount value of all the outstanding shares of a publicly traded company. *Large-caps* are companies with more than $10 billion in capitalization. The really big ones, like Exxon and Apple, are sometimes called mega-caps. Mid-caps have capitalization between $10 billion and $2 billion. Small-caps are under $2 billion.

Sector   The general area of a company's business—for example, healthcare, technology, industrials, energy. Some sectors have more risk or are more in favor at specific times.

Industry   A subdivision of a sector. For example, in the healthcare sector you might have companies concentrating on biotechnology, medical supplies and equipment, or pharmaceuticals.

When it comes to the spectrum of investments, the main thing to remember with regard to risk is that the more risk you assume, the greater the potential reward. The less risk you assume, the less reward you can expect. Write this out and post it above the desk where you carry out your investing activities:

> The more risk, the more potential reward.
> The more safety, the less potential return.

Lost Opportunity Cost

Whenever you choose one thing, you give up the potential of something else. If you take the opportunity to invest in what appears to be a high-flying stock, you lose the opportunity to purchase another one, or the opportunity for safety offered by bonds. Keeping your money in extremely low-risk, low-paying investments represents a lost opportunity to make more money in higher-return investments.

Inflation Risk

This is the risk inherent in extremely safe investments like cash and bank certificates of deposit (CDs). Sure, your original amount (the *principal*) is safe, but its value or purchasing power will be eroded by inflation. In other words, your original investment will not decrease, but what it can buy will be far, far less as the years go by. And it won't be increasing your wealth, because it's earning so little. This is a risk you can control by choosing other investments that do beat inflation.

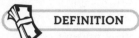

DEFINITION

Principal is the money you originally invested. Earnings, dividends, and capital gains are all based on that original amount.

Market (Systemic or Systematic) Risk

This is the gyration of the entire financial market that you hear about every day on the news. Specific classes of investments respond differently to different events, so you will hear about the "bond market" or "stock market" or "real estate market." You can't control this risk. You will always have some risk depending on what the overall market does, but you can lessen that risk by the mix of investments you choose.

Business Risk

All investments of the same type or within the same industry will tend to have similar problems or benefits. If the bond market is crummy, all bonds will be affected. If stocks are falling like stones, even good companies will usually see a share-price drop. If the technology industry stinks, all tech stocks will struggle. But even if you're buying a stock in a good industry, during a good market, you can still pick one bad company out of a good bunch (and, sometimes, a good company out of a bad industry). The more you invest in one specific investment (one company, one bond), the more business risk you incur. If you *are* buying individual companies as stocks or bonds, concentrate on good companies in good industries. You can lessen this risk by diversifying your investments.

Political Risk

New government policies, changes in tax laws, political unrest, and government takeover can all harm or help specific investments. Outside the United States, political risk is of even more concern, particularly in emerging markets or where there is risk of government overthrow, poorly functioning legal systems, or shaky accounting standards or oversight. Once you put your own money into investments, you will become *much* more interested in factors that could affect them, especially tax policy and international events. There is almost nothing you can do about this risk.

Interest Rate Risk

This is a risk that changes in interest rates will have a dramatic effect on a specific investment, or the market rate as a whole. For example, if you have locked in a low interest rate by purchasing a bond, and interest rates rise significantly, your bond will no longer have a competitive rate, and its price will fall (if you need to sell it before *term*). A rise in interest rates can also have a negative effect on corporations and their ability to borrow, often resulting in stock prices dropping.

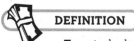

DEFINITION

Term is the length of time the bond is issued for. Remember, a bond is a loan to a company or government. Terms are short, intermediate, or long. Just like a loan, the lender and borrower agree to a length of time in which the loan will be in effect. Just as a borrower can pay a loan off early, some bonds can be paid off early by the issuer, especially if you have a high-interest bond and the lender can now borrow money at a lower rate.

Not all risks can be avoided, but you can lessen the impact of any individual investment choice by careful selection and diversification. Don't put all your eggs in one basket, and choose your eggs and baskets carefully.

Ways to Measure Your Personal Risk Tolerance

You want to take on as little risk as possible to achieve your investing goals. Depending on your goals and your plans, that can range from conservative, low-risk investing to high-risk, very aggressive investing.

If, for example, you have a pension that has inflation protection (a *COLA*) and Social Security that add up to an adequate retirement income, you could probably choose to invest only in CDs or insured savings accounts, because you won't need to worry much about inflation. Or you could choose much more risky investments, because your baseline income is guaranteed. It depends on your own individual risk tolerance or aversion.

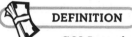

DEFINITION

COLA stands for Cost Of Living Adjustment. This is an increase in a pension, Social Security, long-term-care insurance coverage, or your salary, designed to keep pace with inflation. It can either be fixed (for example, 3 percent or 5 percent every year) or pegged to an index, like the Consumer Price Index (CPI) or the variations of it incorporating different model market baskets.

Since some sectors (nursing home care or college tuition) have risen far more than the average cost of living, if you are a consumer of those products or services you may find that a COLA doesn't cover all the increases you're personally experiencing.

Vanguard.com has a very good risk-tolerance questionnaire available online that I use with my clients. You can download it and score yourself. However, if you're a beginning investor, some of the questions may puzzle you.

I'll suggest a few beginning questions—no scoring, just questions to think about: if you bought a stock and suddenly the market plunged, which would you do:

- Sell it immediately and put the money in a bank.
- Sit tight and wait for it to turn around.
- Buy more as long as it was still a good company.

Which investment would you prefer to invest $1,000 in:

- An investment that might make $20 but could lose $10
- An investment that might make $200 but could lose $100
- An investment that might make $1,000 but could lose $500 (half of your investment lost, or your investment doubled)

Finally, how much money could you afford to lose on a specific investment choice:

- None
- 10 percent
- 50 percent
- Everything

Obviously, if you chose the first set of answers you're conservative or risk averse; the middle set and you're probably fairly conservative to moderately risk tolerant; the final set and you're a more aggressive investor.

Your tolerance or willingness to take risks in the hope of greater reward may change over time. You may gain experience and knowledge that make you more confident in selecting investments, or you may get older and feel the need to consolidate your gains and hold on to what you've earned. You may choose to be more conservative with your retirement funds but more aggressive with your 2-year-old's college fund.

TIP

Don't accept any more risk than you need to; don't take more risk in the hope of getting rich quickly or trying to climb out of financial problems; don't invest so much in a risky investment that you can't sleep at night; and don't focus only on risk—consider benefit and the possibility of reward as well.

Choosing an Investment Mix to Match Your Risk Tolerance

Let's say you took a risk-tolerance quiz and it suggested you should have a mix of 60 percent stocks (or stock mutual funds) and 40 percent bonds (or bond mutual funds). Now what?

Stocks, Risk, and You

Everyone likes to discuss stocks: what's hot, what's not, what's down, what's up. Has the market plunged lately? That means investors are running from stocks by selling off. Is there an industry that is the flavor of the month? Investors will pile into it. We're going to discuss the specifics of stocks in Chapter 11, but for now, let's consider some basic principles with regard to stocks and risk.

First, investing in an individual stock is generally considered more risky than investing in a single mutual fund. Why? Because investing in an individual stock is like putting all your eggs in one basket, whereas investing in a single mutual fund is like distributing your eggs across a dozen baskets. If all your eggs are in one basket and the basket gets kicked over, all your eggs are destroyed. If your eggs are distributed across a dozen baskets, one smashed basket won't destroy your whole stash.

So you should ignore that hot tip you got on your last business trip from the company vice president sitting next to you on the plane. Buying one or two stocks on hot tips is a first-class ticket to losing every bit of your *assets*.

To make investing in stocks a little less risky—to *diversify*—you need about 10 to 20 stocks. Fewer, and it's hard to diversify; more, and it's hard to keep track of them. With at least 10 stocks, not only can you diversify among different companies, but you can also diversify among different-size companies, different sectors, different industries, and maybe even different countries.

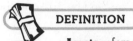

DEFINITION

Assets refers to your money. If you put that money into stocks, bonds, mutual funds, real estate, collectibles, or anything of value, those become your assets. The asset allocation you choose should be consistent with how much risk you're comfortable with. Once you determine how much you want to allocate to specific asset classes, you **diversify,** or choose a mix of investments.

Now, if you can't manage to keep track of that number of stocks, don't feel confident in picking them, or just don't have enough investment cash built up yet, you're probably better off starting with mutual funds.

Investing in individual stocks is risky; you can lose every penny of your investment. But you also have the potential to make far more money than you would by playing it safe. You will probably never see a mutual fund or bond that doubles or triples in value in a short time, but an individual stock can increase 300 percent (or more). Remember, the more risk, the more potential reward.

TIP

Stocks require more attention and monitoring than other forms of investment. You have to pay attention to what the individual company is doing to know whether you should buy it in the first place, whether to hold on to it, and for how long.

Bonds

There are two ways to invest in bonds: individual bonds and bond mutual funds. But therein lies a universe of options. Individual bonds can be issued by corporations or governments. As long as you're not expecting Armageddon any time soon, U.S. government bonds are probably the safest in the world.

There's a wide range to choose from based on type, length of term, and interest rate. For corporate bonds, the creditworthiness of the underlying company becomes important, although in bankruptcy situations, bond holders stand ahead of stockholders when it comes time to pay off, if there's any payoff at all.

Bond mutual funds collect a portfolio of bonds, acting as an average of the type of bond represented by the fund. To achieve your 40 percent investment in bonds, you can choose a collection of specific types of bonds: corporate, mortgage-backed, municipal, international, or so-called high-yield (junk). So for example, if a bond fund's objective is to offer a portfolio of high-quality corporate bonds, the fund will own a collection of bonds issued by different highly rated corporations—not just bonds from *one* highly rated corporation. Thus, you get the advantage of diversity in that segment of your bond investments.

Bond investments are generally considered to be the safer side of any collection of investments. If you buy an individual bond, your rate is guaranteed for the term of the bond (unless the bond is "called," which means cashed in early by the company or government that sold you the bond). While bond funds may offer different total return (interest + change in price) than an individual bond, they can also respond to changes in interest rates. A bond fund smooths out bond returns: it won't lock in the highest rates when interest rates fall, but you won't be stuck with a low-rate bond portfolio when interest rates rise.

Bond prices may not be much concern to you if you intend to hold an individual bond to maturity. As long as you hold on to it for the entire term, and the company doesn't go bankrupt, you will get your principal returned. However, because bond funds buy and sell individual bonds before maturity, interest rate changes can affect them more because of the effect on current prices. In general, bond funds tend to smooth out returns compared to individual bonds.

The problem with bonds is that return is generally low. High-quality bond interest rates are typically not much higher than the current inflation rate. If you bought individual bonds when overall interest rates were low, you have locked in that low interest rate for the life of your investment. If rates go up, you're stuck with it. You may be tempted by lower-quality bonds because they offer higher interest rates (in the hopes of attracting your money). However, they also offer a higher possibility of going bankrupt, so you're risking more to get that possibly better return.

Bond mutual funds can improve their total return by selling off parts of their bond portfolio when interest rates improve, but unlike individual bonds, they cannot guarantee you any specific return.

Bonds may have a place in your portfolio if you need to lower risk. But as always, that safety will come with lower reward. (See Chapter 12 for more on bonds.) The return of bonds and bond mutual funds can be expected to swing less than stocks and stock mutual funds. Their function in your portfolio is to give stability by maintaining fairly consistent value with some total return.

Mutual Funds

Mutual funds smooth out the risks of individual investments by offering built-in diversification, but they also average the return. Even the best mutual funds will never achieve the return of their best-performing individual investment, because that return will be held down by other, less stellar investments in the fund's portfolio.

On the other hand, a mutual fund is much less likely to lose every penny, as you might on one terrible investment pick.

Mutual funds are the most appealing investment choice for investors who have little initial money to invest, are inexperienced in choosing individual investments, and are looking to diversify their portfolio. For most people, they're the place where the majority of a core portfolio should be invested.

Just about every flavor and variety of investment can be accessed through the purchase of a mutual fund. Instead of investing in just one company or a handful of bonds, a mutual fund can make you an investor in dozens, hundreds, or thousands of individual investments.

Before you invest in any mutual fund, do some research to find out what the fund invests in. Fund managers try to put the best name on what they do. High-yield usually means junky investments that offer high interest or dividends because they're so risky. Growth funds sound promising—everybody likes *growth*, right? But over time, growth funds do less well than *value* funds. Be sure you know what you're investing in, and that the mutual fund you choose matches your intentions.

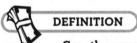

DEFINITION

Growth companies aim to increase in value by reinvesting earnings rather than by paying out dividends. Your total return comes only from increases in the price of the stock and is realized by selling it. **Value** means slow-growing or out-of-favor companies. They generally pay a dividend to attract investors. Some value companies, such as utility companies, may offer little to no growth, but high dividends. Value companies may offer both dividends and the possibility of stock price increases if the company turns around its fortunes or improves its earnings.

You can buy mutual funds that invest in large-caps, small-caps, value or growth investments, corporate bonds, international bonds, or any other segment of the larger market. You can choose a mutual fund that buys investments only in technology, health care, or energy companies. Mutual funds may include an array of company sizes and types, but all with business in a specific area.

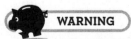

WARNING

If you feel a specific industry or sector has great potential, you may choose sector fund investments. However, by the time you know about them, the market may be shifting away. Try to avoid choosing sectors that are current "darlings."

Owning an array of investments in different sectors is one way to balance stock and bond investments for diversification.

Target Date, Balanced, Fund of Funds, and Life Strategy Funds

Four types of funds to consider are target date, balanced, fund of funds, and life strategy.

Target date funds have become increasingly popular as the default choice in workplace retirement plans. Frankly, this is because the majority of investors in these plans have no idea how to choose investments or what they're actually investing in. Target date funds give employers an easy way to nudge their employees into what can be considered a prudent choice.

Life strategy funds come in moderate, conservative, and growth categories. Life funds will usually maintain a mix based on their stated safety or risk goals. (See Chapter 8 for more on life strategy funds.)

Both target date and life strategy funds are funds of funds. That is, they are funds that purchase shares of other mutual funds, seeking to incorporate a balance of stocks, bonds, international investments, and cash (money market) in a way that offers an appropriate risk level based on the person's age or presumed date of retirement (or college entry, for college savings accounts). These funds become increasingly more conservative as they approach the "target date," meaning they begin to increase their bond and cash holdings and decrease their stock holdings. Life strategy funds will usually maintain the same mix based on their stated safety or risk goals.

Balanced funds may either invest in other funds or in individual stocks and bonds, but attempt to keep a specific balance in their holdings, for 60 percent stocks and 40 percent bonds or another selected mix. Be sure you know if the fund you select has the mix you're looking for. They don't vary much from that balance, so investors can plan that they will have approximately the same level of risk no matter who (or what age group) invests in them.

When evaluating any fund for possible investment, you should determine whether the fund is actively or passively managed. While most target date funds are passively managed, balanced and life strategy funds can sometimes be based on active management.

With *active management*, the manager of the fund uses personal judgment to select investments. He or she will have a philosophy: timing the market, choosing growth or value companies, balancing dividends with growth, or almost any possible investment philosophy.

 TIP

> Individual managers may beat the market over a period of time, but studies show that by the 25-year mark, active managers rarely beat passive management. The trick with active management is to choose a manager when they're on the way up, not after he or she is recognized by everyone as "hot."

With *passive management*, the portfolio manager tries to choose investments that will mirror a specific index. So, if the manager is managing a fund that seeks to replicate the Standard & Poors 500 (500 of the largest stocks in the United States), he or she will buy all 500 stocks, changing them only when a stock is dropped or added to the index. The mutual fund should perform nearly the same as the index it mirrors, with slightly less return to account for management fees (salaries, advertising, office expenses) that it takes to actually operate the fund.

You can't remove all risk from your investing activities, and there are some risks over which you have almost no control. But you can lessen the impact by diversifying your portfolio. You can make careful choices among different types of investments or choose a fund that will give you a collection of investments with a specific focus. Finally, you can choose a broad based fund that will collect a package of investments for you, giving you diversification with only one purchase decision. What will work best for you depends on your individual circumstances, money available, time available, and tolerance for risk versus desire for reward.

The Least You Need to Know

- Don't take any more risk than you have to in order to meet your investment goals.
- If you want a high return, you need to shoulder more risk; greater safety means a smaller return.
- In general, stocks are the most risky investment, bonds the most stable.
- Mutual funds give you a broad range of underlying investments, which may help to make them less risky than individual stock or bond investments.

Protecting Yourself with Insurance

There are two crucial aspects to increasing your wealth: finding ways to make your investments grow, and protecting yourself so that you don't lose what you have to disaster.

Nothing spells disaster like an emergency that's not covered by insurance—an experimental medical procedure, a sudden need for nursing home care, or an accident that prevents you from working. Are you covered if you have to leave your home because of a fire? Will you be reimbursed for the cost of temporary lodging or lost possessions?

In my practice many people come to me for financial advice following a catastrophic disaster. With the right insurance you can keep from having to cash in your investments to survive such crises and will be able to face them from a position of some financial security.

In This Chapter

- Ensuring your auto and homeowner's coverage is adequate
- Short- and long-term disability insurance
- The ins and outs of health insurance
- Keeping insurance costs as low as possible

Protecting Your Home and Your Possessions

One of the most basic reasons to have insurance is to protect what you have. You want to be sure you can replace your most expensive possessions if necessary and that if you accidently do something that injures another person, you are protected from litigation and liability.

Auto Insurance

If you own a car, most states require you to have insurance coverage. (New Hampshire and Virginia are the exceptions.) Insurance can be expensive, but there are a few ways to save on insurance so you'll have more cash to invest:

Choose your deductible wisely   You should only insure against what you can't afford to pay out of pocket. If you have a $500 *deductible* and file a claim for a $750 fender-bender—well, your insurance provider is probably going to consider cancelling your policy. Choose a $1,000 or higher deductible and pay that first $1,000 out of your emergency fund. (See Chapter 1 for more on establishing an emergency fund.)

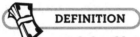

DEFINITION

A **deductible** is the amount you must pay for damages before your insurer pays its portion.

People are often advised to drop collision insurance if the vehicle is older. Be aware, however, that without collision, if your car has an accident and the insurance company determines the cost to repair is greater than the actual cash value, it'll declare it totaled without paying you anything. Even if you would be willing to pay the repair, they generally won't cover the car at all.

TIP

How much auto insurance should you have? At a minimum, you should carry enough to cover the medical expenses of victims and passengers and damage to others' property. Your insurance provider may also have its own minimum requirement, and if you purchase umbrella liability coverage to supplement your insurance, that carrier will require your auto insurance to provide a specified minimum initial coverage.

Re-quote your insurance at least every 2 years   You can easily obtain online quotes from several insurance providers. Want to stick with your current agent because he loves you and takes care of you? Have a couple of accidents and see how loyal he is. The insurance marketplace changes rapidly and is extremely competitive. Keep up with current rates.

Consider whether umbrella liability coverage would allow you to reduce the liability limits on your policy   Umbrella liability coverage is a type of insurance that provides additional protection beyond your car and homeowner's insurance. You can purchase umbrella liability coverage that will kick in after the limits on your auto and homeowner's policy have been reached. Because this type of policy is rarely used, it's generally inexpensive. Such a policy might save you some money on your auto and homeowner's premiums by lowering their liability coverage charges.

Homeowner's or Renter's Insurance

If you're paying a mortgage, your mortgage company is going to require you to have homeowner's insurance to protect their interest in your asset. However, as with auto insurance, you should requote occasionally by going online and comparing insurers. Also consider purchasing umbrella liability insurance, as mentioned earlier.

Homeowner's insurance should include the value of your dwelling, generally, not including land, which persists even if the home is destroyed. You also should have weather- or flood-related coverage if applicable, liability, relocation costs, and personal property and furniture replacement costs. This is by no means an exhaustive list, and you should seek quotes from several companies to see what's offered, at what price. Check out any professional organizations or alumni groups you may belong to, to see if they have affiliated insurance that may offer better group rates. Also, an insurance broker who represents multiple companies may be able to shop coverage for you.

If you rent, you may not feel you have anything worth insuring. I know that in my first couple of apartments, most of my stuff was junk; having someone steal it would probably have been doing me a favor! But you need renter's insurance not only to protect your belongings but for other reasons you may not have thought about, such as relocation expenses. If there were a fire, or your upstairs neighbor left the water in their sink running the entire weekend, creating Niagara Falls in your apartment, the cost of emergency relocation, hotel, eating out, and funds to move what's left and replace the rest could easily reach five figures. Renter's insurance can help cover this.

Whatever policy you have, be sure you understand the *riders*. I once reviewed a policy that had a hurricane insurance rider—in Chicago. Many riders are standard, but some carry an extra charge, and you should be certain they cover what you, personally, need and nothing more.

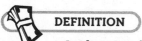 **DEFINITION**

A **rider** is an additional provision of an insurance policy covering specific situations or possessions.

Whether you own valuable musical instruments, jewelry, furs, or grannie's silver service, you should have a rider or separate policy for personal articles. Many homeowner's policies will only cover these up to a small amount (for example, $2,000), so if a burglar leaves with $25,000 worth of silverware, you've lost a pretty good chunk of your assets.

If you have possessions that exceed the usual coverage limits, you need recent purchase receipts or appraisals to establish the value of these items.

Liability Coverage

If you earn a good salary, have any investments, don't like salting your icy sidewalk, or own a dog named Cujo, you have a great big target on your back that says "Sue me." The more you assets you have, the more worthwhile someone might find suing you to be.

I recommend purchasing liability coverage to protect against this possibility. To figure up how much coverage you need, add up all your assets: home, investments, valuables (collectibles, jewelry, and so on), and car. Then estimate your future earnings. A plan that offers $300,000 in liability coverage may not sound so great once you've completed this exercise.

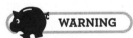 **WARNING**

> Are your retirement plans immune to legal judgments? Your workplace retirement plans are (except for IRS judgments), but the situation with Traditional and Roth IRAs is a little dicier. If you've rolled them over from an employer plan and kept them separate from other IRAs, they are probably safe. Up to $1 million of an IRA is protected in a bankruptcy, but whether it is protected in case of liability such as personal injury depends on your state's laws.

You can purchase umbrella liability coverage to supplement your auto and homeowner's policies. If your car runs into a school bus you're going to be glad for all the liability insurance coverage you have. Get enough to cover your entire net worth and potential future earnings (usually a minimum of $1,000,000). Some retirement plans offer protection from legal judgments and creditors, but for the $100 to $200 a year that umbrella liability will cost—well, get it.

Protecting Your Income

You're young and healthy and nothing is ever going to happen to you, right? Hopefully not. But if you haven't noticed yet, the theme of this chapter is "Be prepared." Protecting your income through disability insurance and life insurance is a necessity.

Disability Insurance

According to the U.S. Social Security Administration, about 1 in 4 of today's 20-year-olds will become disabled before they retire. You are nearly four times as likely to collect disability insurance than someone else is to collect on your life insurance. And the younger you are, the more likely you are to collect disability insurance.

Think you'll be covered by Social Security Disability Insurance? Well, maybe, if you can wait long enough and are disabled enough. If your workplace offers disability insurance as part of your benefits package, sign up for it. (If I worked for an employer who *didn't* offer such a policy I'd polish up my résumé.)

Often, employers will pay for *short-term disability,* but ask you to contribute for *long-term disability.* My advice is to do it. A long recovery from a car or bicycle accident, or a bout of breast cancer, and all your investments could be wiped out—with no guarantee that you won't be laid off as well. Also, check what your policy offers to be sure it covers *own occupation,* not just *any occupation.* If it's any occupation, you may want to consider obtaining some private coverage to supplement your protection.

 DEFINITION

> **Short-term disability** provides coverage for disability up to 6 months. It may include coverage for pregnancy or recovery from surgery. **Long-term disability** generally kicks in after you've been disabled for more than 6 months, and/or the disability is expected to be permanent or result in death. **Own occupation coverage** is the most comprehensive form of long-term disability and pays if you can't perform your usual occupation. **Any occupation coverage** isn't as comprehensive. It pays only if you can't perform any type of work at all.

What if you're self-employed or a stay-at-home parent? Generally, you need a recent track record of employment earnings (or a few years of self-employment earnings) to be approved for individual disability. And if you're currently working but are preparing to start a business, get an individual policy before you leave your job. For people who aren't eligible for private individual policies, there are policies that will pay you a cash sum if you suffer a heart attack, stroke, cancer, or other health issue.

They're better than nothing, and may be the only kind of insurance a self-employed worker or stay-at-home parent can get.

Life Insurance

Auto and homeowner's insurance are relatively straightforward products. Not so with life insurance. There are many variations, and most of them are designed with one goal in mind: to extract a big premium from you.

Do you need life insurance? Not everyone needs life insurance. If you have no dependents, or you have enough assets to take care of those dependents without your income, you probably don't need life insurance. Here are some questions to ask and issues to think about as you consider whether you need life insurance and, if so, how much:

First, check how much your employer provides—usually a multiple of how much you make in a year. A general rule of thumb is that you need at least five times your annual income, but insurance is dependent on a number of individual circumstances.

Do you have a nonworking spouse who could not easily go back to work? Life insurance could help support the spouse for an extended amount of time.

 TIP

Bankrate.com is a great source to check out prevailing rates on all types of bank investment products and loan charges. They also have a free calculator to estimate how much life insurance you need. While you should always take these all-purpose calculators with a grain of salt, it's a good place to start for an estimate.

Could your spouse go back to work after retraining or the kids are grown? In that case you may only need enough life insurance to cover that defined period of time.

Is your mortgage larger than your partner could pay? You may need enough life insurance to pay it off.

Do you have other debts for which anyone else is liable (joint credit card, joint car loan)? Enough insurance can pay these off. If they're yours alone, creditors will try to collect against your estate, but no estate, no collection.

If you have a child or children and worry about whether your spouse could put them through college, you might want to have enough insurance to pay for college. However, you should also consider whether they would be eligible for financial aid without insurance proceeds.

Do you have elderly parents or someone disabled who is or might become dependent on you? The money won't replace you, but it will help them get the care you would have provided.

Do you have obligations for alimony or child support? Insurance should cover those for whatever term they are ordered. Usually this will be specified in your legal settlement.

Does your retirement plan depend on both you and your partner working until retirement? You may need enough insurance to make up for your contribution.

While this is not a comprehensive list of all possible needs for insurance, it should get you thinking about your individual situation.

Obtaining life insurance   If your employer doesn't provide life insurance, or you want to supplement the insurance you have, the easiest and cheapest insurance to purchase is called *term* insurance. You choose a death benefit and a length of time during which the policy will pay if you pass away. So for example, if you make $100,000 a year and purchase term insurance for $500,000 for 25 years, you will probably get the kids through college. If you die after 23 years, your spouse would get the $500,000. If you die in the twenty-sixth year, your spouse would get nothing, but she doesn't really need it anyway because the kids have finished college and she inherits your now (hopefully larger) 401(k).

If term insurance is not offered by your employer, or the amount is not enough (sometimes you can buy add-ons), look to professional and religious organizations and membership clubs for quotes. (If any living member of your family has served in the U.S. military, you might also be able to join USAA, which provides insurance quotes and can help you find the appropriate policy.) Generally, you can find term insurance providers fairly easily. Check a site like USAA.com.

TIP

USAA (originally United Service Automobile Association) was founded in 1922 as a financial services association for U.S. military members and their families. They offer a variety of insurance and investment products. Like any financial service, they're not always the best and not always the cheapest, but if you're eligible for membership, you can get solid comparative quotes and lots of free financial advice.

There are many other types of insurance—whole life, variable life, universal life—but in my opinion you can ignore them (with three exceptions—more on this coming up). These forms of "permanent" insurance are more expensive than term, and generally offer poor returns on the "investment" compared to a diversified portfolio (insurance companies will always model their returns against low-paying investments like CDs and bonds). They also carry high fees, particularly in the early years (which is when you need coverage the most).

There are only three good reasons I can see to consider "permanent" insurance:

You consider receiving a monthly bill a good way of saving money. "Permanent" life insurance may eventually build up some value that you can borrow against or withdraw, but this is obviously not a great way to save money.

Or you know you have a family history of early onset disease (such as multiple sclerosis, early heart attack or stroke, or diabetes) that might disqualify you from insurance in the foreseeable future, when you could need it.

Or you have a net worth of more than $5 million dollars and want to insure that money is available to pay estate taxes and bury you. Insurance settlements are not taxed, so you can purchase enough insurance to pay these for your heirs and preserve the rest of the estate, no matter how long you live.

 TIP

Famous runner Jim Fixx, author of *The Complete Book of Running,* died of a heart attack while jogging at the age of 52. Many people thought it was an argument against the health benefits of running. However, his father had died of a heart attack at age 43, and Fixx had a congenitally enlarged heart. Running may have given him 9 extra years of life. He would have been a great candidate for permanent life insurance, had he been able to qualify.

Protecting Your Health

Since the Affordable Care Act (ACA), we must all have health insurance. But whether your employer provides it or you pay for it privately, a number of choices need to be made as to the options available to you.

Health

In the United States you can't go without health insurance. If your employer doesn't provide it, you must purchase it for yourself. Don't even think about investing until you have health insurance in place—nothing can cause you to lose everything as quickly as a bout of serious illness.

Some drags on how much money you have that's free to invest:

Deductibles   You must have enough money available to be able to pay the deductible. Even if you're normally healthy, if you get a multiyear illness, you could be liable for that deductible each and every year. Make sure you have a backup disaster plan. Unexpected health expenses are one of the biggest causes of bankruptcy.

TIP

Your deductible might range from a few hundred dollars to $10,000. Generally, the higher the deductible, the cheaper the price for the policy.

Noncovered expenses   Check carefully what network your policy plugs you into. Out-of-network excess charges are generally not applied to your deductible. Let's say you undergo an exam for which your doctor bills you $850 (on top of your *copay*). Your insurance only considers $150 as reasonable charges. If your doctor is in-network, he'll get paid $150, or $150 will be applied to your deductible if you haven't met it yet. If you go to an out-of-network doctor, same thing—$150 paid and $150 applied, *except* you'll still owe the out-of-network doctor the rest of the money—$700. Use an out-of-network doctor, or worse yet, a doctor who doesn't accept insurance, and you can end up paying way more than your deductible or *out-of-pocket limits*.

DEFINITION

The **copay** is the share of a bill you must pay, either as part of the payment (with the remainder applied to your deductible) or your share of medical bills after you've met your deductible. Your **out-of-pocket limit** is how much money you must pay before your insurance will pay everything. Generally, this is a limit on how much deductible plus copay you can be liable for.

FSAs and HSAs

Anything that reduces taxes puts more money in your pocket—money you can invest. An FSA (flexible spending account) or an HSA (health savings account) offers this benefit.

If you know you will be needing some type of medical care this year, or know approximately what your medical bills average per year, take advantage of your employer's FSA if one is offered. This benefit allows you to regularly deposit a sum in an account and exclude it from your income. The catch is, you must use what you put aside within the same year or lose it. So don't deduct more from your paycheck than you realistically need—or else plan to get all your dental work done at one time if the year is winding down and your account has a surplus. Another potential downside to an FSA is that the amount you can contribute is fairly low—$2,500 in 2016. If you have a big medical bill, $2,500 is not going to cover the full cost

An HSA is a different animal. You choose a health insurance plan with a high deductible. Then you open a Health Savings Account in which to deposit your contribution (up to $3,350 for an individual and $6,750 for a family for 2016) with $1,000 "catch-up" allowed if you're over 55. These contributions are deductible from gross income, and you can withdraw them tax-free to pay for deductibles, copays, prescription contact lenses, and other qualified medical expenses.

With an HSA there's no requirement that you withdraw the money in the year the bill was incurred—so you can keep those funds until you retire or need the money. If you don't withdraw the money, it grows tax-free until you do, and if you withdraw it now or in retirement for medical expenses, you don't pay any taxes on that end, either. Tax deductible going in; tax-free coming out.

HSAs are a great way to invest for tax-free returns. However, you may have to hunt around for an account that lets you invest in something besides a low-paying bank savings account. Some HSAs will allow you to maintain a minimum balance in a savings account, but transfer the rest to a brokerage account that offers a wider range of investments. Others will open the account in mutual funds, but you will have to pay a monthly or annual fee. Either option is better than a savings account.

Long-Term-Care Insurance

You may not want to picture yourself in a nursing home, but unfortunately, many people will end up needing such services. If you become so sick you can't feed yourself, get out of bed, or get dressed, and your condition is long-term or permanent, you will want to be in the nicest nursing home you can afford. And that could cost you upwards of $100,000 a year. You could require 5 to 7 years of care.

If you think Medicare will cover this possibility, it doesn't. After 100 days of care (and only if you meet stringent requirements), you must pay for yourself. If you purchase long-term-care insurance in your 50s, you probably can qualify at a reasonable price. If you wait until your 60s or later, you may develop health conditions that preclude you from qualifying, or this insurance may become prohibitively expensive. If you have a spouse, do you want them to end up older, sicker, and poorer after expending all resources on you? And what if you both need care at the same time? (It happens.)

If the potential cost doesn't convince you to purchase this insurance, know that people who can pay privately for at least 6 months to 1 year have a much better selection of care options—at home or in a facility. Often, necessary care comes with a very short window of warning—there won't be enough time to sell your house and belongings. And if someone else has to arrange and accomplish an estate sale, accessing your money can take longer.

My advice is to invest in long-term insurance if you want to have anything left in your investments account, or want to leave any sort of inheritance behind. Your children will thank you. However, you may not need to bother with long-term insurance if your net worth exceeds $3 million—you probably have enough assets to liquidate to cover your expenses. The same applies if you have no heirs and enough assets to liquidate to cover 5 to 7 years of care.

Be sure you get several quotes and understand exactly what the insurance will cover: how much per day? For how long? How long before it kicks in? (Usually you have to wait 90 to 180 days.)

 TIP

The National Association of Insurance Commissioners (NAIC) puts out a consumer guide to long-term-care insurance available for download at NAIC.org.

Long-term-care insurance is a relatively new type of insurance, and insurers are in a state of flux as to what products and benefits they offer. Be sure you understand what would be covered before you select a policy.

Insurance is needed to protect against any catastrophe for which you could not afford to pay out of your own resources, or which would diminish your resources to unacceptable levels. Ensuring you're protected against disasters also ensures that your investing program can stay on track.

The Least You Need to Know

- Protecting yourself against catastrophic expenses will keep your investment program on track.
- Auto and home insurance protects your possessions so you can maintain your lifestyle.
- Disability and life insurance protects your income for you and your dependents.
- Long-term-care insurance ensures you'll get quality supportive care when you need it, without overburdening your loved ones and wiping out all your assets to pay for it.
- FSAs and HSAs can save you money on taxes and become additional investment opportunities.

Finding Money to Invest

For many people, the biggest stash of money they will accumulate in any single account will be their workplace retirement account. Because these accounts can build up significantly over time, and may be the basis for how well-funded you will be at retirement, you should understand how these work.

In this chapter, we'll look at understanding and investing your current employer's plan, as well as survey ways to supplement your retirement savings with individual tax-sheltered accounts. Finally, we'll look at other steps you can take on your own to fund your investments.

In This Chapter

- Understanding your workplace retirement plan
- Choosing the right amount to contribute
- Surveying investment possibilities
- Supplementing your income
- Investing windfalls and savings to build wealth

An Overview of Workplace Retirement Plans

When I refer to retirement plans in this chapter, I mean *401(k)s*, *403(b)s* (nonprofits and educational institutions), *457s* (government), and other contribution and thrift savings plans. Although there are different plans depending on the type of employer you have, for the purposes of this chapter we'll classify them all simply as retirement plans.

> **DEFINITION**
>
> A **401(k)** is a retirement program offered by private industry involving contributions from the employee and (frequently) matching funds contributed by the employer. A **403(b)** is a retirement program offered by schools, universities, and (often) other nonprofits. Requirements for withdrawing the money at retirement may be slightly different, but otherwise contributions and match will be similar to a 401(k). A **457** plan is a salary-deferral plan available to government employees and some highly paid employees of private companies.

401(k)s, 403(b)s, and 457 Plans

Your workplace retirement plan is probably the best deal you're going to get in investing. Employers benefit from them too—such plans have enabled them to get rid of the old pension plans that your parents or grandparents depended on. Their "generous" *employer match* to your own savings costs them far less than providing you with a pension. If you don't contribute at all, they don't have to match anything, and since a lot of people don't, the employer is home free. *You* get to assume all the risk. If the investments you choose don't do well and don't pay you enough in retirement, well, that's *your* problem.

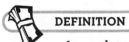

> **DEFINITION**
>
> An **employer match** is an employer's contribution to a workplace retirement fund, often based on the employee's salary or contributions to the fund.

On the other hand, you can't beat the return. If your employer contributes 3 percent of your salary, and you kick in 3 percent, you've just gotten a 100 percent return on your money.

But wait, we haven't even looked at the tax benefit. Contributions to a 401(k), 403(b), or 457 plan directly reduce your taxable income, so depending on your tax bracket, your cost to contribute (your return on investment) is that much higher. And even if your employer only matches part of your contribution, you still receive the tax benefit.

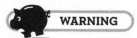

WARNING

If you or your employer contributes to a workplace retirement plan, contributions may have defaulted to a fund or predetermined mix. Don't assume your employer is looking out for your best interests; see what's "under the hood."

For many people, their 401(k) is the largest investment they will ever make.

How Much Should You Contribute?

I hope I've convinced you of the benefits of contributing to a workplace retirement plan. But how much should you contribute?

As of this writing you can contribute up to $18,000 of earnings, with an additional "catch-up" contribution of $6,000 if you're over 50. Your employer is probably not going to match these maximum-allowed contributions 100 percent, but the tax reduction alone suggests that you should do everything you can to contribute.

If your earnings are less than or equal to the maximum contribution, you can contribute up to 100 percent of your earnings—a worthwhile strategy if you can live on earnings from another source (like a spouse).

At a minimum, try to contribute enough to get the full employer match, whether it's 3 percent, 5 percent, 8 percent, or some other number. Next, as soon as possible, you want to up your contribution to at least 10 percent of salary (your retirement savings budget amount, discussed in Chapter 1). As soon as possible means once you have an emergency fund of at least $1,000 to $5,000. It does *not* mean once you've paid off your student loan, bought a house, and so on. The earlier you start contributing to retirement funding, the less you'll have to play catch-up later. In fact, if you begin in your 20s or early 30s, and keep pace with any salary increases, you may never have to worry about retirement income—you'll have enough.

If you can, try to increase your contribution to the maximum allowed by law. When you get a raise, direct at least some of it into increased contributions to your retirement plan. No one has ever sat in my office for financial planning and said they were sorry they saved too much.

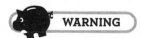

WARNING

If your salary continues to rise, 10 percent of your salary may exceed the maximum 401(k) contribution, currently $18,000 per year (plus $6,000 catch-up for those over 50). Keep saving! Even if it's not deductible, you'll probably have a lifestyle that will require that extra portfolio income potential.

If you're in a high tax bracket, the savings from salary reduction becomes more and more worthwhile. If you have limited ability to save, you should prioritize: first, contribute to the account to the maximum match. Next, perhaps choose to contribute to a Roth or traditional IRA (see "Supplementing Your Workplace Plan with IRAs"), up to your maximum entitlement—this gives you a retirement account in which you can choose your own investments and keep the costs low. After that bucket is filled, you can go back and contribute whatever you can to the workplace account.

The Drawbacks

Now that I've (hopefully) convinced you that your workplace account should be your first- and highest-priority investment, you should know the drawbacks.

First, you probably have mediocre to terrible investment options in your account. Very few workplace accounts allow you to invest in stocks or exchange-traded funds (ETFs), for example.

Second, your choices of mutual funds will be, for the most part, limited. Your employer may have chosen an account provider who offers only high-cost or poorly performing funds (at least compared to the *no-load* fund you might have purchased on your own). You're stuck with the offerings, but do everything you can to convince the powers that be to add low-cost funds in a variety of *asset classes*.

 DEFINITION

> **No-load** funds are funds sold without a sales commission. They will still have management fees, which the investment company charges to pay its staff, advertise, and handle the costs of doing business. **Load funds** are funds that charge a commission to buy or sell them, in addition to management fees. **Asset classes** are the general types of investments with similar characteristics. Stocks and bonds are the major divisions of asset classes, with smaller divisions possible, such as non-U.S. stocks, corporate bonds, government bonds, and so on.

Even with good offerings, many employees make not-so-good choices; employers have moved to making target date funds the default choice. Still, many employees have no idea what they've selected, much less what their target date fund actually invests in.

Generally, target date funds (see Chapter 4) give you a lot of diversity and offer a pretty steady performance over time—neither gaining nor losing dramatically. You pick the year you plan to retire and select the target date fund nearest that date. It will automatically become more conservative as you age. Theoretically, you make one choice and it's set for your entire career.

But that may not be right for you. If you have a large amount of money outside the retirement fund, you may be more interested in higher returns than in a fund that gets more and more conservative. If so, you can pick a target fund with a later retirement date, which will be more heavily invested in stocks. So if you think you'll be retiring in 2040 but know you will inherit some money before then, you might want to choose a 2045 or 2050 fund for the possibility of higher return.

Another drawback of workplace retirement funds is that they can have high costs. This can happen in a few ways:

- Only funds with high management costs or (worse) sales charges (loads) are offered to you.

- You may be charged a yearly fee for having the account.

If you change jobs and want to transfer your account to your new employer or an IRA, you may be socked with a huge transfer fee. Usually the charge is minimal ($0 to $25), but I've seen clients who were dinged as much as $4,000 to move their accounts.

Luckily, the federal government now requires that employees invested in private sector plans be provided with information regarding the costs of those plans. These costs should be reasonable. A fee of 1 percent or less is probably acceptable. More than that, and you should talk with your employer about getting a better plan.

 TIP

Me to client: Wow, most retirement accounts are terrible. How come yours are so good? Client: I work for a university. We have about 10 million economists as faculty. What do you think they pick for themselves? (The options were all no-load mutual funds.)

Given the tax impact and your employer match, it's still worth investing in workplace retirement funds, despite these drawbacks. But you'll need to balance your workplace portfolio with some extracurricular alternatives.

Supplementing Your Workplace Plan with IRAs

If you've maxed out your contributions and still have money to invest, or if you earn outside income, you can enhance your wealth in years to come by establishing an individual retirement account, or IRA.

These are the three types of IRAs worth considering:

- Traditional IRAs
- Roth IRAs
- SEP-IRAs

TIP

With an IRA, you're free to choose your own investments. There's nothing to prevent you from choosing a target date fund or balanced fund for your initial investments, however. You can always change your investments as you become more knowledgeable, more confident, or the amount in the account builds.

Traditional IRA

Traditional IRA contributions, like contributions to a 401(k), are deducted from your income before taxes and therefore directly reduce your taxable income. However, your income limit for deducting contributions is $61,000 (single) and $98,000 (married filing jointly). Earnings in the account grow tax-free until you begin withdrawals. Then, all withdrawals are taxed as ordinary income. You can withdraw from a traditional IRA for college expenses, medical disability, and up to $10,000 to purchase a first home, but you must pay income tax on the entire withdrawal. If you withdraw for any other reasons before 59½ you will pay tax on the entire withdrawal, plus a 10 percent penalty.

Traditional IRAs work very much like a 401(k): you contribute from your income before taxes, and the contribution reduces your taxable income. The difference is that these accounts are entirely under your control and you choose the investments. You can choose mutual funds, target date funds, bonds, cash, or individual stocks. Your contributions and all earnings grow tax-free until you withdraw them in retirement, at which point withdrawals are taxed as ordinary income.

The Feds really want you to leave this money alone until retirement, and you should. At 70½ you must begin required minimum distributions (RMD), whether you need the money or not. After all, the government has been giving you a tax break all these years, and now it's time to pay the piper. The RMD is based on your age and the value of your account on the previous December 31. Wherever your account is housed, the institution should be able to calculate your RMD. Remember, there's no obligation to spend the money; you just have to move the distribution to a taxable account and pay income tax on it.

In order for traditional IRA contributions to be tax-deductible, you must be under certain income limits. This program was originally intended to help the middle class, not help the wealthy shelter assets. You can always contribute to an IRA, it just won't be deductible (but it will still grow tax-free until retirement). You can also contribute for a nonworking spouse.

The following table lists IRA contribution limits.

	Contribution Limit	Catch-Up (Over 50)	Income Limit (Married and Covered by Plan at Work)	Income Limit (Single and Covered by Plan at Work)	Income Limit (Married, One Spouse Covered at Work)	No Coverage at Work
Traditional IRA (deductible)	$5,500 per individual	$1,000	$98,000 to $118,000 (phased out)	$61,000 to $71,000 (phased out)	$184,000 to $194,000 (phased out)	No income limit
Traditional IRA (nondeductible)	$5,500 per individual	$1,000	No limit	No limit	No limit	No limit

Roth IRA

A Roth IRA is a retirement account into which you can contribute up to $5,500 a year (currently) with an additional $1,000 catch-up contribution if you're over 50. Because you've already paid taxes on your deposit, you don't get a tax deduction up front as you do with a traditional IRA. However, earnings in the account grow tax-free, and when you retire and withdraw it, you pay no taxes on those withdrawals. You can contribute to a Roth account as long as your income is below $117,000 (single) or $184,000 (married filing jointly).

You are not legally required to make withdrawals from a Roth as you are from a traditional IRA, so you could leave the entire amount for your heirs, or begin withdrawals at any point after you turn 59½ years old. As with a traditional IRA, you can legally withdraw from a Roth for college expenses, medical disability, and to purchase a first home (up to $10,000). For any other withdrawals before 59½, you must pay a 10 percent penalty and a tax on the earnings (not on what you contributed). After 59½, you can make withdrawals at any time, as long as the account has been open for 5 years.

 TIP

A Roth can be a great place for a backup emergency fund, since you can always withdraw your own contributions. Even if you do need to tap your own contributions, you can leave the earnings to grow tax-free.

As with a traditional IRA, a Roth IRA grows tax-free, but there are several important differences. One big drawback is that you don't get a tax deduction for your contribution. It's kind of ironic, because the higher your income, the more valuable a tax deduction is to you. When your income is under the limits for a traditional IRA, you're probably going to have a harder time contributing to an IRA at all, and the tax deduction won't be as much of a benefit in a lower tax bracket. If you can't save at all without the tax deduction help, then go for the traditional IRA—it's better than not saving at all.

If you can swing it, the Roth IRA offers several advantages. You can always withdraw your principal tax-free. Once you reach 59½ (as long as the account has been open for 5 years) you can withdraw principal and earnings tax-free and penalty free. (See Chapter 17 for a discussion of how the Roth can be used for college savings.)

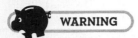 **WARNING**

> While you're holding your investments in either IRA, you don't have to worry about paying capital gains taxes. If you have a big gain on a trade, it's all sheltered. Unfortunately, if you have a big loss you don't get to deduct that either. So only pick investments that go up. (I wish.)

You can also withdraw earnings for heavy medical expenses, disability, or health insurance premiums while unemployed, without penalty. For all other withdrawals before 59½, you'll be socked with a 10 percent penalty on earnings. But remember, you can *always* withdraw your contributions, so a Roth can be a dire-emergency fund. However, you should plan to leave it untouched until you retire.

The biggest downside of a Roth is the limited amount you can contribute, and the income limits. Try to contribute as early in your career as you can, particularly if there's a possibility that your future earnings will rise too high for you to get this tax-free benefit. The Roth has higher income limits, but once you reach them, you can't contribute.

The following table lists Roth contribution limits.

	Contribution	Catch-Up Contribution (Over 50)	Income Limit (Married; Joint)	Income Limit (Single)
Roth limits	$5,500	$1,000	$184,000 to $194,000	$117,000 to $132,000

It is possible (currently) to contribute to a *nondeductible* traditional IRA if your income exceeds the limits, then immediately convert it to a Roth. However, Congress is looking at eliminating that loophole, and there are some tax implications if you also have other amounts in a traditional IRA. See an accountant before you attempt this tactic.

TIP

Some workplaces are beginning to offer the option of a Roth 401(k). You won't get any deduction for your contributions, but you won't pay any taxes in retirement. By the time you retire, there's every chance that taxes will be higher. For pretax (traditional) accounts, you will be paying tax on your contributions *and* earnings at the ordinary income rate, so you'll be taxed on all the money that's accumulated, not just what you contributed. Gulp hard and choose a Roth 401(k) if you can afford it.

The IRA world changes frequently. It's a fertile area for political manipulation, and contribution and income limits can change in any year. Be sure to check with irs.gov for each year's current rules and dollar limits.

SEP-IRA

A SEP-IRA (Simplified Employee Pension) is similar to a traditional IRA with regard to withdrawals and deductibility, but allows higher contributions—up to 25 percent of the salary you pay yourself, with a contribution cap of $53,000 (in 2016). However, these IRAs have more complex rules if you have employees. If you also contribute to a Roth or traditional IRA, the amount you can put in a SEP is reduced by that other contribution. These are great accounts for the self-employed, but you should consult your accountant or financial planner to make sure you comply with all the rules.

TIP

Self-employed people need to be sure they are figuring the cost of benefits into their pricing and income planning. Employers typically contribute 3 to 5 percent of salary to their employees' retirement funds. Be a good employer of yourself and do at least as well!

If you don't earn anything due to business expense write-offs, you can't contribute to an IRA until you actually can pay yourself something.

You owe it to yourself to consider retirement contributions a necessary business expense and benefit. Even if you can't afford to contribute the full amount, contribute something.

TIP

If you're self-employed, you should consider contributing to a retirement fund as a cost of doing business. You can open a SEP-IRA with self-employment income, which will allow you to make larger contributions than to other IRAs. You can contribute up to 25 percent of earnings to a maximum of $53,000—but there are some adjustments to these amounts, so consult an accountant to determine your specific allowable contribution.

Brokerage Accounts

At some point in your life, or for some goals, you're going to want investments you can access before retirement. Or maybe you want to retire before 59½ and would like to avoid tax penalties.

Tax-sheltered retirement plans allow your earnings to grow tax-free, but all except Roth accounts tax your withdrawals (including all gains and earnings) as ordinary income. However, capital gains in regular brokerage accounts (from selling investments) are taxed at a lower capital gains rate, currently 0 or 15 percent depending on income. If your tax bracket in retirement is higher than 15 percent, you'll pay a higher tax on 401(k) or traditional IRA withdrawals than you would by extracting the same sum from a taxable brokerage account through sales.

A brokerage account allows you to access your money at any time, and there are no minimum withdrawals as may be required by some types of retirement accounts such as your 401(k) or traditional IRA. Brokerage accounts give you the maximum flexibility for any type of savings program, but earnings are not tax-sheltered. Brokerage accounts allow you to purchase mutual funds, stocks, and bonds. (See Chapter 7 for more discussion of brokerage accounts.)

Dealing with Past Employers' Plans

If you've worked for a while, you've probably had several employers. At each of them, you may also have had a retirement plan. Generally speaking, you have three choices: leave it where it is, cash it out, or roll it over.

Leave it where it is   When you leave an employer, you aren't obligated to move your retirement account. But you might forget you have it. People lose these things. I've had plenty of clients who come to me for financial planning, and in the course of a deep dive into their files, discover (sometimes several) small employer retirement plans they've forgotten they have. Sometimes they get lucky and the investments have grown. Sometimes the money has been parked in cash and they've earned nothing for years. If you leave it where it is, be sure you keep good records and review the account on a regular basis to monitor its activity and returns.

Cash it out   The most likely thing people do when they leave an employer is to cash out the retirement funds. Please think carefully before doing this. True story: when I quit a job in my late 20s, I had $2,000 in a retirement plan. Not knowing what to do with it, I rolled it over into a mutual fund. I then proceeded to totally ignore it for another 20 years. Sure, I'd get statements in the mail but I was busy with other things, and used to just toss out the envelopes as so much more paper clutter. When I finally got interested and opened one, that $2,000 had grown to nearly $80,000. Glad I didn't spend it at the time.

If you do decide to cash it out, that's considered a distribution and you'll be liable for both income taxes and a 10 percent penalty, depending on your age.

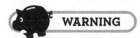

> **WARNING**
>
> Be sure you double-check the age rules for your specific retirement plan if you're considering withdrawals. For 401(k)s, you incur a penalty of 10 percent if you withdraw before 59½ (except for special circumstances). If, however, you've left the employer, you can withdraw at 55 without penalty. For traditional IRAs, you need to wait until 59½. For Roth IRAs, your contributions can be withdrawn at any time, but earnings can't be withdrawn until 59½.

Roll it over   People leaving jobs may feel they could use the money, or there's not enough there to be worthwhile, but they're not thinking about how much that money could grow if properly reinvested. My advice in most cases is to open up an IRA and roll that money over into it. You'll probably change jobs several times in your career. Keep rolling over your 401(k)s into that IRA. A self-managed IRA is going to offer you lots of opportunities to invest—in fact, it may be the first place you start to make real investment choices. Choose a low-cost brokerage firm or a mutual fund company, so you'll have maximum freedom to choose investments. Don't plunk it in a bank—you won't make any money over the long term.

Other Investing Considerations

As you progress in your investing career, and build accounts outside of the tax-sheltered ones, the best management of your accounts also means you will consider asset location—housing your investments with an eye on paying the least amount of taxes.

If you've maxed out your contributions and have money to invest in a regular old brokerage account where you can choose a variety of investments, you generally want to put the ones that pay dividends or large payouts (like bonds and real estate investment trusts, or REITs) where they will be tax-sheltered.

Investments from which you primarily profit by capital gains can be parked in taxable accounts, because capital gains are taxed at a lower rate.

And if you hope to retire early, having some money available that won't be penalized by early withdrawal (before traditional retirement age) can be a great idea.

Augmenting Your Investment Money Through Your Own Efforts

The simple truth about accumulating investment money is that you have to save (or earn) more, spend less, and wisely invest the difference. You can also help yourself by selling any assets you aren't using, getting a part-time job, and being prepared to deal with windfalls.

Selling Your Junk

Do you have unused or excess assets? That's otherwise known as junk. Get rid of it—learn to use eBay, craigslist, hold a yard sale, trade it off to friends. Even a few hundred dollars can help you begin your investing program. Not only can you scare up some capital, selling off your unwanted possessions can also show you the sins of your ways. If it slows down your spending and causes you to more carefully consider future purchases, all the better. Remember, the $100 you spent on that thing you no longer want could have doubled in value as an investment.

Side Income and Part-Time Gigs

I'm a big fan of part-time gigs. They're a great way of investing yourself in something with potential. Most of us waste plenty of time watching TV or reading Facebook—time that could make us some money. Can you think of an idea or business in which you could make $500 to $1,000 a month by working, say, two evenings a week and 4 to 6 hours on a weekend? Maybe not easy, but doable.

It can be a no-brainer type of job, or you can use that time to try out and grow a business idea that might allow you to quit your job someday. As long as you pick something that doesn't require a lot of money up front, it's almost all upside. And if you ever get fired, at least you have some money coming in. Just don't use the extra to, er, enhance your lifestyle. Generating an extra $6,000 to $12,000 won't support you, but it's a pretty nice chunk of change to build your investments.

TIP

Consider easing into retirement. A part-time job, even one you would not have considered when working in your career, can provide supplemental cash. You might be able to stave off withdrawals from your investments, allowing them to grow a little longer. Once the vacations are taken and the repairs on the house completed, many retired people find themselves at loose ends and lonely. A little job can help a lot.

Money from Windfalls

People generally have one of two reactions to big windfalls: I can spend it (all) on something I always wanted, *or* I can't spend a penny of this because I'll never get this much money again.

I'll lean toward the second as my preference, but it doesn't really have to be either. When you get any amount of money, ask yourself what it can do for the plan you've developed. If your goal is to buy a house, and this will get you there, I give you my permission. In debt? Put at least some of it to paying it down. Or let it give you a jump on the long-term investment program you've planned, and maybe you can retire early, or at least have the choice. (See Chapter 19 for more on dealing with windfalls.)

Gifts, Rebates, Refunds, and Other Relatively Small Amounts

Work your plan. You can put the money into your vacation fund, your get-a-new-bike fund, or whatever. Even if it's so small that all it will do is take you out to dinner, choose a cheaper place and spend only half. Remember, wealth isn't what flows through your fingers; it's what you hold on to.

Settlements

Depends on what kind—if you've been injured and it's a big one, they're probably going to want to pay it out in structured payments. You need professional accounting and financial planning help before you agree to anything.

But what if it's a smaller settlement—maybe a couple thousand from a complaint about a product that gave you a minor injury? I really want you to save this once you pay off any medical or legal costs. It's money you never expected to have anyway. Luck has put it in your hands, now invest it and turn it into an even bigger bonanza. You've just received a mini-endowment of your investment portfolio.

Inheritances

This, along with lottery winnings, may be the most difficult kind of money for people to manage. For one thing, since you didn't earn it through your own efforts, you'll spend a lot of time telling yourself you'll never get it again, and that can make you fearful to do any investing at all.

The next problem is that it may be more money than you've ever seen before, and you may not feel experienced enough to make investing decisions with so much. There's absolutely no harm in going slow. Better to forgo some short-term gain than plunge in and take big losses. See Chapter 7 for ideas on where to park it while you're thinking things through.

Finally, you may have a sentimental attachment to the investments Dad or Grandma purchased. Stop! Investments have no sentimental value. The investments don't care anything about you. And any single investment isn't a good one forever.

Whenever you can, attempt to prioritize savings into tax-deferred or tax-free accounts like your 401(k), a traditional IRA, or a Roth IRA. Well-funded retirement accounts are the basis for your future retirement income and the underpinning for financial security. But to improve your wealth, build investments beyond retirement accounts. Try to hold on to as much as you can, and put it to work for you in your investment plan.

The Least You Need to Know

- Contribute enough to your workplace retirement account to get the employer match.
- Contribute as much as you can afford to tax-favored retirement accounts, up to their legal maximum.
- If you're self-employed or have side income, establish a retirement plan—you owe it to yourself.
- Use strategies to earn and save more and spend less.
- Try to hold on to as much of a windfall as you possibly can. Don't rush into investing it, but don't let it sit idle forever.

Where to Save Your Money While Planning

When interest rates are low, people hate to save money they could be investing—their money isn't increasing in value. But one thing their money *isn't* doing in a simple savings account is good: it isn't *decreasing* in value, which is easy to do with a bad investment.

Keeping some money in cash—meaning in a checking account, savings account, or money market account—allows you to have "dry powder," so when the market offers you an opportunity to bag some big game, you'll be ready to fire that musket. But where should you stash your war chest? Of course, you also need somewhere to store your emergency fund (at least 3 to 6 months' worth of emergency cash).

In This Chapter

- Keeping your investment or emergency fund safe while you build your account
- The risks and protections of various accounts
- Which savings accounts earn more
- What you trade off with various savings accounts

In this chapter, we'll look at the different ways you can save money for quick access—regardless of what you want to do with it—and examine the pros and cons of each.

Saving in Your Mattress

Keeping cash, precious metals, or gems on hand is not an investment; it's the ultimate disaster prevention. If the government collapses, or you have to leave the country quickly, or you're trying to hide your wealth from someone, you might consider keeping a stash—maybe those gold coins—at home. But keeping cash, precious metals, or gems on hand is not without serious risks. Apart from the fact that you won't be earning interest on your money, it's subject to other risks. If you're burglarized, have to evacuate ahead of a hurricane or other disaster, or have a fire, your money can disappear instantly. If it's a significant amount, and you or your heirs eventually bring it into a bank or investment house—well, you may have some explaining to do.

A bank safety deposit box is a safer choice, but for investments such as jewelry or art that you may actually want to see or use in the meantime, easy access is a problem. (If events occur that make accessing your gold coins necessary, you're probably not going to be able to get into the bank anyway.)

Please don't keep stock certificates at home or anywhere else. Most companies no longer issue actual paper certificates; it's all electronic now. But you may have inherited some of these ornate beauties from long ago. Just know that stock certificates legally belong to the person who has them in their hands, so if you're burglarized, they're now somebody else's unless you're registered as the owner, have copies of the certificates, or can prove that you owned them.

Many certificates become worthless—the company merges or gets bought out and the certificates must be turned in during a specific period. Unless you monitor this kind of activity very closely, all you'll have is a very pretty relic. If you have some sentimental attachment to your certificates, make a copy and frame one, and bring the originals into a brokerage, where they will be held in the *street name*.

 **DEFINITION**

Street name is used when securities are held electronically at a stock brokerage, custodian, or bank.

If you do want to keep some cash on hand for emergencies, keep a small amount where you can grab it in a hurry.

The Necessity of Banks

You're probably going to need the services of a bank. Banks offer one advantage that no other investment home does: your money is insured up to $250,000. Even if the bank goes bust, the Federal Deposit Insurance Corporation (FDIC) guarantees you will get your money back.

Two types of accounts you will need are checking and savings accounts. You might also want to open a special savings account for money you're saving to invest.

Checking Accounts

Your checking account is for paying bills. But you can also use it to help with savings by setting up an automatic transfer from checking to savings every month. When that withdrawal happens just like any other bill, you're more likely to meet your savings goal.

WARNING

Don't keep either your emergency fund (3 months' worth of expenses) or your investment-building savings in your checking account. It's just too tempting to tap it to cover spending.

Savings Accounts

In addition to a checking account, banks will offer you a variety of savings accounts. While interest rates are low, the *returns* on these accounts are usually dismal, but they're as safe an investment as you can get. Remember the relationship between risk and return? Absolutely safe equals low return.

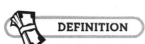

DEFINITION

Return is the money you make from your investments. It can be interest, dividends, or capital gains (money you make from selling your investment). Some investments offer a return only in the form of interest (think bank accounts) or dividends. Some investments have a combination of dividends or interest plus increase in price, referred to as *total return*. If a stock pays a 2 percent dividend and goes up 6 percent in price, you have a total return of 8 percent.

Safety is one advantage in saving at a bank. The other is immediate accessibility. You can walk into a bank any day of the week (except maybe Sunday) and access your money. For many banks with online account services, you can instantly transfer money from a savings account to checking on your computer or cell phone, without having to go into the bank physically.

I recommend you consider a bank as a good place for your emergency fund. This is a fund you want to be able to access on very short notice, and from which you could withdraw actual paper money if necessary. (See Chapter 1 for more on emergency funds.)

Banks will generally offer you a plain vanilla savings account with a very low interest rate. If you're willing to keep a higher, defined balance in the account, you may be offered a slightly better rate. Willing to lock up your money for 3 months, a year, 5 years, or somewhere along that timeline? The longer you guarantee to leave it there, technically purchasing certificates of deposit (CDs), the more interest they will pay you. If, however, you need your money unexpectedly and have to cash in the CD, you will generally lose all your interest and will probably be charged a penalty as well.

Investment-Building Accounts

Consider keeping a separate account for the money you're squirreling away for investing.

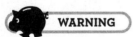

WARNING

Banks only insure you up to $250,000 per individual—the sum of all your accounts in that bank. If you inherit money or sell a house—nice problem to have—distribute the money across several banks so no one bank is holding more than $250,000.

Internet Banks

Internet banks are a relatively new phenomenon. Because they have lower operating expenses, they can offer higher interest rates on savings. Not a lot higher (maybe ½ to ¾ percent), but if you just can't stand to see your funds earning practically nothing, they may be a good option for half of your emergency fund or a place for your soon-to-be invested account. For safety's sake be sure that the internet bank is insured by the FDIC.

Besides paying a bit more interest, internet banks seem to cultivate a hip image. Some of them offer an option to set up separate "sub accounts" for "estimated taxes," "vacation," "investment-building," or "house down payment." It's another way of organizing your saving behavior, and a good one.

Any disadvantages to internet banks? The main one is it can take a little while to get your money—usually about 3 business days. Not all that long if you want to access your investment-building account, but if you need money from your emergency account, not so good.

For example, one lovely Saturday morning a huge tree fell across my sidewalk and front entry and into the street (just missing my neighbor's house, thank heavens). My emergency fund at the time was at an internet bank and I needed the money in my checking account *immediately*. If the money had been in my local bank, I could have transferred it to checking, but instead I had to wait several days to see the funds appear. Luckily the arborist who took care of the situation was patient and could wait a few days to be paid.

I no longer use an internet bank for emergency funds but prefer neighborhood banks. I like the idea that they are controlled by and are investing in the local community, and if I ever need a loan, there's a person to talk to who may have a bit more flexibility in evaluating my worthiness. With an internet bank or one of the big banks, you're part of a formula, so it's all much more impersonal.

 TIP

Check to see if the banks you're considering offer automatic transfers from checking to savings. The less you touch your money, the more likely you are to hold on to it. Also, see if you can deposit checks by scanning them on your cell phone—you'll cut down on your trips to the bank. And read emails about new services with healthy skepticism—they usually mean new fees.

Credit Unions

Something that looks like a bank and quacks like a bank, but isn't a bank, may be a credit union. These are nonprofit financial institutions that return their profits to their shareholders in the form of slightly higher interest rates on savings. Many people like to use them as a way of being more socially responsible, since they invest in the local community and are owned by local shareholders (you!).

It's well worth checking them out if you think you might need a loan anytime soon, because they can be a bit more flexible for their members. And that's the catch—you have to be a member. Credit unions require you to be a member of a group: a specific religious organization, a specific employer, professional association, or even that you live in a specific area.

If you're interested, look around at the membership requirements of the ones in your area—chances are you'll find one you can join.

Your deposits (technically, shares) at a credit union are insured by the National Credit Union Insurance Fund up to $250,000 per individual.

Mutual Fund Companies and Brokerage Houses

Everyone wants to make it easy for you to give them money. Mutual fund companies and brokerage houses will open an account for you in a variety of *money market funds* you can use as savings or checking accounts.

You can choose funds that invest broadly in short-term investments, or ones that invest only in U.S. government *securities* (like short-term treasury bonds), or ones that invest only in tax-free securities. When interest rates are low, the choice between taxable and tax-free may not make much difference, but when interest rates are higher, tax-free securities may give you a better after-tax return if you're in a high tax bracket.

DEFINITION

A **money market fund** is a fund that invests in short-term bonds and other debt securities. When you invest in the money market fund, your deposits earn interest based on the market rate of those securities. Each share generally has a constant value of $1. **Securities** are any financial instrument that gives you ownership in a publicly traded corporation (stocks), show that you are a creditor of government or a corporation (bonds) or have a future right (options).

It's important to note that money market funds (or any mutual funds or stock investments) are *not* insured and in the event of a market collapse you may not get your money back. Also, although only two money market funds have (so far) ever "broken the buck"—share value dropped below $1—there's no guarantee that it can't happen.

WARNING

Beware of offers you get for "private banking." You'll pay high brokerage commissions or top-of-market managed account fees. If you decide you do want private banking services, first check out whether your "private banker" is a fiduciary (legally required to act in your best interests), and whether they will construct your model portfolio with any no-load (no-fee) mutual funds from companies other than ones they own.

The Securities Investor Protection Corporation (SIPC) guarantees against the loss of securities should the firm fold. However, it does not guarantee loss of value—your securities can lose value or become worthless, but you will still be guaranteed ownership. Be sure your investment custodian is covered by SIPC. And keep an eye on what's going on in your account; SIPC does not protect against fraud or identity theft. On the other hand, money market funds are regarded as very safe, based on the type of securities they invest in—short term and usually government based.

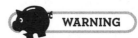 **WARNING**

If you invest in a money market fund as a holding pen for future investment funds, keep your eye on the news. There's interest in passing new laws to prevent instant withdrawals or require higher minimums to prevent "run-on-the-bank" problems caused by people fleeing to the safety of cash in the wake of bad economic news.

You could build up your investment account at a mutual fund or brokerage where you intend to invest in the future. You will be able to make transfers and purchases easily when you're ready. However, you should check out the minimum deposit necessary; some money market accounts can be opened with as little as $500, but others require $3,000 or more. And if you have other investments with the same company, it may permit you to have a lower balance as time goes on.

If you begin investing in other mutual funds or stocks with the same investment house, the institution will generally open a money market fund for you as a "sweep" or "settlement" account. When you sell an investment, the proceeds will be swept into the money market. When you purchase, funds will be tapped out of the money market.

If you have an investment that pays dividends, or a mutual fund that pays capital gains at some point during the year, you can choose to have those received as cash and deposited in the account, where you can write checks to yourself or your creditors, or hold the money for future investments. If you're depending on your investments for income (if you're retired, for example) rather than primarily for building wealth, you can write yourself a "paycheck" from the money market fund.

 TIP

If you have an investment that pays dividends, or pays out capital gains (usually at the end of the year), you can choose to have the dividends reinvested in the same investment, buying more shares. Those extra shares will then earn dividends. Over time, you'll see a better buildup of value than if you took the proceeds in cash, as long as the investment does not decrease in value.

Generally a mutual fund may require that a check be written for a minimum amount (often $250) and that deposits coming from outside also meet a minimum. This does not apply to deposits of dividends, and may also be waived if you've set up an auto-deposit directly from a checking account, which you should consider to automatically save your goal amount.

Some brokerage houses may also offer you a debit card or low-cost credit card as a perk for the account. From time to time some offer a cash bonus or even travel or mileage points if you deposit a certain amount and keep it on deposit for a length of time. If this is important to you, you should consider the benefits that are offered, but be careful that the value offered is worth the strictures on your account activity.

> **TIP**
>
> Many mutual fund companies offer free webinars, white papers, literature, and other education to teach you about different kinds of investments. Sure, they're trying to sell you something, but if you take it with a grain of salt you can learn a lot.

Like banks, brokerage houses can be internet-only or have physical locations. (Most mutual fund companies have only a few or no locations, with the exception of Fidelity.) However, any brokerage with a walk-in office (even the lower-cost ones like Scottrade or Charles Schwab) are doing it as much for their convenience of selling you something as for your convenience. Also, physical locations drive up costs, and guess who ultimately pays those costs? Online-only services will have plenty of people available by phone to walk you through any forms, assist in fixing difficulties, and answer questions.

Ironically, many investment forms will require you to get a *signature guarantee*, so you'll probably need to go back to your bank, anyway.

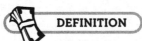

> **DEFINITION**
>
> A **signature guarantee** is when the bank guarantees your signature. They are corroborating that you are who you claim to be (which usually requires that you have an account at that bank).

Other Places to Store Cash

From time to time I get a client who can't bear the idea of "all that money" earning, essentially, nothing. If you're keeping more than 3 months' worth of expenses, and you're willing to take some risk, you might consider short-term bond mutual funds or stable value funds.

Short-Term Bond Mutual Funds

This type of fund invests in bonds with a term of 3 months or less, which means they pay pretty close to what a money market fund pays. However, they do *yield* slightly more. For example, if an internet bank is paying 1 percent interest on savings, a short-term bond fund might yield 1.35 percent.

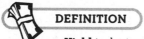

> **DEFINITION**
>
> **Yield** is the interest or dividends paid on a security.

Sounds good, right? Well, we need to remember the concept of total return (see above). Unlike a money market fund, a mutual fund doesn't maintain a constant share price. So let's say you invested your money in a short-term bond fund at a per share price of $10, expecting to get dividends of 13.5¢ per year. But the market share price drops to $9 per share. So you've lost 10 percent and your total return would now be a loss of 8.65 percent. That yield isn't looking quite as good, right?

In any bond investment, the bond price tends to move the opposite way from the yield (see Chapter 12 for a more in-depth discussion). So if the share price is high, the yield will be low. If the share price drops, the yield will go up. This is why bonds tend to maintain overall steadiness, or at least don't vary as much as stocks—price and yield tend to balance each other to keep total return fairly steady. However, depending on when you invest and what the market does after you invest, your return can vary.

In real time, short-term bond funds tend to vary less—if the median price of a share is $10, you're more likely to see it range up or down 20¢. If you plan on leaving it parked for a long but undefined period of time, eventually the dividends paid will build up and smooth over the price variation. But you're taking some small risk for that slightly smaller possible reward.

Short-term bond funds do not have check-writing available. You must sell shares to get your money. The sale needs to settle, which means your money won't be available for about 3 to 5 business days. Then, you will need to transfer the money to your bank, or write a check from your money market account. It can take much more time to access your money from a short-term bond fund than other types of emergency funds.

Stable Value Funds

The other option for investing cash is generally only available in some workplace retirement funds: the so-called stable value fund. These are mutual funds with a guaranteed (by the fund company, not any government agency) minimum (low) level interest rate ranging from about 2 percent to around 3.5 percent. People have piled into them because stable sounds good, right?

However, as with all low-return investments, you're missing out on the possibility of higher return. If you're very near retirement, this can be a place to put your first 2 to 5 years of retirement cash needs (so you can withdraw it with some certainty of how much is there), but because they are currently only available in retirement accounts (and some college savings accounts), they're probably not a viable investment for most cash-need purposes. If you're far from retirement, you should select a better investment to receive your contributions.

Managing your cash, whether for emergencies or to build up money for investing, has a goal of being available on short notice. It's money you can't afford to risk because you need the full amount to be stable, so you give up the possibility of much growth through return to have it available as needed. Sure, you prefer higher earnings—we all do—but your cash is your insurance policy to protect your lifestyle and your ability to make investments once this foundation is in place.

The Least You Need to Know

- There is no perfect or absolutely safe investment—any place you put your money carries some risk.
- Banks and credit unions offer insurance for your principal.
- Internet banks may offer you a slightly higher rate on savings, but accessing your money takes longer.
- Money invested with a brokerage or insurance company should have insurance against fraud, but you aren't protected from market loss.
- Even if your principal is safe in a money market fund, you can lose money to low-return investments because of inflation.

Planning Your Investment Strategy

In this part we look at how to choose investments. We'll consider the broad categories of investments, and how much of your money should be devoted to different categories. You'll understand the different types of investments available to you, and what benefits and pitfalls each offers. You'll learn about different methods people use to select investments with the best potential of success.

We'll discuss how to diversify to help lessen risks to your portfolio no matter what the market does. Selecting and keeping a balance of diversified investments should help improve your overall long-term return.

We'll also discuss how to select an adviser if you need input or a second opinion. You'll learn what the qualifications are of specific types of professionals, and what kind of help you might receive from each.

Balancing Risk by Diversifying

What actually determines how well your investments do? Your brilliant selections? Sorry, no. According to researchers, more than 90 percent of your return is determined by your asset allocation policy. Asset allocation means how you choose to distribute your investments among various investment types in order to balance risk and reward. In this chapter, we'll look at how you might allocate your investments to achieve the highest return you can while still being able to sleep nights.

In This Chapter

- How to allocate your money
- Different kinds of investments to balance risk with reward
- Characteristics and risks of investment categories
- Regularly reviewing your investments
- Buying and selling

Stocks and Bonds: The Basic Asset Allocation Decision

The most fundamental choice you will make as an investor is how you split investments between stocks and bonds (or mutual funds that contain one, the other, or both). The stronger your desire to make the most money possible, the more you should favor stock-based investments. The stronger your desire to protect your principal, the more you should tilt toward bonds or bond funds (or cash).

Stocks: Risk Versus Reward

Stock investments over a long period have always returned more than bonds. During the twentieth century, stocks averaged an annualized return of 10.4 percent. That doesn't mean they made that much every year: some years had extraordinary gains and some years had losses. But over time they've beaten inflation soundly. Inflation over this time period has averaged roughly 3 percent (again, with wide variations by year).

How much variation you can take, for how long, is key to your tolerance for investing in the stock arena. Let's use the S&P 500 as a proxy for "the market." Could you tolerate a loss of .63 percent for a decade (1930s) for a possible gain of 19.28 percent (1950s)? Maybe that sounds pretty easy, but what about a loss in 7 months of 54 percent (September 2008 to March 2009), then a gain of 200 percent (March 2009 to August 2015)? If you have long time horizons, you might be able to sit out such downturns or regard them as stocks-on-sale in bad times, but what if you planned to begin your retirement in September 2008?

For most of us, the most panicky period in recent memory was indeed 2008–2009. During that period, you would even have lost money in bonds—they fell about 8.7 percent. Not great, but a lot easier to survive than a 54 percent drop.

Let's say you had $20,000 invested in the market. Here's what would have happened to your money (theoretically), in that period (September 16, 2008 to March 6, 2009).

Percent in Stocks	Percent in Bonds	Amount of Loss	Percent of Loss	Remaining from $20,000 Original Investment
100 percent	0 percent	$10,800	54 percent	$9,200
0 percent	100 percent	$1,740	8.7 percent	$18,260
50 percent	50 percent	$6,270	31.35 percent	$13,730

Bonds are starting to look a little better, right? In fact, cash would have been even better—you wouldn't have lost anything. Nevertheless, it's easy to see from the table that bonds had a protective effect on a portfolio when the stock market was tanking, and if you'd had a mix of stocks and bonds, even in the worst of times, you would have lost less than if you owned an entire portfolio of stocks. Before you rush out and buy only bond investments, however, take a look at this chart for the next 6 months after the crash (March 6, 2009 to September 16, 2009) and how your $20,000 might have fared.

Percent in Stocks	Percent in Bonds	Amount of Gain	Percent of Gain	Remaining
100 percent	0 percent	$11,687	58 percent	$31,687
0 percent	100 percent	$2,470	12.4 percent	$22,470
50 percent	50 percent	$7,078	35.2 percent	$27,078

Now, you're rushing for the stock market, right? In an up market, you can see the balancing effect of bonds, but also that they are a drag on returns.

TIP

In 1952, Harry Markowitz postulated that there is an "efficient frontier"—that for every degree of risk there is an expectation of greater return, and conversely, for greater safety there is lower expected return. After a certain level of risk is achieved, however, the results begin to flatten out, and taking more risk does not achieve more reward. Markowitz's work is considered a foundation of modern portfolio theory.

While the market in stocks can swing wildly, in the period 1928-2015, the market has been in negative territory only 23 years. So, not only are you likely to make money over the long haul because of higher returns of stocks over bonds, but the majority of the time, the stock market goes up.

The Pros and Cons of Bonds

Bond investments carry another risk—they barely exceed inflation. Here, bond mutual funds and individual bonds can differ. With an individual bond you're locked into the rate you purchased. If you bought at a high interest rate, great, but if you bought at a low interest rate, the return may not even keep up with inflation.

Let's step into my time machine once again. Back during President Carter's term, inflation averaged about 10.4 percent and my first mortgage rate was about 18 percent. Bonds at the time were paying about 12 percent, but many people were happy to keep their dough in money market funds or CDs, which were paying even more. If, at the time, you were the owner of a 30-year bond paying 7 percent, you were really suffering.

In contrast, I inherited a 30-year bond from my dad that he bought in 1997 paying 7.8 percent—in today's low-rate environment, he looks like a genius. Today, 30-year Treasuries are paying about 2.68 percent. (The one I have is lower rated.)

On average, bonds have returned 5 or 6 percent per year. If you subtract out an average inflation rate (let's use 3 percent), you may do at least twice as well with stocks as bonds over the long term, and stocks are going to beat inflation, so your wealth and spending power will actually go up, not just keep pace (or fall behind). Nothing is guaranteed, of course.

Combining Stocks and Bonds Based on Your Age

Maybe you're convinced you should combine stocks and bonds as an approach to investing, but how much of each? There are some rules of thumb you hear all the time:

Your age in bonds:

- At 30, 30 percent in bonds
- At 60, 60 percent in bonds

Your age in stocks:

- At 30, 70 percent in stocks
- At 60, 40 percent in stocks

As you can see, they complement each other—and in my opinion, they're too conservative for many people.

Let's say you need your portfolio to last for 30 years—a decent estimate of the length of a long-lived person's retirement. Studies have indicated that a safe withdrawal rate from that portfolio is about 4 percent or a tiny bit more. But that is only if the portfolio is invested at least 50 percent in stocks, because the portfolio has to make enough over a long period of time to keep up with inflation, weather bad markets, and still allow you to begin by withdrawing 4 percent (plus increases for inflation in subsequent years). A portfolio predominantly composed of bonds isn't going to keep pace, and you will, therefore, need a much more diverse portfolio or a smaller withdrawal rate.

In your 20s and 30s, you're in it for the long haul. Depending on your personality and risk tolerance, and your goals, you may want to invest in stocks 100 percent. If you're looking to build wealth over 20 or 30 years, or you're saving for college and your future student is an infant, you have time to achieve much higher returns by accepting more risk. So what if you lose 50 percent? It might be heart-stopping the first time it happens, but over the course of 20 years (especially since you're going to continue contributing to savings, right?), you'll make it back.

If, on the other hand, you're trying to build up enough money for a house down payment in 5 years, you may want a less risky asset allocation (say, 60 percent stocks and 40 percent bonds). That way, there's a good chance the money will have enough time to grow, but also that most of it will still be there in the event of a downturn right when you hope to buy the house.

Let's look at the other end of the age range. A 60-year-old with no other funds but investments (and a low Social Security payment) might choose a much more conservative asset allocation—perhaps 50/50 or even a 40/60 tilt toward bonds. You can't afford to lose very much, but you still need enough of a return to (at least) keep pace with inflation and survive market downturns. But let's say you have a high Social Security payment, a paid-off house, long-term-care insurance, and maybe even a pension (or have purchased an annuity). You can take a little more risk in the hope of having a little more spending power in the future.

TIP

Often people recommend an extremely conservative approach (say, 70 percent bonds) for the very elderly, but I think an argument can be made against that. If a person is 85 years old and has enough money to last for their foreseeable lifespan, maybe their future investments are not really for themselves, but for their heirs. In that case, their investments could be a little more aggressive to build some worth for their heirs or charity.

Bottom line—your asset allocation is going to be highly dependent on your circumstances as well as your age, and what mix will allow you to sleep at night and not panic when the market dips profoundly. Your asset allocation should be set after some thought, self-examination, and possibly taking a risk tolerance quiz or two (see Chapter 4). You should consider your age and how long it would take for you to recover in the event of a market downturn.

Further Diversifying Your Assets

Okay, so you've figured out how much you're comfortable allocating to stocks and how much to bonds. To accomplish your stock/bond allocation, you could choose two mutual funds—a total stock market fund and a total bond market fund—and put your money in them according to the percentage you established. But you could also choose mutual funds with preselected asset allocations that could accomplish your investing goals.

Balanced Funds

Balanced funds offer a predetermined percentage of assets allocated to stocks and bonds, often 60 percent stocks and 40 percent bonds. Of course, this ratio can vary based on the market and manager decisions; some markets and some managers will alter the mix to 65/35 or another ratio.

Some balanced funds are *funds of funds* and some are invested in individual securities based on what the fund manager believes will perform best in the given market.

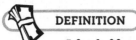

> **DEFINITION**
>
> **A fund of funds** is a mutual fund whose investment holdings are made up of other funds—stock mutual funds, bond funds, international funds, and so on. Most target date funds, life strategy funds, and college 529 plans (see Chapter 17) are funds of funds. You can also purchase a fund of funds outright (outside of retirement plans).

Life Strategy Funds

A third option you can choose with preselected asset allocation is a life strategy fund. These funds are generally labeled "growth" (these are the most aggressive and emphasize stocks with capital gains); "moderate" (these provide a mix of stocks and bonds, with some emphasis on dividend-paying stocks); and "conservative" (these emphasize bonds and safe, dividend-paying stocks).

Target Date Funds

Finally, you can choose a target date fund, which will allocate everything for you based on when you want to retire, and put all your money in it. These can work quite well as a default choice (for example, in your 401[k]), give you quite a bit of diversification, and pick your asset allocation for you. As long as you're comfortable with the current mix, and want your investments to become more conservative as you get older (or your child nears college entry), these are the one-stop shop they're designed to be.

You should look at what's in them, though, to understand what asset allocation has been selected for your age bracket. If you want to be more conservative, pick a date earlier than your retirement; if you want to be more aggressive, pick a date farther out.

The following table shows asset allocation mixes for a sample target date fund.

Target Date	U.S. Stocks	U.S. Bonds	International Stocks	International Bonds	Cash/Short-Term Securities
2020	35.16 percent	28.26 percent	23.37 percent	12.08 percent	1.1
2030	44.67 percent	18.26 percent	29.19 percent	7.82 percent	—
2040	53.23 percent	7.83 percent	35.48 percent	3.35 percent	—

Note: Selections don't all add up to exactly 100 percent because the remainder is diversified into smaller asset picks.

If you look at the mix in the target date fund, you'll see that it's sliced and diced into seemingly more categories than we've discussed so far. Look closer, however, and you'll see that we're still talking about stocks and bonds, but in order to diversify the portfolio's assets, the fund has added international investments to the mix.

Choosing Individual Investment Types

With all of these premade mutual fund options available, why would you want to select your own investments? There are some good reasons.

In any market, some types of investments do better than others. If you have one fund, it's going to average the market somewhat, since the returns of U.S., international, and bond markets will combine to produce the overall return. If you have several and need to withdraw funds, you can choose to withdraw from the ones that are up, and leave the others alone until (hopefully) they recover.

Some types of investments return higher amounts over long periods. For example, small companies tend to increase more over time than do large companies. If you're willing to tolerate greater risk, you may want to have a larger percentage of small-caps in your portfolio; total stock market funds emphasize large-caps. (See Chapter 4 for a discussion of small-, mid-, and large-caps.)

Conversely, you can reduce the risk in a portfolio by spreading your money among different types of investments, especially if they move opposite to each other (that is, have negative or weak *correlation*), so that some always go up while others go down.

You may want to diversify by owning some stocks and some mutual funds. Generally it's easier to research and choose large-cap U.S. stocks than, say, small-cap emerging market companies. You might pick some individual securities and buy mutual funds for ones you can't easily access.

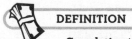

> **DEFINITION**
>
> **Correlation** is a measure of how much different investments move in the same way (positive correlation) or opposite to each other (negative correlation). A perfect positive correlation would be +1; a perfect negative correlation would be -1. A correlation of 0 means that two investments move randomly, with no relation to each other. Since so many investments have some correlation, diversification is usually considered to be achieved with a correlation of .5 or less. Correlations may change over time.

So let's drill down further and talk about diversification. Simply put, to diversify your portfolio within asset classes is to divide those asset classes into smaller subgroups.

Diversifying Your Investments

Perhaps the most popular approach to diversifying your portfolio is to diversify based on size and location (location meaning in or outside the United States). So we might have the following:

U.S. stocks:

- Large-cap: greater than $10 billion market capitalization (Some large-caps are referred to as mega-cap if their cap is more than $100 billion.)

- Mid-cap: $2 billion to $10 billion market capitalization

- Small-cap: less than $2 billion market capitalization

All of these can be divided by whether they emphasize growth, value, or a mix.

International stocks:

- Developed markets (Western Europe, Japan, Australia, and New Zealand): These stocks can be subdivided by Europe and Pacific, by size, and so on. Total international funds will generally emphasize developed countries.

- Emerging markets (generally include Brazil, Russia, India, and China as well as other South American, Asian, and some Middle Eastern and Eastern European countries): These can be further subdivided into specific countries or regions.

- Frontier markets (countries in Africa, some Asian countries): In general these are countries with limited industry; low per capita income; the possibility of political turmoil; questionable accounting standards; and courts and systems of law that may not be well established.

Alternative investments:

These are segments of the market that perform differently from their type of stock capitalization or operate quite differently from stocks. This category includes the following:

- Natural resources (mining, precious metals companies, basic materials such as forest products and chemicals, gas and oil producers, and so on)

- Real estate investment trusts, or REITs (A REIT is a share in a partnership that owns a property or collection of properties.)

- Commodities—generally *futures contracts* on coffee, pork bellies, barrels of oil, and any other actual, physical thing purchased by industries (These differ from natural resources in that you're investing in futures contracts for the substance, rather than in companies that produce the substance.)

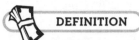 **DEFINITION**

Futures contracts are agreements to buy or sell a particular product or commodity in the future at a predefined price.

While there may be some overlap of companies with other stock categories, in general you might consider investing in alternatives because they move very differently from the rest of the market. Sometimes they can be just about the only investment left standing in otherwise bad markets, but they are highly volatile.

Bonds:

If you didn't have enough categories of stocks to choose from, bonds offer lots of choices by length of term, quality, type of insurer, and location.

By length of term:

- Short term matures (pays off) in 1 year or less.

- Intermediate term matures in 3 to 10 years.

- Long term usually matures in 10 to 30 years.

Usually, long-term bonds are considered the most risky, but may pay higher interest. Most total bond funds end up being intermediate term when all their holdings are taken together.

By quality:

Bond rating agencies rate the strength of the underlying company or government (see Chapter 12 for further discussion). Generally, U.S. government bonds are considered the safest.

Junk bonds pay the highest interest because they are the riskiest. They are issued by companies and governments with low credit ratings. While you may get high interest you run the risk that the issuer will default. Mutual funds average the risk by investing in multiple bond issues and decrease the return you might get by investing in just one high-paying junker.

By type of issuer:

An issuer can be the federal government, corporate, state, municipality, federal agency, backed by mortgage aggregation, and many others. In addition to varying in quality and return, some of these offer tax advantages.

By location:

All U.S., international (outside the United States, known sometimes as ex-U.S.), and global (the whole world including the United States).

A Simple Allocation

Here's a very simple allocation (this is not an investment recommendation):

- One third U.S. stocks/total U.S. stock market mutual fund
- One third international stocks/total international market mutual fund
- One third bonds/total bond market mutual fund

Not too different from a target date or life strategy fund, in that these funds generally contain the same types of assets. No investment recommendation intended.

Don't feel you have to choose all or nothing. Not every one of these subcategories has to be incorporated into your portfolio. In fact, research says that once you reach about 12 different types of investments, you don't get any further advantage from diversification—you've become your own total market mutual fund.

Now let's take it up a notch. Here is a more diversified portfolio:

- 10 percent large-cap U.S. stocks/mutual fund
- 10 percent mid-cap U.S. stocks/mutual fund

- 10 percent small-cap U.S. stocks/mutual fund

- 10 percent international developed stocks/mutual fund

- 10 percent international emerging markets/mutual fund

- 40 percent U.S. bonds/mutual fund

- 10 percent international bonds (or alternatives)/mutual fund

As you can see, there are many ways to stir the mix and emphasize some segments over others.

Diversifying Your Stocks

What if you're planning to invest the majority of your money in stocks? Maybe you have a long time horizon or you welcome risk for the possibility of larger returns. Can you diversify only in stocks or stock mutual funds?

Instead of diversifying by size and whether the company is growth or value oriented, some people diversify by sectors, believing this is another way to capture the market. For example, you might incorporate portfolio sectors you believe will do well (maybe health care or technology) or ones that have done poorly but are currently low priced (perhaps communications or utilities). By distributing your investments among a variety of sectors, you hope to capture the market while emphasizing the sectors you feel have the most potential. Many mutual funds offer portfolios centered on companies in specific sectors.

If you're really worried about how to find the perfect asset diversification, I can tell you right now that there isn't one. It matters more that you diversify than *how* you diversify. As long as you pick investments that are different from each other, and stick to the broad asset allocation that is consistent with your goals and risk tolerance, you'll have some protection and every potential of increased return. See Appendix B for books that recommend different portfolio allocations—and they won't all agree. (We'll consider investing in individual stocks more in Chapter 11.)

 **WARNING**

You're not diversified if you buy several different funds but they all have similar holdings. If you buy Vanguard Wellington Fund, Fidelity Puritan Fund, and T. Rowe Price Balanced Fund, you don't have any meaningful diversity—they all invest in similar companies and asset mixes, even if performance differs slightly. Sometimes brokers load up a portfolio with very similar funds in order to make the client think there's some special, carefully selected, complex mix.

Market Timing

We've considered what types of investments you might buy. Is there any secret as to when is the best time to do so?

Can You Time the Market?

We all would like to think we can "time the market," and that some chart or prediction scheme or careful trend analysis will tell us the moment to buy or sell for maximum profit. I admit that it can be fun to think about, and I'd like to believe it can be done, but I don't think there's any real evidence for the success of such an approach.

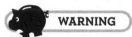 **WARNING**

> Hedge funds are investment funds that pool money from wealthy investors or institutions and use some strategy or scheme to invest money. Hedge funds are filled with smart, highly educated people who have access to the best research and technology. The average survival rate for hedge funds is about 5 years, and within 3 years, about a third of hedge funds disappear (to be replaced by others trying to build a better mousetrap). If they can't time the market, how can you?

In fact, the evidence argues that you do better to establish your asset allocation, get into the market, and stay there. If you have good diversification, inevitably some of your investments will drop the very next day, and some will increase. That's how we expect diversification to work.

It would be lovely if we could buy every investment at its lowest price, after which it goes straight up, but we can't know when that is. If the investment is low, will it go lower? If it's already higher than its history, will it drop or go even higher? Who knows?

Financial adviser and author Nick Murray notes, in his book *Behavioral Investment Counseling,* that for the 20 years through 2007, the average equity (stock) fund had a total return of 10.81 percent. However, the average equity fund investor had a return of only 4.48 percent.

Why? Because we're nervous. We jump in and out of the market, fleeing to cash at often just the wrong moments. We flit from fund to fund when we read an article about some star manager who's produced outsize returns, even though we'll be too late to the party. We allow ourselves, as Murray says, to be ruled by panic and euphoria, and the false belief that we can time the market.

Whatever investment you buy, you probably won't buy it at the lowest price it will sell for in any given year, and you probably won't get dinged for the highest prices. Even if you're unlucky in one investment (and you probably will be at some point), diversification will help minimize the pain of any losses over your entire portfolio. The longer you hold a diversified portfolio, the more your total return will match the total return of the asset class; dividends and capital gains payouts (in mutual funds) will boost your return. But only if you're in there at all the right moments, by staying invested.

Rebalancing

Am I suggesting that you should allocate your investments, then forget about them? Not quite. You should still rebalance your investments to keep them in line with your target asset allocation.

 TIP

Buying low and selling high is what everyone says they want to do. However, most people do the opposite, believing their winners will continue to win (until they don't) and their losers will make a comeback. Or they buy the hottest current investment (which has already peaked) and shun the losers (which have the most potential to improve). Rebalancing forces you to buy and sell most effectively.

Rebalancing is necessary if you're going to maintain your diversification. When you rebalance your portfolio, you sell off some portion of the investments that have increased, and use that money to buy more of the assets that have dropped, returning your portfolio to its designated proportions. This is how you sell high and buy low.

When should you do this? There are two schools of thought: by date and by percent of change.

In the date method, you rebalance once a year, or once every quarter, or even once a month, preferably on the same day. Research seems to indicate that you're better off rebalancing once a year; any more frequently and you're not only jumping around a lot and catching brief trends, but you may be racking up higher trading costs. If you rebalance on approximately the same day every year, conditions such as when dividends are paid, when people are withdrawing to pay income taxes, or any seasonal variation offer some likelihood of being approximately consistent year over year. Whether or not this actually happens, it's a discipline that keeps you hewing to your plan.

TIP
"Sell in May and go away." There is a school of thought that because much of Wall Street vacations in the summer, the market drops. Does it work? Actually, there's some evidence that stocks can be affected, because lower trading volume tends to depress prices. It doesn't work every year by any means, and, as always, a diversified portfolio will balance out the effect.

In the percent-of-change method, you rebalance whenever your target allocation gets out of whack by a specific percentage—for example, if your stock fund allocation is set to 60 percent and you decide to rebalance whenever it veers more than 5 percent from that allocation. Say in May it rises to 68 percent of your total portfolio, so you sell enough to return it to 60 percent, and buy enough of your other allocations, say bonds, to return them to their established percentage (in this case, 40 percent). By September, bonds have done better and they've become 46 percent of your portfolio. Same routine—sell enough to bring the bonds back down to 40 percent, and move the money to the investments that are down.

Using this method, you have to establish just how often you're going to review—for most people, any more than once a month would be too arduous, and again you can incur outsize trading costs (and potential penalties for trading too frequently in some mutual funds).

Even if you decide to stick generally to rebalancing once a year, the percentage method can work quite well for investing new money or regular contributions. Direct your contributions to the investments that are under your target percentage and you'll probably lessen the need to sell and buy existing investments when it comes time for the yearly rebalance.

In any rebalance, I'd leave as is any investment that is 5 percent or less off target. You're never going to get it perfect—even as you place your order, the price will change. Get close and don't sweat the small variations.

Asset allocation is the first, most important decision you will make. It will guide you in choosing what overall mix will result in a portfolio that matches your appetite for risk and goals for return. Once you've selected your asset mix, you'll move on to choosing specific investments to build each asset allocation category.

The Least You Need to Know

- Decide on your general asset allocation approach between stocks and bonds depending on your risk tolerance, age, and timeline for goals.
- Dividing your investments into types of stocks and bonds can give you further diversification and more potential risk/reward.

- You may want to choose an asset diversification mix for yourself, or select a mutual fund whose investments already offer diversification.

- Rebalance your investments on a regular basis in order to maintain your asset allocation plan.

- Once you set your strategy, stick with it. Don't worry about temporary or short-term changes in the market.

Getting Professional Advice

If you have a busy career and an active family, you probably don't have time to do a lot of reading and learning about investing. But if you're facing some big financial decisions—retirement, college funding, investing an inheritance—you may feel you need to consult a professional.

In this chapter, we'll examine the different types of financial professionals available to you and look at their costs and levels of service.

In This Chapter

- Don't believe everything you hear
- Buying from a broker
- Fee-only versus fee-based planners
- Robo-advisers, insurance advisers, accountants, and others

But First, a Word on the Media

Just as reality TV shows don't reflect reality, investment "experts" on TV are more about theater and entertainment than solid advice. How would they construct an interesting show if they continually gave the same boring advice?

Even reputable news and information sources (see Appendix B) spill a lot of words analyzing current events (which you should selectively ignore), short-term performance of specific investments and asset classes (which you should also probably ignore), and changes in government policy (which you should pay attention to, although it probably won't be explained in enough depth to understand).

 **WARNING**

You do want to keep abreast of current events, but you shouldn't radically change your investing principles or plan based on short-term or scare tactics.

Hardly a week passes that I don't get a mailing for a newsletter, an email for a special analysis service, or an invitation for a seminar that promises to let me in on the secrets of super investors. Today, for example, I received one that touted the high returns of the Moo-Cow Discovery Fund (name changed, of course). They claimed a 21.1 percent annualized return for this fund. The following table outlines the current actual results of the fund according to Morningstar, an independent investment research service.

YTD	1 Month	1 Year	3 Years	5 Years	10 Years
−7.03	0.55	−8.34	11.95	10.6	8.93

I'm not saying this is a bad fund. In fact, many people would be quite pleased to have averaged 8.93 percent over the last 10 years. But the fund has nowhere near the performance that the advertisement promised. An author can manipulate the results simply by preselecting the best-performing time period. And if the author knows so much, how come he's still working? Why hasn't he retired on his riches?

Before you believe anything you hear from the media, check it out. Ask yourself what is being promoted, what self-interest the source may have in providing the information, and try to cross-check any advice with reputable sources.

TIP

News coverage of investments often begins with some variation of *this time it's different*. It's *never* different—bubbles come and go; stocks, bonds, and other investments go in and out of favor; some winters have more snow than others.

Different Types of Financial Advisers

No one works for free. The way in which your financial adviser gets paid may have a strong influence on the type of advice he or she gives you. Before you rely on any adviser's advice, know exactly what kind of expertise they have, what their legal duties are to you, and what their self-interest is in the recommendations they provide.

Brokers

Stockbrokers are what most of the public thinks of when they think of financial advisers. Stockbrokers were virtually the only advisers available before the advent of fee-only advisers beginning in the 1980s. Because the term *stockbrokers* has lost some appeal, many brokerage houses (particularly those pitching to the general public) style their brokers as "financial advisers" or "wealth managers." For the purposes of this section, I'll call them "brokers."

Brokers sell you products—stocks, mutual funds, bonds, and other investment vehicles—and collect a commission on the sale. This commission varies depending on the specific product, but is often 5.75 percent of the purchase price.

If you have a small amount to invest (less than $25,000 or so), the broker will generally encourage you to purchase funds he or she recommends, and charge a commission based on what you purchase.

TIP

If you see testimonials on the "financial adviser's" website or literature, or see (in very tiny print) the notation that they are a member of the SIPC (Securities Investor Protection Corporation) or that investments are offered through anything, you're looking at a commissioned salesperson or broker. Fee-only advisers (discussed later in this chapter) do not sell investments and are not allowed to promote testimonials.

A broker has a legal duty to recommend investments to you that are appropriate for your risk tolerance—usually based on your age and answers you give in an interview or when filling out a risk questionnaire. Be careful how you answer such questions, and understand that what terms you use can indicate different investment strategies. The broker must recommend appropriate investments, but what you tell him or her can change the definition of *appropriate*.

Let's look at a possible conversation. You tell the broker that you want "safe investments" and that you "can't afford to lose anything." Normally such goals would suggest a portfolio heavily oriented to cash and bonds or bond mutual funds. But wait! Your adviser asks you some questions. Don't you want growth? Aren't you worried that your portfolio won't respond to inflation? You say yes—and you've now contradicted yourself and opened the door to recommendations of stocks, stock mutual funds, and maybe even junk bonds, nontraded real estate trusts, limited partnerships, and the risky end of the investment spectrum. I don't think it's a stretch to say that the broker is going to recommend investments that pay him or her the highest commissions.

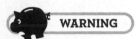 **WARNING**

When selling mutual funds, brokers usually offer three classes of shares (A, B, and C), all of which collect commissions in different ways. I have reviewed portfolios in which the client has been sold all three classes of the same fund, ensuring that no matter what the investor does, the broker collects a commission.

The *appropriate* standard is problematic in other ways. Let's say it's "appropriate" for you to put 60 percent of your portfolio into stock mutual funds. You can be steered to the brokerage house's proprietary mutual funds, or load (commission-paying) funds that will carry not only a commission for the broker, but also much higher management costs—money that is taken out of returns before they are paid to you, and which support advertising, promotion, administrative costs, and the high salaries paid to fund managers. On the other hand, you could buy the same type of funds, no-load (no commissions paid) with much lower management fees. A no-load fund might have a management fee that is .02 percent or .05 percent, and the same type of load fund may have a management fee of 1 percent or 1.5 percent—a big difference. Either fund might be "appropriate," i.e., the right type of investment, but the no-load fund is much cheaper and likely to provide better returns.

There is another standard besides appropriate, and that is the *fiduciary* standard. The fiduciary standard has been fought tooth and nail by the brokerage industry. The fiduciary standard requires your broker to act *only* in your best interest. Generally, your best interest is what costs you the least and returns the most, insofar as it is humanly possible to know. However, I have never reviewed a portfolio designed by a broker that contained no-load mutual funds.

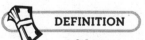 **DEFINITION**

A **fiduciary** is someone legally obligated to act only in your best interests.

A broker may offer to help you with a financial plan. You should consider that plan with some healthy skepticism. What if you ask for input on actions that would take significant money out of the investments placed with the broker? Would the broker encourage you to withdraw funds to pay off your house? Purchase a fixed lump-sum annuity not sold by the brokerage?

I spent a year studying for my 10-hour CFP® exam, took an intensive test prep course, and sat for the exam, which has only about a 50 percent pass rate. (There's a reason the CFP exam is generally regarded as the gold standard for planning.) But be aware that stockbrokers do not need to pass the CFP exam, only some much easier securities licensing.

Before taking the CFP exam I decided to take the exam for the Series 65 license—the minimum you need to open a business as a planner. I spent one afternoon reading the book. You're allowed 3 hours to complete the 130 multiple-choice questions, but it's easy to complete in an hour. In order to sell securities, brokers may be required to pass other series exams—but before you're impressed, understand what the licenses cover:

- **Series 7** Exam to trade general securities (basic exam for brokers); 250 questions

- **Series 63** Minimum a new broker needs in order to pass state requirements on securities regulations, ethics, and procedures; 130 questions

- **Series 65** Minimum to provide fee-based advice based on person's financial needs; 130 questions

- **Series 66** Combination of 63 and 65; 100 questions

TIP

Some brokers do claim to act as a fiduciary when creating financial plans, especially if they've earned the CFP designation, which technically requires them to act as fiduciaries. Be sure you know which hat they're wearing when giving you advice—and when they switch hats.

Are there any good reasons to consult a broker? Well, you won't have to write a check up front, since they work on commission. Also, the plans they create for you are usually offered for free, and you pay only if you purchase the investments.

If you have a large lump sum to invest, if you will never add to it, and if you plan to keep it invested for many years, you may pay less for a broker than if you hire a fee-only planner (discussed later in this chapter). But in real life that's unlikely, because you will get a call from the broker periodically encouraging you to change your investments to some new recommendations, at which point you will be charged, and generate more commissions.

Your broker is likely to be friendly and affable. They'll be glad to talk to you if you're lonely, chat about events in the market, and so on. Everyone who comes into my office suspecting that something isn't quite right with their plan always assures me that their broker is a very nice guy. I always tell them that if he had a forked tail and horns he'd never sell anything. Nice isn't what you need in an adviser so much as honesty and expert fiduciary advice. Also, remember that what your broker recommends is what the brokerage house says he can recommend.

Brokerage houses have battalions of research analysts. But the majority of research and "buy" signals they generate are aimed at encouraging you to purchase and exchange your investments. If you're considering brokerage recommendations, ask your broker to provide you with statistics on what percentage of recommendations are buy, what percentage are hold, and how many sell recommendations are generated—usually only when there's horrendous news, scandal, or the company gives evidence of going bust (and sometimes not even then).

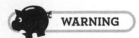 **WARNING**

Many well-known media gurus have websites and programs that offer you an "approved" list of financial advisers. Be sure you understand how these advisers are paid. Just because a guy wrote a good book that seems to offer straight talk, or claims to adhere to religious principles, doesn't mean he's above collecting commissions. Some of these advisers are approved because they paid a big fee to be listed, and are exclusively commission-based.

Brokers' duties to their clients is the subject of a swirl of controversy. The federal government has recently moved toward new rules requiring all advisers (including commissioned brokers) to be fiduciaries when advising on retirement plans. How this will be implemented or subverted is the subject of breaking news. Please keep abreast of the current situation when considering advisers.

Fee-Based Advisers

Some people get a little angry when they figure out their broker is charging them 5.75 percent for a bond fund that returns 1 percent. No problem, the brokerage industry can fix that by fiddling with the terms a little and hoping people won't really understand.

So many people have been told, or have read an article telling them, to look for a *fee-only* adviser, that the brokerage industry came up with the term *fee-based* to confuse the public—er, represent a revised service.

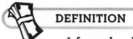

DEFINITION

A **fee-only** adviser is paid strictly from fees for service: either by the hour, by retainer, or as a percentage of assets managed. They collect no incentive for the recommended investments. A **fee-based** adviser is paid from fees and commissions and has a financial incentive to recommend investments that pay a commission.

Fee-based means that you will be charged a fee that's a percentage of the amount you have invested, often 1.5 percent of your total invested portfolio (fees may drop the more you invest). The brokerage will also have some type of arrangement with any mutual fund companies to pay some fees as commissions to the agent selling the investments. A portfolio will be designed for you, and changes will be recommended depending on the recommendations of the brokerage's research department. These accounts are also known as wrap accounts (meaning in my opinion that they've wrapped additional charges around commission-paying sales).

The portfolios that are brought to me for evaluation after these arrangements are often quite complex, sometimes having as many as 40 or 50 different investments (usually mutual funds, although individual stocks may sneak into some portfolios). There's usually a great deal of overlap (several of the mutual funds will hold nearly identical investments), they are never no-load, and it's very difficult to get disentangled—you either have to sell or keep the whole thing. If you want to move out of the firm, you will often be charged a hefty fee to move the investments, or a substantial trading charge for each separate investment, which can really add up. Finally, the complexity of the portfolio all but insures that most investors won't understand what they're invested in.

Fee-based arrangements are only going to be pitched to you if you have enough of a portfolio to make the fees worthwhile. Walk in with "only" $5,000 to invest and you'll be sold a load mutual fund. However, an investment of $50,000 may get you the "services" of a fee-based adviser.

TIP

I don't care how nice the office is (Bernie Madoff's was great). If you need advice or assistance in your investing program, you need to understand what you're really paying for it, and what the expertise and loyalty is of the person who's giving it.

If you're still considering a fee-based adviser after reading this, be sure you understand exactly how much you're paying for the advice, in both commissions and wrap around fees. Ask the adviser if they are a fiduciary and whether the funds they are recommending to you are no-load.

If they are recommending individual stocks, bonds, or other investments, ask them to show you evidence that these investments have outperformed corresponding mutual funds for at least 10 years.

Fee-Only Planners and Advisers

Fee-only financial planners and advisers should not be beholden to any investment company, nor should they receive or pay referral fees from attorneys, accountants, or insurance agents. In addition, a fee-only adviser should not be selling you any investments. Before you spend even 15 minutes in their chair, ask if they always act as a fiduciary for the entire engagement. If not, drink your free coffee quickly and get out of there.

Fee-only advisers get paid in one of three ways:

- Hourly fee

- Assets Under Management (AUM) fee

- Flat fee or retainer

Let's look at each.

Hourly planners and advisers   This type of fee-only planner or adviser will work on your project and answer your questions for an hourly charge. As long as you have clear questions and are able to supply all the background information they'll need, the planner/adviser should be able to tell you approximately how many hours your project will take, and may be willing to guarantee you an upper limit (not to exceed …). Expect that such a project will take a minimum of 3 hours, and possibly as much as 15 to 20 hours, depending on your financial picture.

Most hourly advisers will recommend specific investments that are appropriate for your goals and risk tolerance, but they won't implement it for you. You will have to open accounts, make purchases and sales, and keep on top of the portfolio on your own. You should certainly be able to discuss possible investments with an hourly planner or adviser, but you will be charged for the advice. If you do need assistance implementing the plan, many advisers will sit down with you to do so, but you will be charged for the time.

Advantages of hourly planners:

- They're probably the cheapest way to go, especially if the advice needed is fairly simple.

- They're ideal if you just want a second opinion.

- A project by the hour does not necessarily involve investments, so a fee-only adviser will be willing to discuss insurance, divorce, college aid, long-term-care options, debt, or other issues not related to your having a huge portfolio.

- You will get direct personal attention, but they won't be calling you constantly to sell you things or churn the investments in your portfolio.

- You get sensible investment advice based on independent research.

- These advisers are generally fiduciaries.

 TIP

Hourly planners help you simplify your portfolio and can explain what's in there until you understand it.

Disadvantages of hourly advisers:

- They can be hard to find. Many hourly planners and advisers are solo practitioners operating out of home offices or small offices. They don't have giant advertising budgets.

- It's not cheap. Your project will almost certainly take more than 1 hour and hourly rates are generally north of $200, often much more.

- You have to implement the plan. If you never get around to saving, delay making the investments, or only partially execute the final plan, none of the projected results will work as they should. There's no one who will monitor your actions or progress.

- There may not be much continuity. If you don't update your plan about every year, or when circumstances change, you may get far off track.

- Every time you contact them, you're going to get charged. This can make many people reluctant to seek follow-up advice, even when they need it.

- You may feel that the type of investment advice you get—usually no-load mutual funds—was stuff you could have figured out on your own.

- Theoretically, there may be some incentive to run up the hours charged. You can prevent this by getting an agreement ahead of time as to maximum hours.

To find fee-only planners and advisers, check out these avenues:

- **Garrett Planning Network**　　Must be fee-only. All members must offer hourly planning; some also offer AUM.

- **National Association of Personal Financial Analysts (NAPFA)**　　Must be fee-only and pass a peer review of a sample plan to be a full member.

- **CFP Board**   Be careful here—not all members are fee-only for all functions.

- **Financial Planning Association**   Many members are not fee-only, but you can carefully read their profiles and websites.

Assets Under Management (AUM) advisers   Assets Under Management refers to the method for charging for financial planning or investment management where fees are based on a percentage of your total assets being managed by the adviser.

In this version of fee-only planning, you transfer your investments to the adviser's *custodian*, and the adviser invests your money in a portfolio.

DEFINITION

A **custodian** is a third-party financial institution that holds investments for safekeeping. An adviser may be authorized to trade these investments for you, but should not actually receive the investments or proceeds of the trade.

Your adviser will charge you a fee as a percentage of the assets managed. This fee can be substantial, but it can't be outrageous. Generally you will see fees ranging from .8 percent to a high of around 2 percent of your assets. The fee will be deducted from your account monthly, quarterly, or yearly and will be based on the value of your account on a specific day. The AUM-based adviser benefits when your account increases in value, and the fee is lower when the account and the market are underperforming.

The adviser will meet with you on a regular basis (anywhere from once a month to once a year), discuss any changes with you, and update your investments. Some AUM advisers will charge you separately for financial planning (usually by the hour). Others only charge you for the initial plan, including updates and changes as part of the AUM relationship. Some will include the plan as part of the AUM, at no extra charge.

Advantages of AUM advisers:

- For that money, perhaps the greatest benefit you receive will be that the adviser will keep you on your plan. You won't be jumping in or out of the market constantly, and you'll proceed with a long-term, steady strategy.

- The investments chosen for your portfolio will be prudent and should be low-cost. Generally they will be no-load mutual funds and sometimes individual investments or bonds.

- You can expect that the adviser will take the time to improve your understanding of your investments, and help you strategize a plan to accumulate money or distribute it prudently for retirement income and other goals.

- Your investment plan will actually happen. You won't hold on to investments because Grandpa gave them to you, or you like shopping at that store, or because you never got around to implementing the recommended buys and sells. Your adviser will execute the plan swiftly and certainly.

- An AUM adviser should act almost as a concierge of your financial life—conferring with attorneys, accountants, and your estate planner if necessary to manage your plan. They should be available as questions and the need for decisions (Can I afford to retire? When?) occur.

Disadvantages of AUM advisers:

- Many AUM advisers require you to invest a minimum amount of assets with them. It can be hard to find anyone who will manage a portfolio of less than $1 or $2 million.

- Even if the adviser does not require a minimum amount of assets, they will generally charge a minimum annual fee. For small accounts, these fees can be on the upper end of the percentage range. The adviser still has to carry insurance, maintain software and support staff, continue professional education, and so on, no matter what the size of the account.

- The adviser's fee will cut into the returns of your investments. However, there is significant research evidence that working with an adviser will produce better returns for you than doing it on your own, mainly because of the steadying influence on your decisions. Some studies have suggested that working with an adviser can improve your returns as much as 1.5 percent or more.

- There may be some incentive to discourage you from decisions that will take money out of the portfolio—for example, paying off a home mortgage, making big gifts to charity, or purchasing a fixed single-premium annuity.

 TIP

Fiduciaries are obligated to act in your best interests, so if your adviser discourages you from any moves that would reduce your portfolio, you should understand why. (There may be good reasons, or not.)

Flat-fee or retainer advisers   Rather than basing fees by the hour or the specific value of your portfolio, flat fee or retainer advisers will give you a fixed project or yearly price. This will generally be based on either the size of your portfolio (and what the adviser thinks it will take to manage it) or the complexity of your project.

You also may be charged this way if your money is locked up in a workplace retirement program that can't be managed directly by the adviser, but with which you need help.

Advantages of flat-fee or retainer advisers:

- You know exactly what you'll be charged in a given year.

- You may be billed directly (usually by credit card or through auto-withdrawal from your checking account) rather than having money removed from your portfolio investments.

- You can get the benefits of an AUM adviser even if you don't have a portfolio large enough to manage, or when all your investments are in workplace or other accounts that can't be moved.

- The adviser will be a fiduciary.

Disadvantages of flat-fee or retainer advisers:

- The cost will be very close to what an AUM adviser charges.

- Even if your wealth decreases significantly, you will be charged the same amount. If your wealth increases significantly, you'll probably see your fee increased the next time it's up for renewal.

- As of now, fewer advisers work this way, so you may have to search to find one who does.

Robo-Advisers

In the robo-adviser model, you fill out a questionnaire online, and an investment plan is generated for you. You may or may not be offered a live conference with a real adviser (and if you are, the management fee will probably be higher). I've tried out several of these to see what they'd recommend for a model client.

Advantages of robo-advisers:

- It's usually much less expensive than the traditional broker.

- It will probably give you a solid recommendation of a mix of mutual funds.

- The service will take care of the scary part. They'll transfer your funds, make the trades for you, and rebalance based on the agreed-upon program.

TIP

Robo-adviser fees generally range from .15 percent to .80 percent—although I have seen an occasional quote of 1.5 percent.

Disadvantages of robo-advisers:

- You could, in addition to the robo-adviser, get a personal adviser, but you may get a different one each time you have contact. He or she may not be very experienced. This type of job tends to attract entry-level people who are getting their first experience before moving on. They will be confined to the guidelines of their company.

- The portfolios recommended often resemble a target date fund. If the firm offers target date funds, the recommended portfolio will often contain the exact same funds as would have been contained in the equivalent target date. It's hard to understand why you would pay .3 percent for the exact same mix you could have purchased for nothing.

- Some elements of the portfolio may seem strange. For example, I created a model client with a sample income of $75,000; the service recommended municipal bonds as a component. It's hard to understand why municipal bonds would be recommended without knowing something about the person's tax picture and whether they actually need to sacrifice return for tax relief. It may be difficult to get an explanation for how and why the mix of assets was chosen.

- All the "management" is basically portfolio design. The need for insurance, balancing savings with other life challenges, incorporating real estate investments, the challenges of planning for elders or disabled dependents, and individual quirks and preferences are not part of the plan. Robo-advising is, by nature, impersonal.

- Fees may go up significantly over time. One famous low-cost robo-adviser just doubled its fees, with an add-on if you actually want to talk to someone.

 TIP

It's unclear whether robo-advisers are fiduciaries. Be sure you understand how the funds recommended to you were selected. Are they only from one company that owns the robo-advising?

Insurance Agents

All insurance is sold on commission. While many insurance agents will offer to create a financial plan for you—surprise!—it's going to consist of insurance recommendations. Go to a financial adviser for planning and investment recommendations; go to an insurance agent for insurance.

Some states require fee-only advisers who make insurance recommendations to have insurance certification. If, however, they actually offer insurance, they are not fee-only advisers. Some larger AUM advisers will have an insurance broker in the office, and all advisers can provide you with referrals to insurance agents they have worked with. A fee-only adviser should be available to help you evaluate any proposals.

Accountants, CPAs, Attorneys, and Other Financial Service Providers

All of these people offer specialties you might need, but they're not primarily financial planners. A financial planner acts much like an internist or family practice physician: taking stock of your general health, looking at the big picture, coming up with a treatment plan, and referring you to specialists when needed. You don't see a dermatologist for a physical.

Some accountants have training in financial planning; the Personal Financial Specialist (PFS designation) and some financial planners may also have a background in accounting or taxes. However, accountants are going to see most plans through the lens of tax planning; if that's your primary concern, they're a good choice. Or make sure that your accountant understands your financial plan, and be sure your planner is available to confer.

Many people rely on their divorce or estate attorney for financial advice. But these people are trained in the law, not financial planning, and will (and should) refer you for more expert and involved financial and investment advice.

The Least You Need to Know

- Fee-based advisers, stockbrokers, and other salespeople are required to recommend investments that are appropriate for you; however, appropriate choices may not necessarily be the best choices for you.
- Financial advisers should tell you whether they are fiduciaries, legally obligated to act in your best interests.
- Fee-only advisers should be fiduciaries who charge only for advice and accept no commissions or referral fees. They may charge by the hour, by a retainer fee, or by a percentage of the assets they manage for you (AUM).

- Robo-advisers can offer basic advice, but it may not be fiduciary or personalized for your own situation.

- Accountants and attorneys have specialties that may be valuable and pertinent to your situation, but they are not necessarily experts in financial planning or investment advice.

Where to Invest

Stocks, bonds, mutual funds, and alternative investments have different risk characteristics, different ways of being selected and monitored, and even different ways of being purchased and owned. With some, you may do research once and own them for a very long time. With others, you may need to reevaluate from time to time, keep up to date with the trend of the company, and buy and sell at what seem to be opportune moments.

In this part, we'll look at opening appropriate accounts, deciding if the investment is right for you, and the advantages and pitfalls of each type of investment. We'll consider which investments are more time intensive to buy and monitor, which require the most study and research on your part, and what level of risk and reward they offer. You'll learn how to judge a potential investment, and understand how to evaluate whether it's the good deal you're seeking.

Investing in Mutual Funds

Most of us don't have the time, confidence, or research ability to pick individual stocks and bonds. Assembling a sufficiently diverse portfolio of individual stocks and bonds, then monitoring them for changes in the market and in individual businesses, can require more effort than most people have. (But if that's what you want to do, see Chapters 11, 12, and 13 for how to build your own program.)

Investing in mutual funds is one way to build a diverse portfolio with the least effort. However, even with a diversified mutual fund, one fund is not necessarily as good as another, and you will need to put some research into the ones you choose. In this chapter we'll look at how mutual funds are made, what you should look for in choosing them, and how to use them to build a strong portfolio.

In This Chapter

- What, exactly, is a mutual fund?
- How to purchase mutual funds
- Researching and deciding whether to buy a mutual fund
- A few of the less-common mutual funds

What Are Mutual Funds and How Do You Buy Them?

Simply put, a mutual fund is a collection of investments (either individual securities or other mutual funds) that an investment company puts together and offers to you in the form of shares.

The overwhelming majority of mutual funds are open-ended funds. This means the fund can issue shares at any time. Their shares are priced at the end of the day based on the net asset value (NAV) of all their investments. You place an order for a specific dollar amount and at the end of the day receive shares equal to that amount.

 TIP

> Most funds require a minimum purchase amount. Sometimes it's as little as $1,000. More frequently it will be $3,000, with some specialized funds having minimums of $10,000 to $50,000. Check this first before you waste a lot of time researching a fund.

You have plenty of mutual funds to choose from. There are about 8,000 open-ended mutual funds currently available. Add in the less-common types (unit investment trusts, 5,381; closed-end, 568; and exchange-traded funds, 1,411) and you will have more than 15,000 possible investments. Most beginning investors should stick to open-ended and exchange-traded funds, where information is most available and the funds are easiest to buy and sell.

Purchasing a Mutual Fund

You can purchase open-ended funds in several ways:

By choosing them in your workplace retirement account   Your 401(k) will offer a selection of funds, usually an array of target date funds, perhaps some balanced or life strategy funds, and a usually small array of specific-focus and asset class funds. You choose one or a mix, and your contributions (and your employer's match, if there is one) will go into these funds at whatever share price they have on the day the money is invested. Funds available in your workplace account generally have no minimum investment.

By opening a mutual fund account at an investment company   Go online to the mutual fund company of your choice and you will find that their website makes it very easy for you to open an account. They will also mail you out paper forms if you prefer to work offline. You can open one of these accounts before you decide on exactly what funds you want to invest in. Have your initial deposit placed in the company's money market fund. From there you will be able to transfer funds to purchase mutual funds you select.

By opening a brokerage account   Some mutual fund companies allow you to open one account from which you can purchase mutual funds and individual securities; others will separate the mutual fund account and the brokerage account. The brokerage account can contain mutual funds from other companies, exchange-traded funds (ETFs), individual stocks and bonds, and so on. These accounts generally offer a "fund supermarket" where you can purchase mutual funds from other companies, sometimes with a higher trading cost.

Full-Service Companies and Discount Brokers

Most of the big investment companies offer individuals brokerage accounts. In addition, discount brokers (Scottrade, E*TRADE, TD Ameritrade, etc.) will offer you a full range of mutual funds, ETFs, and securities. Buying mutual funds through a discount broker may cost you a trading charge.

Full-service stock brokerages (Edward Jones, Charles James, Merrill Lynch, etc.) will also offer mutual funds as well as securities, but these will generally be based on their own recommendations and will be primarily, if not exclusively, funds that pay commissions to the brokers. Stockbrokers usually do not recommend investments that don't pay them.

TIP

The largest mutual fund companies are The Vanguard Group, Fidelity Investments, American Funds (Capital Group), JPMorgan Chase, T. Rowe Price, BlackRock, Franklin Templeton Investments, PIMCO, and Dimensional Fund Advisors. If you work for a nonprofit employer or education system, your retirement plan may also offer investments with TIAA-CREF.

Different mutual fund companies offer different focuses. Vanguard Group has historically specialized in no-load *index funds*, although they also offer actively managed funds. T. Rowe Price has focused on actively managed funds. Both Fidelity and T. Rowe Price are huge in providing workplace retirement funds. American Funds are sold through brokers.

If you're thinking of investing primarily in the funds of one company, visit their website to get a feel for how they present themselves. Also, check out the publications and websites in Appendix B to read commentary on the companies.

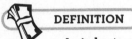

An **index** is an imaginary portfolio of investments that represent a specific segment of a market. For example, an index may seek to mirror 500 of the largest U.S. companies, or high-quality U.S. corporate bonds, or all the stocks in the Dow Jones index. Banking, investment, and analysis services put together these indexes. Mutual funds then seek to replicate (or beat) the index by purchasing all the securities in the index, or sampling similar securities to attempt to reproduce the performance.

Load or No-Load?

Be sure you know whether the fund you're choosing or being recommended is load or no-load (that is, whether it charges a commission or is sold without commission). If you're working through a broker, the fund is almost certainly going to be a load fund for which you'll be charged a commission. Some fund companies offer only load funds, and you must go through a broker to purchase them.

When selling mutual funds, brokers usually offer three types. Class A shares (front-end load), in which the commission is paid when you purchase the fund (and usually, every time you add to it) but no commission is due when you sell (except for trading fees). Class B shares (back-end load), in which the commission is charged when you sell the shares, although this may be reduced if you hold the shares for a specific number of years. These may convert to Class A shares at that point (which have lower management costs). Class C shares (level load), in which you are charged a higher management fee every year you hold the shares and a back-end load when you sell (generally lower than Class B shares).

However, it's hard for me to see why you would go through a broker to purchase a mutual fund. There is a huge selection of no-load funds available in almost any flavor you could possibly want, and opening an account with a mutual fund company or discount broker is easy. So why pay a commission to purchase a near-identical fund, which will often have higher management expenses as well?

Choosing a Company

There's a reason why the Vanguard Group has become the largest mutual fund company—they offer just about any type of fund you might want, and they're all no-load. However, if your workplace account is housed with another company (Fidelity, T. Rowe Price, or TIAA-CREF, for example), you might want to have your individual accounts at the same place for the simple convenience of not having to chase down investment records in several different places. The exception would be if your workplace has gone with a high cost or primarily load fund provider or a so-called private banking service—then, you probably want to select a mutual fund company that offers no-load funds.

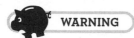

WARNING

Mutual fund investment companies that emphasized low-cost no-load mutual funds used to be the white hats of the industry. However, they're not as consumer-focused anymore. Plastered all over their websites, and in plenty of individual communiqués, you'll be pelted by offers to "partner with an adviser" to buy exactly the same funds, with an asset management fee attached. See Chapter 9 for a discussion of whether you should.

I've also worked with investors who choose one company and management style for their retirement accounts (usually no-load, passively managed index funds) and another for their spouse's accounts, or for an investment account in which they want to try out a more actively managed strategy. There's not a right answer for everyone, but don't let analysis paralysis overtake you—start somewhere.

How Many Funds?

How much of your portfolio should be in mutual funds? Maybe all of it! And why not? You can choose any type of asset (stocks, bonds, real estate trusts, commodities, gold) or any specific focus (technology, energy, health care). Throw in the benefits of diversification, because a mutual fund can own dozens or hundreds of individual securities within those categories, and you've got a complete package.

I generally recommend such an approach to my clients. However, some people still like to try their hand at picking individual stocks. In that case, I encourage them to keep 90 percent of their investments in a well-diversified portfolio of mutual funds, and no more than 10 percent of their investments in the "casino" portion of individual securities.

As discussed in Chapter 8, mutual funds are a great way to establish a balanced asset allocation and get plenty of diversification. You can achieve those goals through a target date fund, a balanced fund, or funds diversified for a specific goal (dividend-oriented funds, small-cap value, foreign, etc.). One fund might be all you need, or you might decide you want to emphasize a different mix than what's chosen by an all-purpose fund.

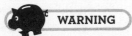

> How much is too much? If you've chosen distinct asset classes, you probably reach the limit of benefit once you have 12 mutual funds. Beyond that, investments in each of the funds will begin to overlap, thereby decreasing diversity.

Researching a Mutual Fund

As you are selecting a home for your investing efforts, it's worth evaluating what kind of research reports a company will make available, and whether the information depends on how much you have deposited. Most investment companies will offer you tools to screen for mutual funds (and individual stocks) based on whatever criteria you set up. If you assemble a sample portfolio, you can usually access a "portfolio x-ray" tool, which will analyze the potential holdings by geographical region, size, sector and industry, and holdings.

Most of these tools are on offer from Morningstar.com, which has become the go-to source for most information and number crunching about mutual funds (as well as other securities). Where investors once needed to comb through company prospectuses and annual reports, you can pretty much turn to Morningstar for all the data you can ponder. Check whether your chosen account home offers just screeners and portfolio x-rays, or whether you can get full access to analyst reports, as well.

> Morningstar's analyst reports are full narrative discussions by a person who specifically follows that company or fund. Generally, you can also read several archived reports to see whether predictions have come true, and how much back-pedaling the analyst has had to do.

Morningstar uses two types of ratings for mutual funds: its traditional one to five stars, and its more recently instituted gold/silver/bronze/neutral/negative ratings.

The star ratings are backward looking. They're based on how well a fund performed compared to peers in its same category based on risk and load-adjusted returns. This is a pretty good assessment of what the fund has done in the past, and how its performance compares to its peers, but it is *not* a prediction of how well the fund might do in the future.

First, be aware that, while a fund may have performed well compared to its peer group, the entire category may have performed poorly, so it would be an error to choose a fund just because it was rated five stars, without consideration for whether the asset category fits into your investment objectives.

Second, as every tiny-print disclaimer will tell you, past performance is no predictor of future performance. The manager of the specific fund may be replaced, the fund itself may alter its orientation, market conditions may change, and so on.

Third, the stars might help you screen out really poor performers, but if you're primarily searching for index funds that mirror a particular index, a three-star rating indicates that the fund is doing about as well as its peers, which is probably good enough—you want an index fund to replicate the index as nearly as possible. If an index fund is far outshining its peers (for example, in an asset category like large-cap), the higher stars may be actively managed funds with much more chance for management missteps that veer far from the index and asset class you're looking for.

TIP

If your investment company doesn't offer you full Morningstar access, check your public library's online services. Many will offer you a portal, via your library card, directly to all Morningstar investment research tools. As a last ditch, you can subscribe directly for access—Morningstar often runs introductory specials and allows you a trial subscription.

Morningstar's gold/silver/bronze/neutral/negative classification was introduced to provide an analyst's forward-looking judgment. Like all analyst judgments, including yours and mine, these ratings may be grounded in numbers, but also depend on a human's assessment of the future. I advise you to take it all in, but don't rely on it completely. I would lean toward funds with a bronze rating or better, but wouldn't choose based exclusively on the rating.

The Decision Process

The first thing you should look at when considering a fund is whether it has a load or not. (All of the following information can be found on Morningstar's pages for each investment.) You already know what I think of load funds, so let's move on to the management fees listed.

Management fees are what the fund company charges investors to run the fund: salaries, advertising, regulatory fees, and so on. You won't be paying these fees out of pocket; they reduce the returns paid to you by the funds. Even though some high-flying funds might have better returns with a higher management fee, studies show that going forward, low management fees are a good indicator of future high performance. And if the content and orientation of the funds are essentially the same, there's no reason to choose one with a higher management fee.

The following table offers a snapshot of what I'm talking about.

	Vanguard 500 (VFINX)	Fidelity Spartan S&P 500 (FUSEX)	State Farm S&P 500 Index (SNPAX)
Management fee	.16 percent	.09	.73 percent + 5 percent load
Value of $10,000 after 10 years	$19,420	$19,517	$18,248 (*not* including load charge)

These fee percentages may look tiny, but consider that the fees charged by State Farm are more than eight times as high as Fidelity's, even before you add in the front-end load. On $10,000 we already see over a $1,000 impact—add more zeros to your portfolio and the difference will have a major impact on your long-term returns.

TIP

As a rule, index funds have much lower fees than funds where a manager is being paid to choose investments based on their own analysis and philosophy. Some types of funds have extremely low management fees (index bond funds), while others require more involvement and selection (small-caps, internationals). Management fees should not exceed 1 percent in most cases.

Once a fund selects the index and the method of replicating it, the only management that's required is to change investments if the components of the index change. For example, if a stock is dropped from the S&P 500 index (or added), an index fund will adjust the portfolio to incorporate that.

The next thing to look at after management fees is the trailing 12-month yield (TTM). This is what the fund has paid in dividends, interest (if it has bonds), and any profit from currency transactions. Not all funds have a yield, or much of one, but I prefer ones that do. Over long periods, most of the growth of a fund will come from dividends reinvested (and then dividends paid on those dividends). Dividends help to smooth out some of the variations in share prices, and if you're retired and need income, you can have those dividends sent to you, perhaps lessening the need to sell shares for income.

Analyzing the Return

Okay, we've noted what analysts think of the fund, how it's performed in the past compared to peers, what it's going to cost us to invest, and whether we're going to see any income from the fund. But how is it doing? You want to examine the *annualized return* of the fund over all available time periods.

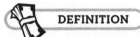

Annualized return is the average return of an investment over a period of years, averaged per year. For example, if an investment has earned 3 percent, 6 percent, and −1 percent over 3 years, its annualized return is 2.7 percent. Annualized return does not tell you how much the fund has *actually* earned each year, only the earnings on average over the time period.

First, look at the 1-month, 3-month, 6-month, and year-to-date (YTD) returns. These figures will tell you what the fund has been doing recently. If a big news event impacted the markets recently, you can see how your fund reacted. For example, if there was a marked change in energy prices in February, check the time period to see if the fund had improved returns or suffered from the news. Bad interest rate news? Changes in short-term return will let you know if that's a factor for your fund. YTD return is probably most valuable toward the end of the year, giving you some indication of whether the fund will finish strongly that year, and maybe a heads-up on whether they will be paying out much in capital gains.

While these short-term returns can tell you how your fund is reacting to current news, don't rely exclusively on short-term performance or you'll find yourself chasing the market. It's hard to resist a fund when it's turning in terrific current results, and hard not to discard one that's currently performing poorly. But in fact, one with a great short-term record will already have its price driven up, probably beyond future performance, while recent losers may offer buying opportunities. Or will a good performer continue to perform, while a loser has significant market headwinds against it? You won't know without doing a little research to see what the news, and analysts who follow the fund, are commenting.

Don't be afraid to view the annual report of the fund (available on each one's website) and any explanatory excuses—er, commentary—offered. You'll have to do your own thinking and sometimes wade through a lot of happy talk, but several different analysts' opinions will help you form your own.

Once we understand what a fund has done for its investors lately, we want to look at the mid-term record: the 3- and 5-year annualized returns. These can give you some indication of how the fund is likely to perform for some of your short-term goals. If you're considering the fund for medium-term goals, you also want to look at the year-by-year returns for 5 years. If, for example, the fund has an annualized return of 8 percent, does that mean that most of those 3 to 5 years it's returned 7 percent, 8 percent, or 9 percent, or does it have a record of −1 percent, 16 percent, 3 percent, 8 percent, and 14 percent? With the latter record, the fund might be too volatile to produce results for you in the year you might need your money.

When I'm judging a fund for long-term investment potential (and most investing should be long term), I look at the 10-year annualized return—even longer, if available. Some mutual funds haven't been around that long, but you should be wary of those with very short track records. Since the recession of 2008 and 2009 was the worst we've had since the Great Depression of 1929, it's useful to check how your potential fund did in a really horrible market. I especially like to look at how a $10,000 investment did over 10 years, paying attention to how close it dipped to the baseline in 2008 and 2009, or how far below $10,000 your investment would have dropped. It's not a given that you should avoid losers from that period, but it's certain that it can happen again. Can you tolerate that?

What's in the Portfolio?

Next, I look at what's actually in the portfolio—what are the top 10 holdings? Index funds will simply hold the companies in the index. But if I'm looking at an actively managed fund, I think about whether I would be willing to hold the top 10 or top 25 holdings individually. Do I think these are interesting picks, or do I wonder if the manager has his head under his wing? Do the holdings seem consistent with the fund's stated objective?

 TIP

> Mutual funds can be a good source of ideas for your individual stock picks. If an active manager is known for success, you might want to examine the picks in the fund's portfolio. Particularly for small-caps or specific sectors, you might spot a stock you'd like to acquire individually.

How big is the fund? An index fund will have a predetermined set of investments, and the size may be due to low fees or prevalence in retirement fund offerings. But an actively managed fund that has become outsize for its type indicates that many investors are piling in because of past performance (which is not necessarily the point where you want to join the herd). An active manager who suddenly experiences overwhelming investments may have a difficult time steering the ship—what used to be a swift and nimble sailboat may have become the *Titanic*. It can become so large, and take such large positions, that buying and selling a very large position can take time and produce different results (as the market gets wind of the activity). These funds sometimes shut down to new investors, and moving in and out of the fund may become more difficult.

On the other hand, a very small fund may not survive. Once it falls below a minimum level of money invested, the parent company may either close the fund or merge it with another, possibly changing the style. For small-caps, that level is below $800 million; mid-caps below about $3 billion; and large-caps below about $18 billion.

Finally, I review the Morningstar analyst report to identify near competitors. Is an index fund performing on par or slightly exceeding its peers? If it's doing far better, it may not actually be an index fund. Is an actively managed fund consistently doing better than its competitors *and* a comparable index fund? If not, why pay the extra fees?

Other Types of Funds

We've talked about open-ended mutual funds in general, including index funds. Now let's look at a few other types of funds: exchange-traded funds, unit investment trusts, and closed-end funds.

Exchange-Traded Funds

Exchange-traded funds (ETFs) are a relatively new development in the fund field. These are mutual funds that trade like stocks. Generally, they're index funds that focus on all the types of asset classes and sectors that are available in mutual funds. However, rather than waiting until the end of the day to establish a price based on the underlying investments (the net asset value), ETFs can be bought and sold throughout the day for a specific price from minute to minute, depending on the market.

In some companies (Vanguard, for example), ETFs are siblings of specific mutual funds—simply a different share class. Other companies have devoted themselves exclusively to packaging investment collections as ETFs, while some companies don't offer them at all, preferring to stick to traditional mutual funds.

Advantages of ETFs:

- You know exactly what the price will be the moment you purchase them.

- You can set a specific price at which you'll sell or buy.

- They're usually more tax efficient—the share price increases, rather than a manager paying you capital gains at the end of the year.

- There are no minimum investments. You can buy $25 worth if that's what you want to invest. (But you will usually pay a trading charge.)

Disadvantages of ETFs:

- If the market is in turmoil or market sentiment suddenly turns against a specific type of investment, the share price of ETFs can vary substantially from its net asset value. The market is acting like a voting machine, not a sensible weighing machine. ETFs can be whipsawed during daily trading.

- It takes 3 to 5 business days to access your money. As with stocks, you have to wait for settlement, whereas mutual fund money is available the next day.

- ETFs don't not have a long performance history, so we don't know how often their share price might vary from their NAV.

- So far, they are generally not available in workplace retirement funds, because they, like stocks, require a brokerage trading account.

Closed-End Funds and Unit Investment Trusts

Closed-end funds and unit investment trusts (UITs) are investment options that are probably too risky or esoteric for a beginning investor, but in case you come across them or inherit them, I'll mention them.

Both of these mutual funds are somewhat equivalent to ETFs, in that they sell shares, and once those shares are sold, they can be resold on an exchange. UITs generally have a specific term (5 years, 10 years, and so on) after which they are liquidated. They are most popular as a package of bonds.

Closed-end funds resemble ETFs in that they're sold like stocks, with a share price set by the market. However, whereas ETFs are generally index funds (required to disclose their holdings at the end of every business day), closed-end funds are managed by an investment manager and generally concentrate on a specific industry, sector, and so on.

Both of these investments faded somewhat in popularity when open-ended mutual funds and ETFs became available. You may still see them if you have a legacy or inheritance portfolio, but your investing is probably better concentrated in more readily available and easily traded funds.

 **WARNING**

Be extremely wary of anyone trying to sell you master limited partnerships (MLPs), which are shares in a company, usually some type of natural resources, and nontraded real estate investment trusts (REIT). Publicly traded REITs are a valid investment for those seeking risk for return. But anything not traded on an exchange has no real way to sell and recoup your investment. Because these are privately held, the actual value can't be determined except for what the company tells you.

Mutual funds are a great way to own a piece of many different types of investments, harvesting the benefits while avoiding some of the drawbacks and risks. They're not a no-brainer choice, however. You should do your research so you're not just picking something with a good name.

Take a little time to make a plan, and you have a good chance of growing your investments and still sleeping at night.

The Least You Need to Know

- Mutual funds are a package of investments put together by an investment company that diversify your portfolio's risk and return by owning a variety of securities.

- Morningstar offers extensive research and data to help you analyze mutual funds.

- No-load mutual funds put more of your money to work as you don't pay a commission to buy or sell.

- Funds with low management costs generally perform better over time than the same type of fund with high management costs.

- Examine fund returns over various time periods to see how your fund has performed under different market conditions.

- ETFs are mutual funds that trade like stocks: the value changes based on the price investors are willing to pay, and they can be traded any time during the trading day.

- Don't get hoodwinked by types of funds that you don't understand and that are privately traded.

CHAPTER 11

Investing in Stocks

Millions of books have been sold detailing various surefire schemes to beat the market, most of which make more money for the author in book sales than they ever make for the investor.

In this chapter we'll examine methods of evaluating stocks, from the crazy to the technical to the fundamental, and determine which one is best.

In This Chapter

- Should you invest in individual stocks?
- Diversifying your portfolio
- Using different strategies for choosing stocks
- Resources for gathering information
- Developing your own strategy

Deciding Whether to Invest in Stocks

Back in the days when the young Warren Buffett was learning at Benjamin Graham's knee, stocks were one of the few investments available to the individual investor (the others being insurance and bonds). Stock ownership was primarily an activity of the affluent middle class (or the truly affluent) and the majority of people saved in a bank, had a pension from their job, and bought insurance to cover burial expenses and leave a legacy. Students put themselves through college, or parents paid out of then-current income. Endowments and pension funds bought bonds. We all know those days are gone.

Beginning in about the 1980s, the scene began to change, and it wasn't good news for individual investors. We saw the rise of mutual funds, hedge funds, and big endowments that were able to take advantage of technology to make massive investments according to algorithms; invest in horrendous amounts of number-crunching analysis; and move the entire market by their decisions and nano-speed trading. In addition, we saw the disappearance of pensions, allowing companies to shift investment decisions and all investment risk to their employees at far less cost than providing pensions. It was David against Goliath.

Nevertheless, in the story, David wins. He wins by being nimble and thinking through his strategy using the materials at hand. If the individual investor has any advantage, it is that they can be more nimble, play individual best-guesses, and maybe beat the big guys.

As I discussed in Chapter 10, I believe that most investors can get all the investments they need through a diversified portfolio of mutual funds, and do well with them. But some of us just have that yen to see what we can do, and whether we can produce better results than the big guys. If you are so inclined, I urge you to learn as much as you can before investing your money, and to devote only a small portion of your total net worth to individual investments.

Before you begin investing in individual stocks, you should be certain that you have an adequate emergency fund, are fully funding your retirement savings, and don't need the money for at least 5 years. It's just a prudent standard—remember, although stocks may reward you to a greater degree than mutual funds, they are also far more risky.

 TIP

Stocks are listed and traded on an exchange. The largest is the New York Stock Exchange (NYSE), which generally lists larger and more stable companies. The NYSE requires that stocks trade consistently for at least $1/share. The National Association of Securities Dealers Automatic Quotation service (NASDAQ) is an electronic-only exchange of generally smaller or newer companies. The Over the Counter (OTC) market is where stocks that don't make the standards of the exchange are traded—generally dealer to dealer. It is far less regulated and there are no standards or listing requirements.

A Word on Diversification

Before deciding on an investing strategy, let's return to our principles of diversification (see Chapter 8). Whether you choose to orient your portfolio to growth, value, or income, or use crazy, fundamental, or technical approaches, you should aim for a sufficient number of stocks to diversify your risk.

Let's say you've purchased Pfizer, Novo Nordisk, and Merck and Company. You have three different companies, but very little diversity: they're all giant (large to mega-cap) drug companies. The only diversity you have is that one could be considered an ex-U.S. (international) stock: Novo Nordisk.

 **WARNING**

> Companies and stocks are mentioned for illustration purposes only. I haven't necessarily evaluated these stocks and am not recommending the purchase or sale of any of them.

Now let's say you've purchased Whole Foods, Air Lease, and IPG Photonics. Now you have diversified by the following:

- Size (large-/mid-/small-cap)

- Sector (consumer defensive, industrials, technology)

- Industry (grocery stores, rental and leasing services, semiconductors)

 TIP

> You can find these classifications for individual stocks on the quote overview page of the company's Morningstar description.

There's no diversity by location—all of these stocks are headquartered in the United States, although they do business around the world. As you get started, it's not critical that you have a fully diversified portfolio, but you should aim toward diversification. You can balance the portfolio by allocating money to mutual funds in areas where it's harder to evaluate and purchase individual stocks—for example, emerging markets, or internationals in general.

Wait to begin buying individual stocks until you can invest in three to five stocks with a reasonable number of shares. If you've never invested in stocks before, you might want to begin investing with a relatively small amount—say, $1,000 per company. Although it doesn't really matter if you own one share of stock that trades at $1,000/share (if it's a good one) or 20 shares of a stock that trades at $50/share (if it's also a good one), I recommend that the beginning investor choose stocks whose price is under about $50 to $60/share. Prices whose share price is quite high discourage other investors, and there's some psychological satisfaction in having a nice chunk of stocks. There's plenty to choose from in that category.

A nicely diversified portfolio clocks in at about 10 to 20 companies, chosen for diversity in size, industry, and sector. More than about 20 stocks and you're going to have a really hard time keeping up with the news, regularly evaluating them, and making informed decisions on when to buy and sell. But how do you find these stocks to evaluate?

Choosing a Stock-Purchasing Strategy

You'll need to choose a method of stock analysis, and an orientation that you believe in to finding stocks that meet that method's buy and sell signals, then work that plan. There are three general methods of purchasing stocks: the crazy methods, the technical analysis method, and the fundamental analysis method.

The Crazy Methods

If you are thinking about a method that relies exclusively on someone's opinion, promises quick money, or espouses a "foolproof" system that "guarantees" you high returns with little effort, the system you're considering belongs in this category.

The hot tip   This one comes from your brother-in-law, a guy at church, somebody you sat next to on an airline, or (worst of all) a guy on a television show. If you listen to these people as one source of ideas, be sure to check out the company using an evaluation method you apply to all potential stocks. (By the way, if the hot tip comes from somebody inside the company, or someone who has insider knowledge, that's called a federal crime. Don't act on it or you won't have much need for income in the future—because you'll be in jail.)

Buying what you like   Just because you like a product doesn't mean others will. I, personally, loved clothes from a specific store, but that didn't make it a stellar investment for me, alas.

A kissing cousin of this is a method once propounded by Peter Lynch, who produced great success for investors when he managed the Magellan fund, one of the best-known actively managed mutual funds of all time. He alleged that he would sit at a mall and watch what stores had the most business, and what people were buying, to choose companies to invest in. I'm skeptical. And even if it worked for him (many people believe the then-success of that fund was simply that the whole market was doing quite well), there are several problems with this method:

- You'll end up with a narrow portfolio of mainly consumer goods and retailers, because that's what most of us know.

- Just because a product is popular doesn't mean the company is well run. In my misguided investment in the clothing retailer, I noticed that the store was always packed. But my daughter got a job there, and that was when I realized that the store never had the right sizes in stock. You can't make sales if you don't have the right stuff.

- By the time you know about the company, everyone else has already figured it out and run up the share price.

Media recommendations   You have absolutely no idea how these were selected. Remember, television, radio, magazines, and newspapers are in business to entertain and sell advertising space. Imagine if they told you the same boring advice month after month. And even if they could predict the future, by the time that advice goes out to millions of people, the "news" is already factored into the price of the stock. Financial magazines in particular have a record for horrible predictions, and many have moved away from forecasts and focused on consumer articles, where they actually do add some value.

Super-special insider newsletters   Some of these are decent sources of possible ideas, and insiders in the investment business do read them. The more reputable ones follow a specific analytical method, and show you that analysis so you can make your own judgments. The more hype in the promo letter or email, the less I'd be inclined to subscribe. Why? Because if the author is so good, why is he even still working? If the ideas are so good, why does he need to hire a direct mail company to bulk mail 100,000 people with his exclusive ideas?

The worst of these are the penny stocks promotions. Unsophisticated investors are lured by the idea that there's a low price to investing in these because they literally sell for a few cents a share. A few problems with that:

- In order to make any meaningful amount that's worth the time you're spending and the trading costs, you have to invest a pretty big chunk of change.

- These companies go belly up a lot.

- They're often not traded on an exchange, or trading is so sporadic that you may not be able to sell them at any price.

- It's often impossible to get any information on them, and no analyst follows them.

My other least favorite type of newsletter is the kind that tells you how you can make a fortune in day trading or playing the options market. Trust me, you don't have the computing power, speedy access, or market knowledge to day trade. And neither do the hedge funds, which go out of business regularly with these so-called strategies. Options are a very sophisticated and complex strategy, and anyone reading a book on beginning investing should not even attempt this without a lot more experience and a huge war chest.

TIP

> If, despite my warnings, you're still interested in options, get your basics straight from the horse's mouth—the Options Institute of the Chicago Board of Options Exchange (CBOE). They offer tons of online instruction geared to your level and progress. Of course they're industry sponsored, so they take quite a positive view, but at least you'll be getting industry advice and many courses are free.

Schemes of all sorts   There are lots of schemes and methods that claim that if you just follow them, you'll beat the market. They'll usually follow some specific buying method that won't require you to actually dig into the quality or potential of the company. Their popularity waxes and wanes depending on how they're currently performing in the market.

The one I see most often is *Dogs of the Dow*. The idea is that once a year you buy the 5 or 10 highest-yielding stocks out of the Dow 30, hold them for a year, then switch out the following year for the current 10 highest yielding. The idea is that the worst performers will yield the most (because the price is depressed), and since they're the worst, they have the most potential to improve. Unfortunately, they may also do so badly that they get thrown out of the Dow, and no matter how much yield a stock pays, if the price drops, your total return can be tiny or negative (meaning you've lost money).

Be highly skeptical of anything that promises a simple system, needing no judgment or effort, which promises to help you get rich quick.

Technical Analysis

Technical analysis is the idea that if you follow certain markers and indicators, you can predict what a stock will do, and the best time to buy it. I'm not a believer in technical analysis because I don't think research supports it. Time and again research has shown that past performance is no indicator of future performance. In addition, market timing studies have shown that the best investing results are obtained by being in the market and staying in. If you guess wrong and are out of the market on the few best days, you can lose most of your potential earnings.

Technical analysts don't much care about the fundamentals of the company. Instead, they study and produce charts showing changes in sales volume of the stock, price ranges, and a variety of movement indicators. Hedge funds and some mutual fund managers are very much into various proprietary algorithms that they believe will predict the stock's performance and allow them to pinpoint appropriate buy and sell points. They're wrong, and the regular demise of so many hedge funds and the underperformance of active managers demonstrates this. If the big guys can't make it work, with all the computing resources in the universe, I don't think the individual investor has much hope.

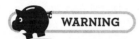

WARNING

Back testing is a method of using historical data in the construction of investment models to determine how well they would have worked had they been implemented in the past. The only data we have is from the past, so we'd like to think it can model the future. There is no reliable proof of this, however, and many unforeseen events can affect the future of an investment scheme. It's interesting, but not reliable.

Fundamental Analysis

The orientation I favor is fundamental analysis. It's based on a belief that you can, with research, identify and buy good companies at good prices that are currently being undervalued by the market, but whose value (and price) will improve over time. Depending on your own beliefs, you select companies based on their growth potential, their being currently undervalued by the market, or their dividend/income potential—or a combination of these factors.

Warren Buffett is a successful example of someone who uses fundamental analysis principles. While none of us has the wisdom, depth of knowledge, and access to information that Buffett has, I believe it's possible to make a reasoned and researched choice of companies the market has so far ignored. Analysts have been known to be wrong, and the market does not always behave rationally. In fact, I once owned stock in a company that Warren Buffett bought out. Note, however, that Buffett advocates that most investors should invest in index mutual funds.

There are many, many sources of information on the internet for stock data, but the four I use most frequently are Morningstar.com, Value Line, S&P Capital IQ, and BetterInvesting.

Morningstar.com   Morningstar has almost replaced the need for most investors to read annual reports, because all the numbers and graphic representations are easily available on the site. With the premium service (which you purchase or access through your library) you can review analysts' opinions as well. Morningstar will show you the price history of a stock, give you a rundown on what the company does, who its competitors are, the latest news, and all kinds of statistics and financial information.

I particularly like a section in the analyst's report that details what the *bulls* and *bears* say— a summary of reasons to have a positive (bullish) or negative (bearish) outlook on the stock. That, plus a look at the stock's competitors, can give you an inkling of its prospects.

Morningstar offers a lot of stock-screening tools: you can see their 5-star picks, stocks in specific sectors, international stocks, and so on. They also offer portfolio tools to survey the balance and return potential of a group you're thinking of buying (just create a model portfolio), and tons of articles on any topic you might want to learn about. As with all advice, test their analysis against your own judgment—analysts can be wrong.

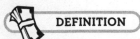

DEFINITION

Bulls are individuals or analysts who are optimistic about an investment, or the market as a whole. A bullish market is one that's on the rise. **Bears** are pessimists who believe the market or the investment is deteriorating, or see reasons why it will. Bear markets generally encourage investors to flee to bonds, and analysts who are bearish on an investment will likely recommend a sale.

Value Line   Value Line is a terrific, albeit pricey service. However, it's available in nearly every library, and if you're serious about investing in stocks, you should make a Saturday morning trip to learn about what it has to offer. Value Line may have a different take on a stock than the Morningstar analyst, so it's well worth getting this second opinion. Individual company reports are crammed with data.

Value Line can give you lots of ideas for stocks you may want to consider—they issue lists and reports of hot stocks in hot industries. They also offer sector reports, their opinion of sector or industry potential, and rankings of stocks for timeliness and safety (1 being the best and 5 the worst). Unless I had a good reason to disagree with Value Line, I'd be very reluctant to choose a stock that didn't rate at least a 3 on both factors.

Reviewing their lists is a terrific way to build a list of companies you might be interested in, as well as identifying companies you might never have heard of but which offer potential worth examining. You can choose several sectors that would offer you portfolio diversification, then review the best companies in those sectors.

Value Line is a treasure trove of market commentary and instruction. You won't understand everything you read at first, but you'll learn a great deal over time.

TIP

Your results will never exactly match the results of Value Line or Morningstar or any other model. You will always be buying at a slightly different price, on a different day, or at a different time. Over long periods, these differences tend to flatten out, and your return will grow closer to published returns, but it's never going to be a perfect match.

S&P Capital IQ   S&P reports are usually a service of your brokerage company, but they provide another analyst opinion, lots of data, and a rating by S&P (Standard & Poor's). It's worth getting these opinions in order to weigh them against your own judgment.

BetterInvesting   BetterInvesting used to be known as the National Association of Investment Clubs, and I still highly recommend joining an investment club and learning their methodology (see Chapter 22 for more information). However, even without joining an investment club, you can be a member of BetterInvesting, attend online training and stock study seminars, and access a vast amount of information on how to analyze stocks. They publish a magazine that highlights their stock selection of the month, stocks they feel are undervalued (with numbers analysis), and articles on current issues in the market. (Full disclosure—I write a quarterly mutual fund column for them and sometimes write cover articles.)

BetterInvesting offers a software tool to produce a Stock Selection Guide. It takes a while to learn but is the best tool I've found for evaluating stocks based on fundamental analysis. It's available online or as a complete software package called Toolkit. BI's method involves choosing stocks that have growth potential based on previous performance, growing sales and profits, and improving price ranges. You also seek out factors that appear to indicate the stock is undervalued (a low price-to-earnings ratio, or *P/E*), determine a high and low potential price to estimate risk, and add in dividend payments to determine total return potential.

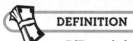

DEFINITION

P/E stands for price-to-earnings ratio. It's calculated by taking the current price of the stock and dividing it by the current earnings per share. It tells you how the market currently values the stock, and gives you some idea whether it's a bargain. For example, if the S&P 500 average P/E is 23, a stock with a P/E of 45 means the market so values the future potential of the stock that it's willing to pay more, even though earnings are relatively low, because there's a belief that the stock will produce much higher earnings in the future.

One slogan popular at BI is the five stock principle: for every five stocks you analyze properly and purchase, three will do about what you predict, one will do far worse, and one will do far better. I've found that to be true over the long haul, and it's pretty good odds. But you do have to be prepared that you'll select a few stinkers, even with the best effort at analysis.

Obviously, each of these resources has a method they use for evaluating a stock, but I've referred several times to "using your own judgment." How would you go about that? Here are some questions to ask while looking at the above resources.

Do you understand what the business does? You may not understand the details of every product line or service, but you should be able to explain the nature of the business, understand the sector and industry, and have some idea of how the company would make money, and what events or conditions would affect the business.

This is one place where it's really worthwhile to take a look at the annual report. Generally, annual reports will have a letter from the chief executive officer (CEO) of the company, explaining how the business did, what challenges it faced in the previous year, and how the company will be affected in the future. You can decide whether this is accurate information or just happy talk. A CEO is almost never overly pessimistic. If he or she says something is wrong, it's probably worse than that.

Does the business make sense to you and do you believe it has potential? A clothing store has to have fashionable clothes in enough supply and at the right time. A restaurant has to deliver tasty food without making people sick. A firm that books travel around the world will probably be hurt by terrorism, bad weather, and economic downturns.

When the company's offerings are business to business rather than business to consumer, potential may be harder for you to judge, but you should still research the industry and analyst comments to get a better understanding.

Does the company do business in an area you feel comfortable with? Warren Buffett has said he avoids technology stocks because he doesn't understand them. Personally, I don't like fashion or restaurant stocks because I think they go in and out of style too rapidly. Many people have purchased health care companies on the promise of baby boomer demand, but that demand has turned out, in some cases, to have a much longer time horizon than investors expected. After you invest for a while and have some successes and failures, you'll develop your own yardstick.

Is the company actually making money and does it have forward momentum? Many growth stocks have seen fantastic price increases but have no actual underlying earnings. This is particularly common with tech stocks and pharmaceuticals, where promise and investor hope may run up the price far beyond the worth of the company. Maybe you'll catch the wave and ride it upward, but I view trading on growth potential alone as a gambler's strategy.

I like to see stocks that have steadily increasing sales. But even if they sell a lot, they still have to make a profit, and the two don't always go together—the company may experience runaway costs, poor investments in infrastructure or real estate, or roiling labor unrest. You can have steadily rising sales, but flat earnings. As with all wealth building, if you don't hold on to what you make, you aren't going to profit.

I like sales and earnings that are both steadily increasing, with no surprise dips. If you graphed the sales and earnings, they should look like railroad tracks climbing a hill.

Is the stock price increasing and is it reasonable now?   Stock prices trade within a band every year. Morningstar gives you the 52-week range the stock has traded in, and you can look back at many more time periods. The stock should have a steadily increasing price band. Of course you're going to be sorry you didn't buy it way back when, but we're looking for things that can still go up. It's always hard to know whether a high price will continue to increase (pricing you out of the market, perhaps) or whether the stock will take another dip and allow you to snap it up. BI's Stock Selection Guide projects a buy-hold-sell range based on your expectations of the forward high and low price and P/E ratio. Generally, in an initial screening you might look for stocks that are currently priced in the lower half of their 52-week range, but know why the price is currently low.

What's the price/earnings ratio?   Google the average P/E of the market, the S&P 500, or the Dow. I don't think it matters all that much which one you use, but it helps to know how your proposed investment compares.

Growth investors don't necessarily look for a low P/E, and in fact may feel that a high P/E indicates the potential for explosive future growth. Value investors are much more wary of high P/Es, and generally seek companies whose P/E is at or below the market average. Value seekers look for low P/Es as a signal that the market has undervalued or not recognized the company's potential.

What's the stock's beta?   Beta is a measure of how much the stock swings compared to the overall market. A beta of 1.0 means the stock moves in synch with the market. Less than 1.0 means the stock moves less than the market—a fairly placid and stable stock. More than 1.0 and the stock is much more volatile (and risky) than the market. Once again, the higher the beta, the more potential risk and reward. You shouldn't necessarily avoid one or prefer the other, but it should be consistent with your expectations for the stock.

Does it pay a dividend, and has that dividend steadily risen?   Dividends, reinvested, will account for the majority of the increase over time in your overall portfolio. In general, value investors want to see a dividend, while go-go growth investors will ignore the absence of a dividend. A company that pays no dividend is likely to be reinvesting everything in the business. However, at some point investors get fed up, especially if the balance sheet shows a lot of cash, and demand that some of the earnings be paid to them as dividends.

Certain sectors tend to pay higher dividends—utilities and other low-growth industries and companies generally pay dividends to encourage and reward investors who hold them. Real estate investment trusts (REITs) are required to pay out 90 percent of earnings to investors. But too high a dividend compared to others in the industry may indicate a company in trouble. Either they're paying out too much in earnings to sustain over the long run (and perhaps fool investors) or they may even be borrowing in order to meet the expected dividend. In any case, a high dividend is worth investigating to make sure the earnings can sustain it, and to determine whether the company has concluded that it has no real growth or investment use for the earnings.

Seeking dividend stocks is certainly a valid selection strategy, especially if your investment goal is to provide a steady and stable income for such goals as retirement. Just know that you're probably not going to make a killing on capital gains.

Investors generally like to see steadily rising dividends—maybe not huge increases, but a sign that the company is steadily growing earnings. Be wary, however, of huge share buybacks. This is sometimes done because the company believes too many shares outstanding are hurting the stock's price, but it can also be a sign that the company is seeking to prop up the dividend by paying a perhaps higher amount on fewer shares.

 **WARNING**

A company that is forced to omit a dividend will generally see share prices plummet as a sign that it's in deep trouble.

How much debt does the company carry?   Some industries traditionally carry a lot of debt, while some companies have none at all. It's important to compare the debt load to the average of the industry (data for which can be found on Morningstar).

Have you established a target price?   Based on your research and analysis, you should have a goal price in mind for when you would consider selling the stock as having met your expectations. Similarly, you should consider how much of a drop in price you could stomach before you would want to sell. BI suggests having a goal of a stock doubling in value in 5 years, but this is aggressive. You should have lower expectations for bigger companies. Large companies generally do not move as much in price or have as much earnings growth as smaller companies. On the other hand, they should be more dependable.

Just because your stock has increased or dropped does not mean you should take immediate action. It's time to go back and reevaluate the reasons for the change. Generally, investors should let their winners run and get rid of the losers. Just because a stock was once priced a certain way doesn't mean it will ever return to that price—it doesn't have any memory. And just because a stock has doubled doesn't mean it has stopped growing; some companies have explosive growth. I remember when Apple Computer sold for $15 per share. And it could again.

Buying individual stocks is indeed risky business, but it can have thrilling rewards. You should do what you can to inform your judgment with as much information as possible, while still using your personal experience to reach independent conclusions. There's nothing wrong with sticking to a portfolio of diversified mutual funds, and they should be your core portfolio. Keep stocks as a small segment of your overall investments, building experience over time to choose what's right for you.

The Least You Need to Know

- Invest in individual stocks only if you can afford the risk and have time to research companies.
- Be sure to diversify in order to protect yourself against stocks that decline in value.
- Don't buy a stock based on random or unreliable recommendations.
- Fundamental analysis evaluates the nature and quality of the business to reach a decision about the worth and potential of the company.
- Use multiple information sources such as Morningstar.com and BetterInvesting to guide your analysis.
- Begin making a plan for how you will analyze a stock and make buy and sell decisions.

Investing in Bonds

Individual bonds were once part of every rich person's portfolio, and many independently wealthy people relied on them for guaranteed income. When interest rates are extremely low, new bonds fall out of favor because they pay so little.

Rewind a few decades back, especially during the Carter administration, and people were reluctant to snap up bonds even though rates at the time were quite high. Short-term money market accounts and 1- to 5-year bank certificates of deposit were paying extremely high rates, so why lock up your money in a bond? Those who had the foresight to purchase long-term, high-quality bonds at the time had the good fortune to collect a now-unobtainable rate of guaranteed return. Let's look at whether it's worthwhile to buy bonds, and how to go about doing so.

In This Chapter

- Should you invest in bonds?
- The pros and cons of bonds
- Different types of bond investments
- How to buy bonds

Should You Buy Bonds?

As with all the investments we're considering, whether you should buy bonds depends on your appetite for risk, the money you have available, and market conditions.

Generally, bonds and stocks move in opposite directions: when the market is hot, interest rates are low, and bonds are unpopular. When the stock market tanks, people "flee to safety" and bonds become popular. Because of this negative correlation, you can diversify the overall risk of your portfolio by including some bonds to balance stocks.

 TIP

Bonds won't give you a high return, but they won't desert you in a pinch. Think of stocks as your hot date who takes you great places, while bonds are your steady-Eddie cousin who's boring but will loan you some money from time to time.

You'll want to balance your bond holdings with your needs and risk tolerance too. An all-bond portfolio won't generate enough growth to allow you to keep up with inflation and still withdraw enough cash in retirement to maximize income from your portfolio. An all-stock portfolio can be so risky that you might not *have* a portfolio in retirement.

Why do bonds provide stability? Besides their negative correlation with stocks, they offer two forms of return: their price (if they are sold) and their yield. Price and yield move opposite to each other. When bond prices go up, the yield goes down. When prices are down, the yield goes up. This combination is not a perfectly equal exchange, but it tends to smooth out returns in mutual funds devoted to bonds. If you hold a portfolio of individual bonds to maturity, as long as you hold the bonds (and they're of decent quality) you'll receive rock-steady income from them, with a return of principal at the end.

How many bonds are enough? If you have a long time horizon for your investments, maybe none at all. By now you've heard of the 4 percent rule: that you can withdraw about 4 percent of the value of your portfolio each year in retirement and expect it to last about 30 years (at least). But that rule is based on your having at least 50 percent in stocks, and no more than 50 percent in bonds, in order to get the growth that stocks provide over the long term. For very elderly people, investment managers will sometimes select a predominantly bond mix—say 70 percent bonds, 30 percent stocks—because this group has a strong need for safety and probably a shorter time horizon for inflation to erode buying power. But this, as with all other investment decisions, is dependent on the individual's financial picture.

Bond Basics

A bond is a loan you make to a government entity or corporation. In return, the borrower agrees to pay you interest for a specific period of time. At the end of the bond's lending period (the *term*), the borrower agrees to pay you back the original sum (the *principal*) you invested.

Depending on how good the borrower's credit rating is, they may have to pay you more or less interest to make loaning them money attractive. The safest bonds pay the least. The most risky bonds will give you the most income.

The longer the time you agree to lock up your money, the more you will generally be paid, because you're sacrificing access to your money for a longer period of time and you're running the risk that interest rates could go higher or the borrower could default, in which case you would lose your principal.

 TIP

There have been a few historical periods where short-term interest rates were actually higher than long-term interest rates (called an *inverted yield curve*). Why? Generally these were periods of high inflation. Experienced investors may have realized at the time that all rates were at uncharacteristic highs, and long-term bond buyers were trying to lock up those relatively high rates for the long term—thus, issuers could attract buyers with somewhat lower rates. Watch for that opportunity!

When bonds are offered to the marketplace (individuals, pension funds, endowments, etc., all buy bonds) they are referred to as an issue. Governments and companies (the issuers) use them to raise money at a predictable cost (rate of interest), while delaying payment until sometime in the future, when hopefully the money will be available to repay bond holders. If a company does default, bondholders are ahead of stockholders for distribution of any remaining assets of the company.

New issues are sold at a specific price, for a specific guaranteed interest rate (the coupon rate), and a specific term, or period of time, until the principal must be paid off (the maturity date). So you might purchase a $10,000 30-year bond with an interest rate of 2.5 percent. You'd be paid $250 in interest every year, and at the end of 30 years you'd get your money back, provided the issuer was still in business.

The example I'm using is the current rate on U.S. Treasury bonds, so they'll likely pay off.

TIP

Some bonds are sold at a discount to their face value (U.S. Treasury bills) or as zero-coupon bonds. These bonds pay no interest. You buy them for a lower price and at the end of the term you get the whole amount. The difference between your purchase price and your final value is the interest rate you've made.

Bond Quality

Bonds are rated for creditworthiness, to give you some idea of how likely you are to get your principal back, and to determine how much the issuer is likely to need to offer you in interest in order to entice you to lend them your money. Three different services—Moody's, Standard & Poor's, and Fitch—provide bond ratings, using slightly different numbers (and occasionally rating a specific bond differently). S&P's ratings are the most frequently referred to. Bonds are divided into Investment Grade and Non–Investment Grade, with divisions ranging from safer to riskier, as shown in the following tables using the Standard and Poor's rating system.

Investment Grade	
AAA	Prime
AA+, AA, AA-	High-grade investment
A+, A, A-	Upper-medium investment grade
BBB+, BBB, BBB-	Lower-medium investment grade
Non-Investment Grade/High-Yield/Junk	
BB+, BB, BB-	Non-investment-grade speculative
B+, B, B-	Highly speculative
CCC+	Substantial risk
CCC	Extremely risky
CCC-, CC, C	Default is imminent with little recovery potential
D	In default

AAA bond ratings are granted only to extremely stable governments (e.g., United States, Australia, Canada) and very stable companies (e.g., Automatic Data Processing, Johnson & Johnson). Well-run corporations and less-stable governments can be found in the lesser grades. Once below BBB-, interest rates paid will be much higher but the risk also increases.

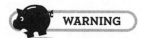

WARNING

Unscrupulous brokers sometimes pitch low-rated bonds to unsuspecting investors, especially seniors, with the claim that these bonds will yield a good income. They will, until they default. In that case, you lose your income and your principal. Be sure you understand bond ratings before you purchase an individual bond, and know the average rating of bonds in any bond mutual fund in which you invest. High yield means junk.

Once a bond is issued, its rating can decline if the creditworthiness of the underlying issuer declines. As you might imagine, this makes it very difficult to sell the bond, and puts the holder of the bond at more risk of future default. These formerly higher-rated bonds are called fallen angels.

Other Bond Risks

New bond issues typically track inflation. When inflation is very low, so also are bond rates. In eras when inflation has exploded, bond rates have been very high as well. People will often refer to the good old days of high bond rates, forgetting that inflation was much higher at the same time.

But let's say you were smart enough (or will be smart enough in the future) to purchase some bonds at high interest rates. Can you sit back and collect that interest for the term of your bond? Maybe; maybe not. You need to know whether the bond you are purchasing is callable. This means the issuer can call back the bond before the term is up, paying you back your principal and any interest owing up to the point of call. If interest rates drop substantially, and the company can afford it, they pay off the bonds costing them high interest payments, and refinance with new issues at lower prices (or possibly they are doing well enough to just pay the bonds off).

This is not good news for you. Although you do get your money back and therefore have no risk of default, you now have reinvestment risk, meaning that it's highly unlikely you'll be able to find the same interest rate at the same credit quality, in the current market.

As long as the bond is not called (or is not callable), you can sit back, collect your interest, spend it or invest it in something else, and collect the principal at term. However, what if you need the money before the term is up? Unlike annuities, you can sell a bond in the *secondary market*.

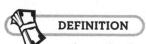

DEFINITION

The market for used bonds is called the **secondary market.**

Generally, the current value of a bond will have some correspondence to now-current rates. For example, let's look at the way an individual bond might change. In our example, John Elder bought $15,000 worth of BBB rated 30-year bonds in 1997. They paid 7.8 percent at purchase. In 2027 he or his heirs will get their $15,000 back, and in the meantime he collects $585 twice a year ($1,170 per year total) in interest. In retrospect, given current rates, it looks like a great deal.

But let's say John needs that money now. He can sell the bonds today for $129.679 each, or a total of $19,451.85 (approximately). He won't collect any more interest—his buyer now gets the interest. But, given the purchase price, the interest is worth only 6 percent to the buyer, the term is shorter, and the bond is still callable. (In real life, the buyer is also going to pay a commission, and any accrued [pro-rated] interest due to the original purchaser up until the time the bond is actually sold.) The buyer is taking more risk for less reward than the original bond owner, but compared to current market returns, it may be worth the risk. This is called the current yield.

However, there's another way to think about the worth of a bond that you're selling or buying, called the yield to maturity. This is a combination of the current income generated by the bond, plus any change in its value when it's held until maturity. You'll need a financial calculator to calculate the rather complex formula, so I'm not going to go into it here (and if you're buying, the investment house should be able to tell you). On the earlier bond, the yield to maturity is about 4.38 percent. It's generally thought to be a more accurate estimate of the bond's return (of course, conditions can change) and is more in line with competitive current rates for the same type of bond.

Finally, there's the yield to call, which is the yield if the bond were to be called on the earliest possible date. Weigh all three of these to scope out your potential return, depending on your time horizon and intentions for the bond. Services like Morningstar or the brokerage you're using for trading can supply you with all these figures based on the day-to-day trading price of the bond.

Buying Bonds

Buying bonds is a bit different than buying stocks. There's no specific exchange (like the NYSE or NASDAQ) for bonds, but they are traded between brokerages in an over-the-counter, or dealer-to-dealer, market. U.S. government securities can be bought directly from the feds via their website (TreasuryDirect.gov), or at banking institutions.

We're going to look at the general characteristics of bonds, considering primarily corporate bond behavior. Then we'll note some differences between corporate bond and government bond investing.

TIP

When buying bonds, it's not quite as important to evaluate the underlying company as it can be with stocks, because the bond is going to carry a credit rating, and should be competitively priced based on the rating and the yield. Obviously, if a company or government authority has been in the news recently for credit problems, their bonds are more risky, but in general this is not as big a concern as it is when evaluating individual stocks.

Characteristics of Corporate and Government Bonds

An investment house is going to have specific bonds on offer, and you choose the type, then the specific bond. There will be a difference between the bid price (what buyers are offering) and the ask price (what sellers are asking). You may be told there's no commission, but we know there's always a hitch, right? So the bond's price will be marked up to include a commission. Look up the price at Morningstar to see what they are quoting to know whether the marked-up price is in line.

 TIP

The big investment companies, both full-service brokerages and discount brokerages such as Charles Schwab, Vanguard, Fidelity, and TD Ameritrade, will have the ability to assist you with bond purchases, and you should take advantage of their live help and online demonstrations and tutorials before purchasing individual bonds.

You usually need a fair chunk of change to purchase bonds. Most U.S. government issues have fairly large face values of $1,000, $10,000, or $1,000,000. For corporate bonds, you will usually need to make at least a $5,000 investment, even if the bonds are denominated in $1,000 face values.

It's not prudent to put all your money into one bond. Sure, U.S. government bonds are as safe as you get, but what about changes in interest rates in the future? In a low-interest-rate environment, you don't want to commit yourself to all low yield.

People who invest in individual bonds generally build what is known as a bond ladder. You purchase a set of bonds with differing maturities, depending on when you will need them—5 years, 10 years, 20 years, and so on. As you need cash, these mature and pay you a return on your investment. Problem is, when current rates are low, locking up a significant amount of money for a long time may have you kicking yourself in the future.

How do you know when rates are right to purchase bonds? It depends on your goals. If we estimate inflation to average about 3 percent, and you wanted your withdrawals from an all-bond portfolio to give you 4 percent a year, you're going to need bonds paying 7 percent, at least, not easy to find these days.

On the other hand, you might consider locking up some guaranteed money when bond rates are at or about their historical average of 5 or 6 percent or better. Because bonds are not going to be your entire portfolio, securing a solid return (based on historical averages) for some part of your portfolio may be worth considering.

Or you might consider a bond mutual fund. Bond funds can emphasize specific classes of funds (emerging markets, international, long-term, short-term, intermediate term, U.S. government) or can be a combination of all types (total bond market fund). You can get an initial reading of the risk level of the fund by examining its *duration*, and the mix of credit ratings or average overall credit rating of the fund. (See Chapter 10 for more on mutual funds.)

DEFINITION

Duration is a calculation using present value, yield, maturity, and call features; luckily you don't have to calculate it yourself. The mutual fund or sources like Morningstar will include this in its standard information. The longer the duration of a mutual fund, the more risk (in normal interest rate environments). Total bond market funds generally clock in at an intermediate duration because their short-term, long-term, and intermediate-term bonds will tend to balance to the mean.

Advantages of a bond mutual fund over bonds:

- Easier to buy and sell. There's a share price every day, and the funds are either sold and redeemed by the company or listed on an exchange (for exchange-traded funds), so there should be no difficulty in finding a buyer or seller.

- Well diversified. Bond funds contain hundreds of bonds, and you can choose the level of quality, type of bond, and average term. You'll hold far more bonds and spread the risk far better than if you held a few individual bonds.

- More responsive to market. Bond managers can sell and buy much more easily than you can, and shape their portfolio for maximum total return.

- Having a bond called won't affect you very much. The risks and returns are all averaged.

Disadvantages of a bond mutual fund over bonds:

- Return is not as dependable. If you're holding high-interest-rate bonds to maturity, you'll get that yield. Bond funds will tend to drift to the current bond market.

- Yield differences. Yield will probably not be as great when a large number of bonds are averaged as it would be if you owned a high-return bond (when they're available).

Types of Bonds

There are myriad types of bonds: U.S. government, corporate, municipal, mortgage, and foreign, to name a few. The U.S. government uses different names to denote the various fixed-income securities it offers:

Treasury bills are debts sold in denominations of $100 to $1,000,000, maturing in 3 to 12 months. They are sold via auction (you enter a noncompetitive bid) at a discount, so a $10,000 bond might sell at $9,700, which would give the holder 3.1 percent interest for the holding period. These are also the type of short-term securities that underlie some of your investment in money market mutual funds.

Treasury notes are intermediate-term debt (1- to 10-year term). They are sold in denominations of $100 to $100,000.

Treasury bonds mature in more than 10 years and are sold in denominations of $100 to $1,000,000.

Notes, bills, and bonds can be purchased through TreasuryDirect.com, or from banks and brokerages.

In addition to these three bonds, there are two familiar, consumer-oriented options: EE bonds and I bonds, otherwise known as savings bonds. Savings bonds were originally issued (as E bonds) to help finance World War II. There is no resale market for EE bonds, they can't be used as security for a loan, and they can't be transferred as a gift. They can be redeemed at banks, and pay 90 percent of the average rate paid by 5-year Treasury securities in the past 3 months. They used to make a popular gift at a baby shower or graduation, but it's hard to justify investing in them at present because of the low interest rates and inability to sell them before term.

I bonds sell in denominations of $50 to $10,000, and interest rates are set twice a year by the Treasury, adjusting every 6 months. The rate combines a guaranteed minimum fixed rate and an adjustment for inflation. Maturity date is 20 years from issue date and is exempt from state income tax.

TIP
Both EE and I bonds are exempt from federal tax on interest if the bonds are used to pay qualified higher education expenses (see Chapter 17). There are better ways to save for college, but if you already have some of these bonds, using them for college expenses might be a good way to maximize their value to you.

Treasury Inflation Protected Securities, otherwise known as TIPS, are bonds designed to overcome one of the difficulties of other bonds: that they don't rise with inflation. TIPS pay a pretty modest interest rate, but if the Consumer Price Index (CPI) goes up after issuance, the principal that the government owes goes up. If the CPI goes down, it's possible that the bond would lose money. Obviously, these bonds are much more volatile than other bonds, and TIPS mutual funds have seen some wide swings in share prices. Probably no one would put all their bond investments into TIPS, but for some inflation protection they are worthwhile contenders (particularly as mutual funds).

Ginnie Maes are bonds backed by Federal Housing Administration and Veterans Affairs mortgages. They were flying high not so long ago, but when mortgage rates are low, they're not so popular. They have a face amount of $25,000 and have an expected term rather than a term-certain (because mortgages can be retired early). The payment you receive is a combination of interest and principal, and you won't get a payment at the end of the term (so payments will seem much higher than other types of bonds). Again, these are probably easier to invest in via mutual funds.

There are other types of U.S. government bonds, but they are beyond the scope of a beginning investor. If you have determined to invest in bonds, these are the most common securities you'll find individually or in bond funds. All-U.S. bond funds will contain a mix of government and corporate securities (unless they are specifically designated as only U.S. government or corporate).

State and municipal government bonds are exempt from federal taxation, and may be exempt from local taxation if you live in the jurisdiction. You won't be surprised to learn that therefore these pay a lower rate of interest. Whether it's worth it depends on your tax bracket: if it's high, these may have a better net return than taxable bonds. State or municipal bonds can be either *general obligation bonds* or *revenue bonds.*

However, there's no reason to hold these bonds in 401(k)s, Roths, or traditional IRAs, which are already tax exempt. Hold municipal bonds, or municipal bond funds, only in taxable accounts. It's also very important to pay attention to ratings on these bonds—many states and municipalities are in bad financial shape and some may even default on these bonds. Once again, you can spread the risk by investing in a mutual fund.

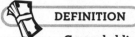

DEFINITION

General obligation bonds are backed by the general revenues (taxes) of a state or municipality. Since the government has the power to raise taxes, these bonds are regarded as safer than **revenue bonds,** which are used to raise money for a specific project, like a toll road, which will then produce its own income. If the project goes bust or loses money, the bond will be in trouble.

It can be worthwhile to diversify bond holdings into non-U.S. bonds. Depending on the strength of the country's government, foreign government bonds can range from very safe (with low interest rates) to very risky (poorly governed and/or emerging market countries). As with international stocks, international bonds do not directly correlate with the U.S. bond market. While you might want to diversify your portfolio with an investment in foreign bonds, this is an area where you should almost certainly stick to investing in them via mutual funds, given the difficulty of evaluating them and having a sufficient number, in addition to your U.S. bond investments, to achieve diversification.

International bond mutual funds are available in just about every flavor—total international bond market (usually weighted toward the developed countries); developed markets (Europe, Australia, New Zealand, Canada, Japan); and emerging markets. However, you have an additional choice with international bond funds: *hedged* or *unhedged*.

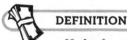

DEFINITION

Hedged means the fund has invested in currency instruments to protect against the blow if the dollar varies significantly, so that returns are only dependent on changes in the actual bond. **Unhedged** means no protection is in place with currency risks. Unhedged funds will offer more diversification to your overall portfolio (because they'll be less correlated with U.S. bonds) but more risk and volatility. Hedged bonds are less volatile, but will act closer to U.S. bonds.

In my opinion, individual bonds are more complicated to invest in than individual stocks, but can provide a safety net for your other, more aggressive investments. In high-rate environments, you might consider locking up returns with purchases of individual bonds. But for any investor interested in bonds as part of their portfolio, bond mutual funds can offer easy access to many of the benefits.

The Least You Need to Know

- A bond is a loan you make to a government entity or corporation, in return for which the borrower agrees to pay you interest for a period of time.
- Bonds provide a safety check on your portfolio, because their price usually moves opposite to stocks.
- Bond mutual funds can diversify your risk and give you a portfolio of bonds, but they don't lock in returns like ownership of individual bonds does.
- Bonds come in many varieties and can be issued by governments and corporations. Whatever the variety, return will be determined by risk and current market rates.
- Some bonds (and bond mutual funds) are safer than others; know the bond's rating before you invest.
- Bonds can be sold before they mature, but the price and yield will likely be different from what they were when the bond was originally issued.

Choosing Alternative Investments

Investing in alternative investments can produce another source of potential wealth whose market and value can operate far differently from more usual investments like stocks, mutual funds, and bonds. However, there are complexities and considerations unique to these investments that you should be aware of before committing significant wealth to any investments in this category.

Before investing in alternatives, you should have an in-place savings plan, be contributing regularly to retirement savings, and be well diversified in your core portfolio. If these factors are in place, you might consider satellite investments in some or all of these categories.

In This Chapter

- Understanding the market for alternative investments
- Investing in collectibles
- Investing in gold, precious metals, and gems
- Investing in natural resources and commodities
- Investing in REITs and MLPs

Concerns Common to Alternative Investments

Alternative investments, by definition, are out of the mainstream. They require more investigation than more widely traded investments like securities and may be harder to buy, sell, and evaluate. Almost certainly, they will require more of your time invested, a higher degree of expertise, and more risk tolerance.

The Nontraditional Markets

Investing in alternative investments means you're investing in nontraditional markets. When there's an established exchange (as for stocks and ETFs), large companies backing securities (mutual funds), or an established trading system (bonds), it can be easy to buy, sell, and value your investments.

Not so with most alternative investments (gold, publicly traded REITs, and MLPs being partially excepted). You may need to purchase and sell these investments to a dealer, find a private buyer or seller, or consign them to an auction house. Any of these alternatives take far longer and are far more uncertain than simply selling your stocks online through a brokerage. In fact, for certain select pieces (antiques or other collectibles or works of art) it can take years to accomplish a purchase or sale.

It can be very difficult to assign a value to some alternatives until a sale is actually transacted. Some items are so unique that few comparables may exist. In that case, you're at the mercy of whatever buyers or sellers are in the marketplace when you want to make the transaction, and whatever valuation this inefficient marketplace offers at the time.

In addition, particularly in collectibles, markets are subject to fads and herd mentality. Crazes strike this marketplace regularly, until the fad passes and late buyers are stuck with a rapidly devaluing collection.

Many of these investments are luxury purchases or are only accessible to individuals with great wealth. When the securities market or general business environment is in decline, these investments may lose value more rapidly because of fewer potential buyers. And if a style or tastes change (especially in antiques, art, and some collectibles like dolls or stamps) you can see a long-lasting precipitous decline.

 TIP

Shirley Temple dolls were once quite popular with doll collectors. However, many dolls tend to be popular with people who played with them as children, and as that subset of collectors ages out of the market or acquires a complete collection, the market drops for the dolls.

The Cost of Selling

Because it's not as easy to value or sell many alternatives, the selling is not a simple transaction like entering a buy/sell order online at a brokerage. Consequently, agents or auction houses can charge very hefty commissions to facilitate the transactions.

We're all spoiled nowadays with the very low commissions charged for selling securities. Not so with many alternatives. Residential real estate commissions are typically 5 or 6 percent; dealers who will sell your art or collectible on *consignment* may charge 30 to 40 percent of the sale price. If you do consign a piece, be sure you understand what the commission is, whether there is a return charge if the item doesn't sell, and whether the item will be covered by insurance (either yours or the dealer's).

In the case of auctions (usually for art and collectibles), both buyer and seller are charged a fee or commission based on the final sale price. Auction houses such as Sotheby's and Christie's charge the seller 2 to 15 percent, and the buyer 10 to 15 percent (over and above the actual selling price).

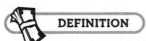

DEFINITION

Consignment is an arrangement in which a dealer or shop owner (online or bricks-and-mortar) takes your item, handles display and marketing, and perhaps even takes it to live shows. If and only if the piece sells will you receive any proceeds. Many dealers limit the time period during which they will continue to attempt to sell the item before returning it to you.

Taxation Issues

Taxation on alternatives is complex and specific to the type of alternative. The capital gains rate on collectibles and art can be up to 28 percent (unlike the maximum rate of 15 percent on securities gains); for REITs, MLPs, and any partnership taxation is even more complex. See the specific type of investment in the follwoing sections for further information. And plan on consulting an accountant who's familiar with your type of investment if you plan to make this a feature of your investing.

Usage and Ownership Costs

Collectibles, art, wine, and other alternative investments require maintenance costs while you own them. For the item to retain its value, or continue to be in desirable saleable condition, you must maintain them in optimal environmental conditions: proper lighting, temperature, humidification, protection from any environmental damage. For example, a wine collection requires temperature-controlled and humidified conditions; musical instruments require protection from dust, dryness, and physical injuries and in some cases may need to be continuously played; coins and stamps cannot be scratched or abraded.

Some items must be stored in a rented safety deposit box. Some (such as gold) can be stored with a dealer, but you will also pay charges for that.

Finally, any valuable collection must be insured. Your homeowner's insurance may cover some value (less the deductible), but to fully cover the value of an item you will probably need a separate personal articles policy or add-on rider for specific coverage. In order to obtain and maintain this coverage, the insurer will almost certainly require up-to-date professional appraisals on all items. Appraising a collection, or even, say, a few musical instruments can cost hundreds of dollars. As the value grows, you should update the amounts of coverage.

> **TIP**
>
> If your collectible is something that may be moved or damaged (for example, musical instruments), you should check that your insurance coverage is for "all perils," which covers damage or breakage.

To accurately evaluate alternatives as an investment, you must calculate all these factors as "costs of doing business." We all fantasize about buying something at a garage sale and finding out on *Antiques Roadshow* that our item is worth many times what we paid. But if we add in all the costs (probably not yet paid if we didn't know it was valuable) and factor in what it would take to sell it, it may not be quite as great an investment.

Let's say I bought a drawing at a rummage sale in 1976 for $100. I take it to *Antiques Roadshow* and they astound me by telling me it's worth $2,000. Of course I'm excited. I decide to auction it in 2016 and get $2,000 for it. I have to pay, let's say, 10 percent to the auction house, so now I have $1,800. My capital gain is $1,700, so I'll pay $476 in taxes, leaving me with $1,224 in profit. That looks excellent, but is it? The annualized rate of return for that $100 was 6.5 percent. That's not bad—but if I'd carried insurance on the drawing, or paid to have it framed with archival materials and so on, it would not have been as astounding an investment as it first seemed.

Collecting Collectibles

Jane buys a necklace at a high-quality antiques show from a well-known dealer who's an expert in the field. She pays $5,000 for it in 1993. She's told it's 14-karat gold, Italian, and dates from the 1860s. In 2015, she takes it to *Antiques Roadshow,* where they test it, tell her it's 15-karat gold, English, dates to the 1880s, and is worth $8,000. Jane is relieved that it's at least worth what she paid, but realizes that in 23 years it hasn't been a good investment. However, she decides she needs to increase the insurance on it and hires an appraiser for $100 who tells her the original well-regarded dealer knows better than the guy from *Antiques Roadshow* and that the necklace is indeed Italian, 1860s, etc., although he'll go with the $8,000 valuation.

This story illustrates three important points about collectibles:

- Part of the value of many collectibles (including art and antiques) to the owner is the sheer enjoyment of possessing and owning. Collectibles cannot be strictly valued at market value alone.

- A great deal of expertise is required to truly evaluate unique objects, and the experts don't always agree.

- There is risk inherent in identifying and valuing a unique piece, and no way to realize a precise value without finding a ready and able buyer.

- Buying retail may make it harder to realize any gain.

One of the most entertaining versions, for me, of *Antiques Roadshow* is when they show a clip from an old show, then place a current value on the item. A significant number have either stayed flat or lost value (with a few spectacular increases). Anyone investing in collectibles should realize that fashions change and that even certain long-established collectibles (for example, antique dolls or certain painters) can experience price drops.

TIP

Sometimes your interest in or purchase of one item can lead to an active business. I've seen people who began with an interest in a specific type of collectible become so expert and active that they turn it into a business. This, like investing in rental properties, requires a great deal of time and effort and should be considered a business venture (and evaluated accordingly) rather than pure investing.

The capital gains tax rate on collectibles parallels your income tax rate up to 28 percent maximum, as long as you have held the item for at least 1 year. Otherwise it is a short-term capital gain, taxed as ordinary income. You can offset other losses against the gain, but this is an area in which I urge you to get professional tax help. Also, be sure to keep purchase receipts—there's no brokerage house to go through electronic records to establish your cost basis. And if you ever expect to sell the item, keep track of any insurance costs or commissions pertinent to it. If heirs inherit, their cost basis should be established as of your death date, so a current appraisal is in order.

I've discussed the difficulties of what is a very inefficient market. Because of this, there are two other cautions you should consider.

The first is that it can be just plain hard to sell a collectible. Similar to real estate, you have to find a buyer with enough money and interest, and that buyer may take some time to appear. This is not an investment area where you can raise cash immediately.

The second is that, because the market is essentially unregulated, there's no real government oversight to protect against fraud. Unless you're an expert (and even they have been fooled), you may find you've purchased a very good fake. That's why *Antiques Roadshow* is always talking about *provenance*. In some cases (looted artworks, items made from parts of protected species), you may be prohibited from selling them at all, and they may be confiscated. Collecting physical objects is a case where a buyer must beware.

> **DEFINITION**
>
> **Provenance** refers to the established and documented history of a collectible.

Gold, Precious Metals, and Gems

You can invest in gold, precious metals, and gems in two ways: by owning the physical items, and by *speculating* on prices through investment instruments. Many people want to own the physical objects as a hedge against disaster, while others like to speculate through gold-based investment shares.

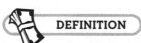

> **DEFINITION**
>
> **Speculating** is gambling that you can purchase something at a low price (perhaps below market) and sell it, usually quickly, for a far higher price—either because the market will change rapidly or you can find an eager buyer. If you're an expert investor, you may take a calculated risk, but be prepared to be wrong on some of your bets. Speculating is a high-risk venture that can (rarely) produce outsize rewards.

Gold as a Disaster Hedge

Gold, especially small gold coins, and gems have been a traditional way to hoard wealth, especially in dire economic and political scenarios, and be able to transport at least some wealth from place to place. Plenty of people in wartime would have starved to death without some gold coins hidden under the floorboards, and people have escaped war-torn countries with gems sewn into the hems of their clothes.

Gold coins purchased because they are antiques or are rare are collectibles, and my cautions in the above section are more applicable. Coins kept as the ultimate disaster hedge should probably be selected in small sizes so they're easy to transport and use to transact during Armageddon.

For those of us who don't believe the world is ending, having gems and precious metals in the form of jewelry is probably more enjoyable. Again, however, the value of these items depends more on artistry and fashion than simply on the weight of the metal or size and quality of the gems. And as anyone who has ever tried to sell a diamond ring after a divorce knows, you're going to take a real bath on the price. Gems are somewhat an artificial market, where major mining and producers have historically conspired to keep the price higher than what market supply would otherwise have achieved.

Gold Coins and Bullion

Investing in pure gold can be achieved by purchasing Canadian Maple Leaf coins. The coins are .9999 pure gold. They are minted by the Royal Canadian Mint, and while they are legal tender and stamped with a face value, their actual market value varies with the current price of gold. They must be kept in untouched condition in order to maintain value. (The Mint also sells other precious metal coins, and commemorative sets, which fall into the category of collectibles.) Coins are available through dealers; be certain you're purchasing through a reputable one.

TIP

There's some indication that the price of gold goes up during Indian wedding season (September to December), when large amounts of gold jewelry are purchased and given as gifts.

You can also purchase bullion, or gold bars. These aren't very functional as an end-of-the-world hedge, but if you're determined to speculate on the price of gold, they're available. Generally, you have your choice of taking delivery yourself, storing them in a safe place, insuring them, and facing the burden of proving their worth. Certificates are generally provided corresponding to the stamps on the bars. If you lose the certificates, you'll have to pay to have the bars assayed to prove their gold content. Once you take possession, you have to prove the gold content and quality. You can store the bars with the dealer to avoid this, but you will still need to pay storage costs and insurance. You will be charged a premium over value to buy (often 10 percent) and the same to sell, meaning you will have to achieve a sale price 20 percent higher than your purchase just to break even.

Gold-Based Investment Shares

If you're just speculating on the price of gold, you can also purchase ETFs that own gold, and the shares are marketable in the same way as any other ETF. The price basically tracks the price of gold. However, like other commodities funds, these shares pay no yield, so the only increase in value is based on share price. There are people who believe passionately in gold (especially brokers who want to sell it to you), but in general, gold tracks inflation. Frankly, I'm not a fan of it except when it's made into things I can enjoy.

You can also invest in mining stocks and gold mutual funds. With mining stocks you're making a bet on not only the demand for a specific natural resource (precious metals), but also both its price as a metal and the demand for that metal in industrial uses.

Gold mutual funds invest in gold mining companies, various forms of gold, and other assets (like silver) that are complementary. They're more diversified than other precious metal investments, but I'm happier with a general natural resources fund, which will contain a diversified portfolio of the stocks of these companies along with many other products or materials—chemicals, forest products, energy, and so on.

 **WARNING**

> Be aware that gold mutual funds are very volatile and that you can lose a lot of money investing in them. For example, as of this writing, if you had placed $10,000 in one specific gold and precious metals fund 5 years ago, it would now be worth $3,876. If you had placed $10,000 in it 4 months before this is being written, it would be worth $16,567. You have to be willing to live with that kind of volatility, but why would you? It's a gamblers stratagem.

Natural Resources and Commodities

For years I've thought natural resources mutual funds and commodities funds and ETFs should be part of large, diversified portfolios. Now I'm not so sure about commodities.

Commodities funds are considered as part of a portfolio because they are negatively correlated with just about every other kind of investment, meaning they tend to do well when everything else stinks, and stink when other market segments are doing well. Commodities funds invest in futures contracts on oil, timber, corn, soy, hogs, and so on.

There are several problems with commodities funds: they can veer far from the actual commodities markets because of the complexity of trading and financing futures contracts; they pay no dividends so you never build up the fund by reinvestment; and they can lose and lose and lose.

The consensus among financial advisers in the last several years is to get out of investing client portfolios in them at all. Finally, commodities funds have complex taxation and should probably only be held in tax-sheltered funds where, unfortunately, you cannot deduct their sometimes-crushing losses.

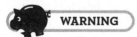 **WARNING**

> While commodities funds are often selected because of their negative correlation with other asset classes, the one asset class they do correlate with is emerging markets. Emerging economies are often dependent on basic materials production. When commodities sink, so do emerging markets, but perhaps to a lesser degree. An investment in emerging markets may be all the exposure you need.

Natural resources funds are a somewhat different story. They are very volatile as well, but here you're also investing in the health and efficiency of corporations. For example, a fund that holds Dow Chemical is already diversifying among a number of chemical products. In a well-diversified fund, at least some of the companies should be doing well in different market environments. These funds also usually offer decent yield (2 percent or more) so you have some chance of building over time.

However, if you own stock funds, you already have an investment in natural resources companies. If you add specific natural resource funds, you're overlapping—tilting your portfolio more strongly toward them. Take a look at your stock funds to determine what percentage they're already invested in natural resources companies.

Real Estate Investment Trusts and Master Limited Partnerships

I mentioned these investments briefly in my discussion of mutual funds in Chapter 10, but let's look at them in more detail.

REITs

Real estate investment trusts (REITs) are an investment in which, technically, you're part of a partnership rather than a stockholder. They are operated by the general partners (who actually run operations) and the investors (you), who are limited partners who provide the cash. The partnership then owns and operates any variety of real estate: storage lockers, industrial or office parks, skyscrapers, hotels, and so on.

An individual REIT usually focuses on a portfolio of similar properties. A REIT mutual fund or ETF will hold partnerships in a portfolio of individual REITs, so you get broad diversification to many possible types of real estate. REIT performance doesn't necessarily correlate with the individual housing market—in 2009, not a banner year for homeowners, REITs returned (as a class) 28.60 percent.

Because they are a partnership, REITs come with more complex taxation. They must distribute 90 percent of earnings to limited partners in order for the general partners to avoid federal taxes. Guess whose obligation that is? REIT dividends aren't considered the same as corporate dividends and are taxed at your marginal tax rate. For this reason, REITs and REIT mutual fund investments are usually most tax efficient if you hold them only in tax-sheltered funds such as 401(k)s and IRAs.

It can be extremely difficult for the individual investor to evaluate the quality of a REIT. If you're a beginning investor, I urge you to stick to REIT mutual funds and ETFs, which are publicly traded, and where there's a better chance that the manager has selected a diverse portfolio of (hopefully) reputable REITs. These are volatile investments, but they throw off a lot of income, so many people find them worthwhile to incorporate into a diversified mutual fund portfolio.

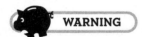

> **WARNING**
>
> Whenever you contemplate an investment you don't thoroughly understand, repeat to yourself, *If it looks too good to be true, it is.* Nearly every investor in Ponzi schemes and investments later investigated by the SEC would have avoided getting scammed if they'd just paid attention to that one principal.

Nontraded REITs are another story. I probably read more scandals involving these than any other type of investment news that crosses my desk. These "investments" are packaged in glossy brochures detailing the beauty and popularity of the underlying properties, and often pedaled to unsophisticated investors seeking large income payments. Nontraded REITs will often offer twice the yield of a publicly traded REIT, which should already cause you to smell something coming from Denmark.

They can look great until you try to sell them. There's no way to establish a market worth—they're "worth" what the company says they're worth, but since the shares can't be sold except to the company (always at a big discount from what you paid, if they'll buy them back at all) there's no way to know how the market will value them. There's virtually no secondary market in nontraded REITs.

Eventually they will have what's known as a liquidity event (after anywhere from 2 to 10 years), when they're brought to public trading. Just before the liquidity, the company will offer to buy back shares, almost invariably at less than you paid, while the agent will encourage you to keep the shares because they have "every chance" of selling for more at liquidity. Yeah, right. They're not totally worthless in most cases, as long as they have profitable underlying properties. But the chances of you getting a capital gain are pretty slim. Don't buy them, do what you can to get out of them if you're already in, and invest your money in something else.

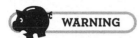

> **WARNING**
>
> Ponzi schemes, sometimes known as pyramid schemes, are one of the most common ways investors are defrauded. In this scam, the organizers must continually sell new shares, or investments, and use the cash to pay off previous investors while skimming off huge amounts for themselves. It all eventually collapses when no new investors can be found. The method is featured in Charles Dickens's novels *Martin Chuzzlewit* and *Little Dorrit* and is named after Charles Ponzi, who scammed investors in 1920.

MLPs

Master limited partnerships (MLPs) have just about all the same factors and cautions as REITs, except they're invested in something different, usually energy producers such as oil and gas drilling and pipeline transportation. When the price of oil is depressed, they can look cheap, but before you jump at the "bargain" you should think carefully and do research on the future of fossil fuels compared to the movement toward clean energy sources. Venerable companies, such as Bell and Howell, once looked quite cheap—just before the entire camera and projection industry collapsed.

Taxation on MLPs is complex, and you really should have a session with your accountant before plunging into any investment. MLPs pass through income and depreciation and depletion to limited partners, so in order to realize tax benefits they should probably be housed in taxable accounts.

These are another investment often targeted at retirees and people seeking income, but they can vary greatly in the strength of their businesses and volatility. It's not an investment you should make on a short conversation or the undocumented recommendation of a broker. I don't think MLPs belong in the portfolio of a beginning investor, but if you decide they're of interest, you've got a lot of study ahead of you.

Alternative investments probably are the place where the most questionable investments surface. It's easy to see why: there's usually an inefficient marketplace (so it can be hard to verify claims of value); they are often complex products or hard to value (so investors don't really understand what they're investing in); and they go through waves of fashion and market whipsawing (so a few people make a lot of money and bring tales to others, too late to profit).

No one needs to include alternatives as part of their portfolio in order to achieve diversification, although many reputable advisers recommend some investment in publicly traded REITs for the income received and exposure to a different sector of the market. Go slow and be careful to understand what you're investing in.

The Least You Need to Know

- Alternative investments can be difficult to value because the market for them is less efficient.
- Collectibles can have value as an investment, but they may have a hard-to-quantify value of enjoyment for the owner.
- Investing in precious metals has two functions: as a personal hedge against disaster, and as speculation on the direction of the price of the metals.
- Commodities pay no dividends and are very volatile.
- Stick to publicly traded REITs and MLPs.
- Understand how the investment will be taxed, and choose appropriate accounts (if applicable) to house the investments.

Investing in Real Estate

Once upon a time I was a real estate broker, and my territory was one of the wealthiest neighborhoods in Chicago. Who bought those ultraluxury homes? Generally, people who had made their money themselves. These homes were often sold for cash, to people who had started and sold a successful business or invented something astounding; personal injury lawyers who had settled a big case; and people who had *invested in real estate*. (This was some time ago, so I'd probably add in tech millionaires who cashed stock options, nowadays.)

Some began by buying, living in, and selling their homes at a profit. Some invested in apartments, office buildings, or occasionally land and were able to generate a combination of rents and gains at sale. But be warned: investing in real estate is far more difficult and requires far more time and attention than most other investments. Despite what get-rich-quick seminars would have you believe, real estate investment can be just as risky, if not more so, than investing in securities.

In This Chapter

- Should you invest in real estate?
- Real estate agents and how to work with them
- How to treat your primary residence as an investment
- Calculating whether the investment can be profitable

Buying a Home as an Investment

In this chapter, I'm going to briefly consider your home as an investment. Chapter 16 covers your home purchase as a goal—as an end to your investing program, rather than as part of a wealth-building program.

Your Primary Residence

Let's say you need a place to live, but you want to use your home as a stepping stone to all your future, improved homes. You're going to treat a home purchase and ultimate sale a little differently than if you just want a nice place to settle into for the rest of your life, or at least the foreseeable future.

Most people's first home is not their dream home. What you buy for investment needs to be someone else's dream home, not necessarily yours (because you're going to be moving on, right?). Figure out your target price range—how much of a mortgage you can get (or less) and how much of a down payment you've saved. As long as you live in the property, you will probably be able to get an owner-occupied mortgage rate. Financing strictly investment properties often requires a higher down payment and different financing. No matter how much a lender might be willing to loan you, think carefully about what you can actually afford in the context of your own lifestyle. You might not want to borrow the maximum.

Your first step is to understand the market. Choose the area you would like to purchase in, and start going to open houses. Be sure you see not only properties in your price range, but cheaper ones. The owners of lower-priced homes may be your future buyers and will want something better than they have now. Or you might find a good deal. Also see more expensive properties, so you can begin to understand what kind of amenities and finishes make the difference.

You should look critically at purchasing condominiums and townhouses. Depending on where you live (center of a big city, for example), they may be the principal type of affordable housing available. However, because they are part of a larger complex whose value is well established, it will be hard for you to sell this type of property for much more than the average sale price, unless you find a wreck or a distress sale and intend to improve it while living in it.

Be particularly careful to understand why the unit is distressed (developer problems? estate sale? big assessment coming up?) and how condo rules might affect anything you contemplate doing to the unit. Don't buy a condo without studying a copy of the declaration and rules, and find out whether the assessments or homeowner's fee has gone up dramatically, or whether a special assessment is contemplated or planned. None of these things will necessarily kill your purchase, but you should be able to scope out what your ownership costs might be. No surprises.

You should also understand the history of sales in the building. Have they sold steadily? Have sellers had their unit on the market for years? How much did prices drop in a downturn, and have they recovered? One advantage of condo buying is that you will be able to assess the price track record better than a more unique single property.

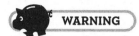 **WARNING**

> Many people think that if they can't sell their condo immediately they can just rent it out. Not so. Many buildings have imposed restrictions on rentals because they've found that if units are not primarily owner occupied, the quality of life, the commitment to the space, and the type of fellow residents quickly deteriorates. Know what the rental rules are in a building if you're thinking of rental as a plan B or source of future income.

When you buy a single-family or small multi-unit (more about that in "Small Multi-Unit Properties," later in this chapter), you're more likely to have more freedom in selling or renting, but check with the local government of the area to understand if there are regulations or requirements for single-family rental.

Buy the Worst House on the Best Block

Once you've scoped out what's available in your price range, the price range just below yours, and the price range just above yours, you want to narrow it down to which are the worst homes on the block.

Are you saying to yourself, *I saw this adorable place. Sure, the neighborhood is a little dicey, but I can get so much more for my money?* Wrong, wrong, wrong. You're thinking like a homeowner, not an investor—a homeowner who is going to live in that place a long, long time waiting for the neighborhood to catch up with what you paid.

You want to do the exact opposite. You want the tiny house, the ugly house, the neglected house, the 1950s house in a sea of vintage homes, the old home in a sea of new ones. This strategy has several advantages:

- Your new neighbors will be thrilled to see you. They'll welcome with open arms someone who's going to improve the eyesore.

- Your upside potential future sales price will be higher because the neighborhood pricing will support it.

- Future buyers who would like to live in the neighborhood but can't quite afford it will be interested. Some will move into the neighborhood just for schools, proximity to transportation, or safety (three factors you should consider when purchasing).

Understand the Real Estate Business

During your travels in open-house land, you're going to meet a lot of real estate *brokers*. It can be a great way to find someone to work with, guide you through all the listings for sale, and help you with the contract, finding a lender, and suggesting inspectors and repair people. Do you need one?

It depends. I'd never sell a house without an *agent*. I wouldn't want to be available at all hours to answer calls (they aren't either, but more than I would care to be), or make appointments with potential buyers. I don't have an ability to prequalify a buyer, and I simply don't have the connections to arrange the closing, deal with sometimes hostile negotiations face to face, or promote the property to other agents. In my view, they earn their commission.

DEFINITION

What's the difference between a real estate **agent,** real estate **broker,** and **Realtor?** In popular speech, they're used interchangeably. But technically, an agent is a salesperson, while a broker has more education and can supervise agents. Realtor is a specialized term, properly written with an uppercase R, that indicates the person is a member of the National Association of Realtors.

Real estate agents tend to fall into three types:

The professional who understands her segment of the market   She has the contacts and the understanding of value and financing to help you out. Be aware that if she specializes in high-end homes, or starter bungalows, she's probably not going to know much about properties at the other end of the price spectrum, and probably not much about small multi-units or investment properties. She may have an assistant, and if you're small potatoes, that's who you'll probably be working with. She's out trying to get more lucrative listings. Real estate agents live in the moment for short turnarounds, so you're not going to get her excited by the promise that one day you'll be a seller.

The socialite   Real estate is filled with part-timers and, often, wives of rich and influential men. These people cycle through the job very quickly when they find out how much work it really is. They may turn out to be quite good—or they may know absolutely nothing about property. True story: an agent and I were once standing in the basement of a home with a client, looking at a furnace. The client asked what kind of heat the house had. A blue flame was clearly visible through the door of the furnace. The agent said, "Really, I have no idea—oil, I think." She was right about one thing: she had no idea.

TIP

Meeting agents at an open house allows you at least a first impression of whether or not they are any good. Again (as with brokers), don't choose one simply because she seems nice. They all are. If they aren't, they don't sell anything and they're quickly out of the business.

The newbie   Don't immediately select an agent just because he or she has total sales in the millions or is the top seller in their office. The agent may have a turn-and-burn policy, and if you don't quickly generate a sale, they could lose interest or hand you off to an assistant. People cycle through the profession rather quickly, but if you find a hungry newbie who behaves professionally (follows up, keeps in touch, shows you what's out there, and gives you honest advice), you might be working with someone who will put much more time and effort into you than a more experienced agent. You're more valuable to this new agent.

TIP

Did you call in on a "For Sale" sign? You will likely be connected to whoever's on the floor that day, unless the listing agent is actually in the office. This person's mission will be to convert you into a client, not necessarily for that specific property. There's no harm in this, but you won't know who you'll get. Give 'em a chance, but don't feel obligated to work with that agent.

Get an Inspection

Unless you're extremely well versed in housing construction and know what can go wrong, get a qualified home inspector to go over your proposed purchase, and make sure your offer has an escape clause in case the inspection goes poorly. This is less necessary in a condo, where common elements are common problems, but you should thoroughly test appliances and plumbing, look under sinks and at walls and ceilings for signs of leakage, and so on.

TIP

Most real estate agents can recommend an inspector, but you may want to find your own. If an inspector nixes a deal, they won't be recommended by the agent again. You want someone who owes their allegiance only to you.

Just because the inspector finds things wrong (and they almost always do), it doesn't mean that you should discard the property. Just be aware of what a repair might cost. The agent and the seller might not like it, but you can go back with a contractor for an estimate. If they won't let you do that, be very wary. You can sometimes negotiate for a higher price and cash back at closing, which may allow you to finance the repair. Just be aware that that will increase your mortgage and closing costs based on the higher purchase price.

On the other hand, even the best inspector misses some things. You need to have at least a small emergency reserve to cover things like the bottom dropping out of the water heater, or a sewer line that hasn't been rodded out in a while.

Be Canny with Improvements

Improvements that you make when you're an investor planning to sell may be different than what you'd do if you planned to live there for 30 years.

Since you've done your homework on what buyers expect in properties at the level you hope to sell this one, you'll know whether granite counters, custom cabinets, tile, oak floors, or highly upgraded bathrooms are expected or not. If you're still friendly with the agent after the sale, ask for suggestions on what would improve the property. What would she like to see done if she were to re-list it? Agents know what sells: when I sold my dad's house, mine made a terrific suggestion for flooring that was quite inexpensive. Just about every person who viewed the property commented on the beauty of the flooring.

 TIP

The more you can do yourself, the more you'll keep your outlay small. Just about anyone can learn to paint an interior (which often makes the biggest single difference in appearance), but replastering a wall is a serious skill. Some things, especially those requiring inspection (electricity and plumbing), should be done by a professional.

Don't fail to research what permits might be required in your jurisdiction for specific home improvements. Mess up and you could find your job shut down, yourself slapped with some big fines, and even your eventual sale halted. It's just not worth trying to sneak by. Put it in your budget.

Keep the place neat and clean (and get the pets out).

If you're going to be an owner-occupant who wants to sell the place eventually, learn to be spic-and-span and super neat. Buyers hate clutter—the less you have, the more they can picture their own things in the space. However, totally empty rooms read smaller, because there's nothing to scale the eye against.

Most Realtors will advise you not to be home when prospective buyers are viewing the property because there's too much chance they'll ask you something or you'll blurt out something that will turn them off.

Don't Neglect Maintenance

You may end up living in the home longer than you think. Trees still need to be trimmed, roofs repaired, lawns edged.

 **WARNING**

Many people think of their home and the built-up value as their ultimate fallback emergency fund. However, over the course of years, maintenance can be deferred, and the décor can become familiar but out of date. Recognize that if you plan to sell, some money will need to be invested in updating to current trends, at least visually.

What About Staging?

In big cities you can hire professionals for a consultation on how to make the home look more attractive. Often they are decorators, but what you want is someone who can help you make dramatic but inexpensive improvements—select paint colors, rearrange furniture, distribute candles, flowers, or potpourri about the house, and so on. They'll help you get rid of clutter you don't notice. These people can literally make a $10,000 difference in the selling price, and speed up a sale.

If you can't find someone, bring in a couple of real estate agents and ask them to be brutally honest. Here's where you absolutely want the top sellers with experience—they know what sells. Agents won't charge you for this because they're hoping to get the listing, and to be fair you should at least consider them when you do sell.

Have an Exit Timeline in Mind

An investor has a plan. If you just settle in until you finish, you'll still be there when your kids graduate from college. Set yourself a deadline based on how much improvement you can make, what repairs you can afford over that time, and what additional cash you can save, if any, to kick into the next property.

Let's say you want to sell in 3 years. Do the structural repairs first, then the exterior, and finally the freshening up of the interior so that everything will look new to the buyer and you haven't had 3 years to beat it up.

 TIP

A real estate investor is always looking at properties in order to keep current with the market. Be sure you keep looking so you're abreast of trends and prices.

What's a Good Profit?

I don't know your local area, but I can say with certainty that your profit won't be as much as you hoped and as much as those real estate seminars would like you to believe. Some areas are so up-and-coming that in a few years your sale price can double. Not as likely anymore, but it still happens.

I'd feel pretty darn good about a purchase if I got my down payment back plus double the cost of what I'd put in for repairs. You got the tax deduction for owning the place and lived there for all that time. Of course, some sellers do far better, but you're probably going to need to do it a few times before you can spot the perfect house needing the most cost-effective repairs.

Other Considerations

While you can probably get a better return from buying owner-occupied housing, improving it, and selling it, you're going to be putting a lot more time into this type of investment than you would simply going online and trading mutual funds.

It can be hard to raise enough money to handle the down payment and the needed repair costs. Most people tend to buy the most expensive house their down payment funds will get them, and neglect to keep a reserve for repairs and upgrades. You may be able to get a construction loan, which will temporarily loan you money at a fairly high (often variable) interest rate with a balloon payment at the end of the (short) term. Then you have the house reappraised at its now higher worth and refinance the mortgage, paying off the construction loan. If you do this, the carrying costs of the loan need to be accounted for and figured into your sale price and profit analysis.

 TIP

The market can take a turn for the worse and you may not be able to sell your house for anywhere near what you've put into it. Or, you may not be able to sell at all, and need to sit on it hoping that the market will recover. This is a little easier to do when you're the owner-occupant rather than someone who's just renovating to sell quickly.

You may be wrong in your estimate of what your house can sell for, and your improvements and hard work may not return what you hoped. Bigger risk, bigger rewards, remember? You can control some of the risks because the investment is being run by you, not some far-off CEO or the government of Krakistan. At the same time, it's you who must make the choices, do the work, and live with the consequences. Or hopefully, reap the profits. What might they be?

Let's say you purchase the home for $250,000, putting 10 percent down and allowing $5,000 for closing costs and moving your stuff, putting down deposits on utilities, and so on. You plan on putting $35,000 into repairs, but you end up spending $50,000 instead. Three years later you sell it for $350,000. How much have you made? We're going to confine our first look to the cash gain or loss and leave the tax factors for your accountant to advise on (and you should have that conversation if you're seriously evaluating a potential investment).

Your total investment:

> $25,000 down payment
>
> $5,000 closing costs
>
> $50,000 repairs
>
> $38,670 in mortgage payments ($225,000 at 4 percent interest)
>
> $118,670 = your total cash cost

What did you make?

> $350,000 sale price
>
>   −$118,670 your cost for home purchase and upgrade
>
>   −$35,000 closing costs, transfer taxes, and real estate agent commission
>
>   −$212,622 mortgage payoff
>
>   −$16,292 = loss

Not exactly get rich quick, right? But wait, you've lived there for 3 years—3 years you would have been paying rent somewhere else. You also got a tax deduction for the interest you paid on the mortgage (and it's mostly interest in the first few years.) You'll walk out of the closing with about $102,378—which will give you a start on a much bigger purchase. Fiddle with the numbers a bit—sell for more, put less into repairs, sell it yourself without an agent (good luck) and the returns can come out quite differently—in either direction.

Is this type of investing worth doing? For some people, yes. Personally, I've never had the time or courage to make it work, but I see people who do. Often, they are people who are full-time real estate agents who see tons of property, can judge value, and have a flexible work schedule that allows them to meet the plumber when he calls asking where you want the bathtub that was just delivered to your front porch. One agent I know had set herself a goal of purchasing a property a year, renting it, and selling it when the appreciation allowed a profit and she could upgrade to a better property. She managed 10 in 10 years. Not all of them were profitable, but once the portfolio grew large enough she had enough portfolio diversification to absorb losses. And a tidy retirement income base.

Purchasing Small Multi-Unit Properties

People who buy small multi-units (four apartments or less) with the intention of living in one while renting the other(s) have a somewhat different orientation. The worth of these properties is based more on rent collected than the renovate-and-sell model.

In this scenario, the main obstacle is coming up with the higher down payment for what is nearly always a more expensive property than a comparable single-family home. As long as you will live there and the building is four units or smaller, you should qualify for owner-occupied lending rates, and the lender will take into account the actual rents as income on the rental unit(s) when figuring out if you will qualify for a higher mortgage. Depending on the property and the neighborhood, you may qualify for a low down payment FHA loan, or be required to come up with 10 percent or 20 percent for a down payment.

The second obstacle is actually finding a property. Some neighborhoods are filled with these properties—they were particularly popular with immigrants and people who had large families or expected their children to move upstairs when they married. Other neighborhoods and suburbs have practically none. Especially in older properties, these units can be spacious and quite nice—they were built to be owner and family occupied.

The idea in investing in one of these properties is that you live in one, getting help with paying the mortgage by applying rent from the other units, and over time you increase rents until the tenants are buying the building for you. If your plan is ultimately to move into a single-family home, you can rent the unit you now have, providing more income; sell the property with increased value based on now higher rents; or borrow against the property for whatever amount the increased rents will support, and add another property.

The main pitfall with this strategy is that the tenants can drive you crazy. A small property will probably need to be self-managed (so you need at least rudimentary fix-it skills) because it's too small to support professional management fees. Also, maintenance and repair costs may be higher on a bigger property. Multi-units can experience market reverses also, and rents can deteriorate. Major, unexpected repairs can gobble up all your projected profits. The fewer the units, the more a vacancy will hurt your income.

The main advantage is the flexibility. You can live there, you can increase income, and you can sell it at a profit. There's not as much pressure to move in a hurry, and no restrictions on renting it. There's some economy of scale over renting a single-family home, and even if one stays vacant for a few months, the other unit(s) will still be paying rent and covering some of the costs—less risk of vacancy or destruction than renting single-family properties.

In the early years, you'll be lucky if the property pays the mortgage (figure your unit in at a reasonable market rent) and covers repair costs. These properties are usually priced at break-even or a little less (figuring you should also count your tax deductions). But as the years go on, they can be very profitable.

> **TIP**
>
> When I see clients who own multiple small properties (often in partnership with other family members), they're usually quite happy with the income and value if they've owned them for fairly long periods (10 years or more). However, almost all of them at retirement are looking to transition out of them—they just can't take the tenants any more. Buy while you're younger and more tolerant!

Apartment Buildings, Offices, and Other Real Estate Investments

Larger apartment buildings are a whole different ballgame. You need different kinds of financing and a much bigger down payment. A lender will evaluate their worth based on the property's balance sheet, carefully evaluating costs and rent collected. Special care needs to be taken to ensure that the current owner isn't providing a statement based on a lot of deferred maintenance, or that the cost of those basic repairs is factored into your purchase offer. This is really beyond the scope of beginning investing, and I suggest you either get your toes wet with smaller properties to gain experience, or get a reliable partner who can help you learn the ropes while investing with you.

> **WARNING**
>
> Office buildings and industrial buildings are for investors who understand the peculiarities of the market—not beginners.

The one purchase that many beginners make, or find themselves inheriting, is vacant land. You might have the luck to buy a great piece of land in the path of development, but these opportunities have become far fewer in recent years as city sprawl has diminished. In the meantime, land produces no income and requires you to pay taxes. Unless you plan to build on it in the near future, or use it for some profitable purpose, it's a liability, not an asset.

I've seen a fair amount of clients who have inherited farm land, often rented. It can be quite hard for the city-dwelling heir to evaluate and manage the investment. If you find yourself in this situation, get an appraisal. County extension services can tell you what the estimated price per acre for the county is, but a professional on the spot can do a better job of evaluating the value based on both the land and the rents collected (if it's being farmed by someone).

If you inherited the property free and clear (without any loans), you'll have to take into account the appreciation potential and the collected rents. Is it a worthwhile investment? Well, compare it to a decent dividend-paying stock—are you making at least 2 percent on rents for the total worth of the property? Does it have steady value or solid appreciation value? Whenever you keep your money in one investment, you give up the opportunity to invest in another. Be sure holding the farm is actually a decent investment, and don't retain it only because of childhood memories or loyalties to a deceased family member.

Investing in real estate can bring you good returns—if you learn how to manage costs and use a sharp pencil when figuring income and outgo. Be prepared to put far more time and hands-on labor into this type of investment, and be sure you have the personality to cope with contractors, tenants, and house hunters.

The Least You Need to Know

- Work with a real estate agent who's right for your needs.
- Treat your primary residence as your first real estate investment.
- Choose the most cost-effective improvements that will help you sell at a profit.
- Get an inspection to protect yourself.
- Consider small rental properties as an alternative to renovating and selling.

Investing for Specific Goals

Just as no investment is truly all-purpose, no one's goals are exactly the same. Depending on your age and financial circumstances, you may be more concerned with retirement, or college funding for your kids, buying or upgrading your home, or investing for a special dream. You might have come into "sudden money": a lump sum that both delights and scares you.

In this part we'll discuss how to tailor your individual investment plan to match your goals. While you still need a big-picture asset allocation strategy, there are special considerations to consider for specific goals. Even if retirement is a long way off, you still want to incorporate planning for it into your overall financial life. Conversely, if you're near retirement you might want to help out grandchildren, or invest in educational services.

It's always useful to have an understanding of the issues related to different goals. The more you know, the better an investor you can be.

Investing for Retirement

The old reality was that Social Security provided a base to guarantee minimum living expenses. The new reality is that even if you collect the maximum monthly payment at full retirement age (currently $2,639/month), you'll have a tough time living on it. Of course, most people don't collect the maximum—$1,335/month is the average collected benefit. You're probably going to want, or need, more than Social Security will provide.

It's likely that investing for retirement is the most long-range, expensive goal most of us will ever face. Yet we put it off, push it out of our minds, and begin investing later than we should or maybe not at all. That's really unfortunate, because nowadays it's all on you.

In This Chapter

- How much will you need to retire?
- When can you retire?
- Maximizing guaranteed income
- Protecting your funds
- Withdrawal strategies

Many of our parents and maybe grandparents could count on a pension from their jobs, coupled with Social Security payments that went a lot farther. If they saved above and beyond that, they had guaranteed income plus a little extra. But retirement looks very different nowadays. Let's dial back a little and think about the good old days and how the new reality immediately suggests steps you should take.

Estimating How Much You Need

Retirement income can best be balanced if it's designed like a three-legged stool (which one way or another always balances):

- **First leg**   Guaranteed income through Social Security, pensions, and certain types of annuities

- **Second leg**   Taxable income from retirement accounts and other investment accounts

- **Third leg**   Tax-free income from Roth IRAs (and possibly some annuities)

The closer you are to retirement, the easier it is to estimate your living expenses, and the harder it becomes to save enough. So the best advice is to start early and keep it up.

I discussed how to get a rough estimate for your retirement savings goal back in Chapter 2. You're not going to be able to pinpoint exactly how much you can withdraw until you're very close to retirement, because at that point it's going to depend on inflation, how well your investments have done, and what your spending needs have become.

Many retirement income calculators assume you'll need 70 percent of your then-current income as retirement income. I've yet to discover why that figure is near universal. It seems to assume that you're saving 10 to 20 percent of your current earnings, that your taxes will be lower, and that you won't be spending as much on transportation, clothing, or other work-related expenses. Of course, if you're not saving much now, you'll need close to what you're earning. If your taxes won't go down in retirement, there'll be no reduction in need. And if you've been dreaming about travel, or pursuing hobbies you didn't have time for, or upgrading or repairing your home, your expenses could actually go up.

The better web calculators will estimate the effects of inflation (use at least 2.5 percent to 3 percent per year if you can choose) and estimate your return on portfolio low—say, 6 percent to 8 percent. Check out Kiplingers.com, aarp.org, Quicken software, and any brokerage house where you have an account—they'll all have calculators. Admittedly these enterprises have an interest in getting you to save more, but I can almost guarantee you'll be stunned by the figure.

Employer Plans

The moment you get your first job you should begin contributing to your workplace's retirement program. (See Chapter 6 for information on workplace retirement plans.) At a bare minimum, you should contribute enough to get the employer match to your contributions. Some employers will match 3 percent or 5 percent or whatever percentage of your salary as long as you're contributing an equal or greater amount; some will match half of your contributions up to a certain maximum. Contribute that amount—it's the best guaranteed return on investment you are ever likely to get. What other investment guarantees you a 50 percent return on your money the moment you invest it?

Besides the employer match, your workplace retirement plan offers a direct reduction to income, which will lower the income tax you need to pay. Depending on your tax bracket, that makes the savings hurt a lot less. For example, if you're currently in the 25 percent tax bracket (about $75,000 to $151,000 for a couple), every dollar you save is only going to cost you 75 cents in lost spending power. It's really an investment return that's impossible to pass up.

It's not easy to avoid the tax man, but some jobs (especially government) offer other income deferral programs. Be careful to read the fine print and consider whether it will work. If they require a lump sum distribution at retirement, you could be hit with a gigantic tax bill in your first year.

One other strategy that people use to save with tax-deferred benefits is a variable annuity. You make contributions to the annuity, and the earnings on your contributions grow tax-free until you begin withdrawal at retirement. At that point, your payout consists partly of your own contribution (not taxed) and partly earnings (taxed). You don't get any deduction for your contribution, but it theoretically improves your earnings potential.

I'm not a big fan of variable annuities for several reasons:

- They often come with huge commissions or fees that eat into the money you have to invest.

- They're hard to get out of if you change your mind, and may have surrender charges and tax consequences.

- Your investment choices are limited by what the annuity provider offers—often their own high-cost, low-performing funds.

Usually, people would be better off simply investing the money in a brokerage account of mutual funds, chosen with an eye to tax efficiency. But if you're absolutely rabid about avoiding taxes, and have maximized your workplace retirement and IRA contributions, you might seek the advice of a fiduciary investment adviser or financial planner to evaluate any variable annuities you're considering.

Guaranteed Income

Investment returns in retirement accounts are always subject to risk and variability. But there are sources of guaranteed income to keep in mind: Social Security, pensions, and single premium fixed income annuities (SPIAs).

Social Security

Social Security is valuable for two reasons: it's money you can never outlive and it has a guaranteed cost of living increase so it has some chance of keeping pace with inflation. While I'll agree that it's not enough for most people to live on, without it most of us would really be in a fix. And what is it really worth? If you get the average $1,335/month payment, you'd need an extra $400,500 in investments in order to withdraw that same amount. Eligible for the current maximum? You'd need $807,900 to withdraw that amount of income. That's in today's dollars, without cost of living increases. It's not chump change.

Sadly, most people begin collecting Social Security at 62, which reduces their benefits by about one third. Your best strategy is to wait as long as possible, ideally until age 70, to collect maximum benefits.

There are a few good reasons to collect benefits at 62:

- You're unemployed with no prospect of getting another job. If you do start earning money before your full retirement age, you lose $1 of benefits for every $2 you earn.

- You have a terminal illness—but it will reduce your survivor's benefits.

- You have very young children and collect Social Security for them as dependents.

On the other hand, waiting until 70 will give you benefits almost twice as high as what you would have collected at 62. Also …

- You'll receive the highest benefit possible—about one third more than you would have received at full retirement age.

- Your cost of living increases are based on the higher dollar amount.

- Your surviving spouse can have higher benefits.

- As long as you continue working, you may increase the basis of your benefits.

Sometimes I'm asked whether it would be a good idea to take the benefits and invest them instead. Bottom line, no. Let's look at an example.

Let's say you'd get $1,000 a month at full retirement age, but decide to collect reduced benefits at 62 and invest the money.

- "Safe" portfolio withdrawal rate is about 4 percent.

- At 5 percent return = $39,761 ($132/month extra from portfolio).

- At 8 percent return = $42,262 ($140/month extra from portfolio).

But wait!

- Waiting *guarantees* about a 6.25 percent return from 62 to 66 (and about 8 percent yearly for the years between 66 and 70).

- Social Security is indexed to inflation.

- You would have received an extra $250/month.

So as you can see, it doesn't make any financial sense.

Would you be better off taking Social Security and withdrawing less in the early years from your portfolio? Only if you're certain your portfolio will grow more than 8 percent a year plus a cost of living increase.

In waiting, you're betting against the house. Social Security was calculated on an average life span, and benefits are paid based on those calculations. Trouble is, they've turned out to be wrong—people are living much longer than expected.

If you don't expect to live very long, take benefits at 62. If you think you might live to be older than about 77, you'd be better off waiting until full retirement age (66 or 67, depending on when you were born). If you wait until 70, you win if you live past 83. Average life span in the United States is 76 for a male and 81 for a female. However, that average includes infant deaths and people who die young. If you manage to make it to 65, you have 15 to 18 years more expectancy (male) and at least 19 (female). It's your call, but waiting at least until full retirement age is a pretty good investment.

Pensions

When people who have a pension retire from their jobs, the company will almost always offer them a lump-sum payout in order to forego monthly payments. Should you take the lump sum and invest it, or should you stick with the pension? Not an easy answer, but here are some points to consider:

- Does the pension payout go up with inflation? If not, it's going to be worth less each year. However, if it allows you to delay withdrawing from your own investments, your investments may grow enough to make up the difference in the future.

- Do you have high interest debt with no way to pay it off? If you can relieve some high-cost payments and this will allow you to live on much less, it *might* be worth running some numbers.

- Could you use the money to buy a single premium annuity that would pay more than the pension (probably not, but you could check)?

- Is it important to leave money to heirs, and this is all you have? When you're gone, the money's gone (but you can elect for lower payments to be made to your surviving spouse for their lifetime).

For most people, projections will indicate that they are better off with the monthly payments than the lump-sum payout, but there are exceptions. This is an issue where you need to consult a fiduciary financial planner. Scrutinize the numbers to determine what rate of return they're using to make the projections. (It should be conservative.) If they recommend you take the lump sum, be very sure that they're not just trying to get you to invest it with them, and that they are acting in your best interest.

SPIAs

If you're not lucky enough to have a pension, you can buy your own. It's called a single premium fixed income annuity (SPIA). It's a pretty simple operation: you give the annuity provider (usually an insurance company) a lump sum and they agree to pay you a monthly (or quarterly or yearly) sum for as long as you live.

 TIP

SPIAs have many options. Any except single life (payments made on one life only) will reduce your monthly payment. *Joint and survivor* means full payment for your lifetime and reduced payments for a spouse for life if you pass away. *Period certain:* if you die before 10, 15, or 20 years your beneficiary gets payments for the remainder of the term. *Cash balance:* if the annuity hasn't paid out your initial investment by your death, a beneficiary gets the remainder in a lump sum.

As with all investments, SPIAs have advantages and disadvantages. If you understand that providers are assuming some people will die young, you'll understand better how these work.

Advantages of SPIAs:

- You can never outlive the money if you choose a lifetime annuity. Even if they've paid you everything you originally invested, the payments will keep coming.

- A SPIA will give you more income for your investment than you could withdraw from a portfolio of the same size. If you could withdraw 4 percent per year from a portfolio, a SPIA might pay out anywhere from 5 percent on up, depending on what options you select and your age when you purchase it.

- As long as you choose to purchase from a high-quality insurance company, even if the company's investments lose money, you will still get payments. It's much less risky than depending on your own portfolio.

- It can give you more spendable income in the early years of retirement, when you may want it for travel or other goals. As you get older, you may not have as much need for income (especially if you're protected for long-term care or other health needs).

Disadvantages of SPIAs:

- Once you give the annuity company the money, you can never get it back. There will be no inheritance for your heirs from this money (unless you choose a specific provision that continues the term or pays out a balance).

- If you die young, the money's gone. Once you're gone, it's gone.

- If you need money for an emergency, you can't get it from the SPIA.

- If markets are good, you won't get any more money—the insurance company takes the profit.

- Usually your payments won't increase over time. Inflation will erode the value of your payment.

- Even if they refund the remainder of your principle to heirs, you won't get the earnings that money generated.

- Generally SPIAs should be purchased with money from taxable accounts. If the only money you have is already in retirement accounts, you should be sure that the SPIA payment will meet the RMD.

SPIAs make higher payments the older you are when you begin them, so it can make sense to wait until you're in your late 60s to evaluate your health. If it's good, 70 years old may be a good age to begin a SPIA. If your health is poor, you may not want to invest a large lump sum.

TIP

Deferred annuities are similar to a SPIA in that you invest a lump sum (or a series of payments) with the promise that at some future date you receive an annuity payout. All the same advantages and disadvantages apply, with one more caveat: check out the actual compound rate of return you're getting from time of investment to payout. These are generally lower than you might get in a diversified portfolio. You'll need to weigh guarantees versus growth. These are complex products worth having evaluated by a fiduciary financial adviser (not the same person who's selling the product).

It's a quirk of our natures that people love to have pensions but hate to purchase annuities, when in reality they're about the same thing. We all hate losing control of our money, but if we never had it, it seems like a benefit to receive guaranteed payments.

If having an income annuity would make the difference between not enough income or just right, you should consider a SPIA. If you're concerned about investment risk, or outliving your investments, an annuity might give you peace of mind. No one should put every penny into a SPIA, but if you can purchase one that, with Social Security, will guarantee your minimum necessary living expenses, it's a worthy investment for a portion of your retirement savings.

Realigning Your Portfolio to Produce Retirement Income

When we're accumulating investments to build retirement income, we focus on growth of the worth of those investments, saving to the best of our capabilities, and reinvesting dividends (and mutual fund capital gains payouts) to build shares. In retirement we still need to be concerned about growth, because our investments need to give us enough to withdraw but still keep pace with or exceed inflation. However, we are also in a withdrawal or distribution phase, so we need income. A portfolio can provide income in several ways, so let's look at the options for withdrawing money from the portfolio.

Continue to reinvest income, rebalance yearly, and take money out of investments for the next year's withdrawals. From a purely financial standpoint, this method has the potential to generate the best increases. You're still reinvesting income, and future dividends are based on building that pyramid. However, you have to have the fortitude to rebalance and sell investments, taking out a lump sum and putting it in a cash account you can withdraw from. Also, in a market where your investments are tanking, the reinvested dividends go downhill with the rest of your shares.

A variation of this rebalancing method is the bucket approach, where you designate at least three buckets:

- One for current (2- to 5-year) expenses you keep in cash

- One for safe investments (like bond mutual funds, and stable and dividend stocks) for 5- to 10-year needs

- One for high-potential but more volatile investments (stocks and stock mutual funds) you can leave alone for 10 years, especially if they're not performing well

Each year you rebalance and fill up the cash bucket from the safe investments, and possibly the safe investments from well-performing risky investments. If it's a bad year, you can wait to replenish and not be forced to sell poorly performing investments.

Also, realign your portfolio to emphasize dividend and interest paying investments. Instead of reinvesting earnings and rebalancing to withdraw earnings, the income dividend approach means you refocus your stock and mutual fund purchases to favor ones that generate dividends or interest. (See Chapters 10, 11, and 12 for more specifics.) Rather than reinvesting dividends and interest, you have them deposited in your cash account or sent as checks and use that as your spending money. If you emphasize this, you may be able to collect about half (2 or 3 percent) of your safe portfolio withdrawal (remember, around 4 percent total). You then depend on capital gains in your investments to provide enough overall gain to beat inflation and tide you over in bad markets. You'll still need to rebalance and take the rest of your needs out of the portfolio (unless you have a SPIA or enough income between Social Security and dividends).

 **WARNING**

As discussed in Chapter 11, don't go overboard and choose all your stocks only based on dividends. Unusually high dividends don't do you any good if the investment itself loses money. You still need to be aware of total return, and at least some of your portfolio needs to produce enough growth to beat inflation.

The traditional solution for retired people was to purchase quality, well-paying bonds. It's not so viable at the moment because we're in a low-rate environment. See Chapters 10 and 12 to parse out whether some portion of your investments should be in bonds or bond mutual funds. It's more of a safety move than an income move at the moment.

Reevaluating Your Risk Tolerance in Retirement

How safe do your investments need to be? Is this a period where you should emphasize bonds, to be sure you don't lose your principal? Or should you be worrying that your money will be eaten by inflation?

Well, both. You need some growth and some safety in a portfolio. People with a good pension or annuity and high Social Security payments can probably afford to emphasize stocks (and stock mutual funds) in order to get that growth, either for themselves or for their heirs.

People who have moved into the stage of life where they may be becoming more frail, and for whom health issues and long-term care are bigger concerns than travel or a new car, may be inclined to tilt their portfolios to safety with bonds (and bond mutual funds) and cash. Because you would have a shorter time horizon (perhaps 10 or 15 years rather than 30), inflation erosion of spending power is a less predominant concern.

However, in old age, especially if you have adequate income and provision for long-term-care needs, should they arise, you might decide that you are investing not so much for yourself as for your heirs. If your heirs are relatively young, you may feel comfortable orienting at least some of your portfolio to produce maximum possible gains for them. We're back to stocks, again!

What If It's Just Not Enough?

Maybe you've done everything right, but some disaster has struck and you can see that Social Security, any pension, and your investment portfolio will just not produce enough income for your retirement. It's not an easy situation to solve, but there are some steps you can take:

Work longer   This doesn't necessarily mean in your current high-pressure job. Even a part-time job can provide you with supplementary income and delay depletion of your investments.

Consider moving   Many, many people have too much investment in their home. It's possible to have great net worth and be unable to pay your bills. A smaller place, a cheaper neighborhood, or a cheaper city may give you a better housing situation and lower property taxes. It costs more even to make repairs in Manhattan than it does in Indiana.

Consider renting   Can you rent out your current home and de-camp to another country for a few years? You've always wanted to travel, right? Sometimes the rental on your current place would support you in style in another country.

Live with the kids   It all depends on your family, but in some cases this can be a mutually supportive relationship—which works for most of the rest of the world.

The golden key to retirement is savvy saving. Maximizing your savings, taking advantage of tax-favored accounts and employer matching contributions, and putting together a sensible portfolio that grows over time are necessities for a stable and secure retirement.

The Least You Need to Know

- Determine how much guaranteed income you will have from Social Security, a pension, or an investment in a single premium income annuity.
- Your investment portfolio must grow in order to keep pace with inflation, especially if some of your guaranteed income does not.
- You'll withdraw from your investment portfolio to make up the difference between your guaranteed income sources and the remainder you need to support your retirement income.
- In retirement, structure your portfolio so that you will not be forced to sell investments in a bad market to cover spending needs.
- Your risk tolerance may change depending on the size of your portfolio, changes in needs and spending priorities, and your desire to leave an inheritance.

Investing for a New Home

The holy trinity of personal goals is usually buy a home, send the kids to college, and have enough for a decent retirement. In this chapter we'll discuss building investments for a home purchase, ways to accomplish it, and what costs you should anticipate.

In This Chapter

- How much money do you need for a down payment?
- How much should you borrow?
- What loan options are available?
- Ways to increase the value of your investment
- Knowing when to sell
- Working with a real estate agent to sell your home

How Much Money Will You Need?

There are two main challenges in purchasing a home: having an income that will qualify you for the mortgage necessary to purchase your desired home, and saving enough down payment as required by your mortgage.

My advice is *you* need to decide how much of your income and funds you're willing and able to invest in a home, and not necessarily let the mortgage lender decide. Sometimes lenders are willing to loan you more than you can comfortably pay. They judge you on (total) debt to income, often allowing up to 45 percent of your income to service total debt (auto loan, education, credit cards, and mortgage). In my opinion this is way too high if you're going to do anything else with your life but make payments.

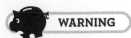 **WARNING**

I would never recommend that more than 33 percent of income go to all debt service. Higher than that and you're going to be standing outside your bank waiting for your paycheck to clear.

One of the biggest ways to enhance wealth building is to keep your housing costs low. Your fixed costs drive your budget, and the lower they are, the more discretionary money you will have to invest (and spend). Housing costs are the biggest part of fixed costs for most people. You don't have to buy the biggest house you can possibly afford.

Your monthly cost includes not only your mortgage payment, but also property taxes and the homeowner's insurance your mortgage company will surely require. Depending on the type of property, you also may need to pay condominium or homeowner's association fees.

 TIP

You'll see mortgage lenders refer to your monthly cost as *PITI*. PITI stands for principal, interest, taxes, and insurance.

Deciding How Much to Invest

In the old days (the late 80s and early 90s when I sold real estate) it was easy to figure out what someone could buy. You simply multiplied their income by 2.5, added on their down payment, and voilà! As long as interest rates stayed low—lucky you! Now, it's still based on a percentage of your gross income. Right now, you can probably get a mortgage based on a payment of 28 percent of your income (and that's a doable payment for most people). The lower the interest rate you can secure, the higher your purchase price can be.

Let's look at how this might work. Let's say your income is $76,000 per year. Find a mortgage with interest of 4.5 percent and you can buy a house with a purchase price of $350,000 (with a monthly payment for principal and interest of $1,773.40).

But let's say you can find a loan of 3.75 percent. Now you can buy something around $380,000, with a monthly payment of $1,759.84—more for less. Now you know what all the shouting is about concerning mortgage interest rates. By the way, that's 5 times your income—more than twice the house price you could have purchased 20 or 25 years ago. Low interest rates make houses more affordable.

But let's look at the flip side—interest rates go up to 5 percent. Now the house you can buy is down to $330,000, and generally that's a different kind of house than you can buy for $380,000. Obviously, if at all possible, you want to buy when interest rates are at their lowest.

Try not to exceed the 28 percent of gross standard for your monthly payment, even if the lender will make a larger loan. I'll relent a little if you have no other debt, and have a generous emergency fund. Because you probably already have tapped the maximum loan possible on the property, you're not going to be able to get a home equity line of credit (HELOC) to fix anything that goes wrong.

WARNING

> Really unexpected things can happen when you own a single-family home or other property for which you are solely responsible for repairs and maintenance. When I bought my current home, I had an inspector go over everything, and I also had some experience in renovations. Three days after closing, I heard a loud crash. Two thirds of the stucco on an exterior wall had peeled off and crashed to the ground. It was not inexpensive to fix, and it had to be done immediately.

You don't want to invest your entire net worth in the home. It doesn't generate income, and even if the value improves significantly, you have to sell it to realize the gain, and that may not be easy depending on the market. When you sell, you will still need to live somewhere, and in real estate all boats tend to rise on the same tide. Anything else you can buy will also have risen.

If you're under 40, real estate is probably going to be your major investment, although I hope you've been consistently contributing to your workplace retirement account (and if you haven't, you probably shouldn't be buying a house yet). As long as you stick to the 28 percent guideline, you should be able to start saving for other goals as soon as you recover from the closing.

However, once you're halfway to retirement age, real estate should become less and less a percentage of your portfolio. Ideally, I like to see your residential real estate investments (including, perhaps, a vacation home by then) constitute no more than a third of your total net worth. Whether you count what you paid for the property, or use a figure for what it's worth now, the rest of your investments will be the only ones that can generate income for you in retirement. Unless you plan to sell your home at some point in the future, it's not going to help you pay for things, although, especially if the mortgage is eventually paid off, you may not find another place to live that is as low-cost as your home. (More on deciding when and if you should sell later in this chapter.)

Unless you have an inheritance or some other source of a large amount of cash, you're probably going to be financing the balance of your purchase. There are several common types of financing. In general, the less down payment you make, the higher your monthly cost will be, not only because of the amount financed, but because low down-payment loans will generally require you to have some type of mortgage insurance. After all, the less *equity* you have in the property, the easier it is to walk away from it.

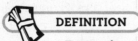

DEFINITION

Equity when used to describe real estate investments means the amount of investment or ownership you have in the property above the liability (loan). As you own a property over time, you should have more equity, because some of the loan principal will be paid off, and the property's value will grow. If the property's value drops, you could have negative equity, referred to as being *under water*—the property is worth less than what you owe.

Sources of Housing Loans

Two sources of low down-payment loans are U.S. Department of Veterans Affairs (VA) and the Federal Housing Administration (FHA).

VA loans can be a terrific deal if you're a member of the U.S. armed services, a qualified veteran, or the surviving spouse of a veteran. VA loans permit a no-money-down purchase, although you'll be charged a funding fee of 1.25 percent to 3.3 percent, which can be rolled into the loan. The VA doesn't make the loans; it simply guarantees them, so you'll have to find a lender that works with the VA. There are limits on the purchase price by area in which you live, but these loans can be a great way to purchase and still have money left for renovations or other investments. And if rates go down after you purchase, they provide a streamlined process to refinance into lower rates.

FHA loans require a minimum down payment of 3.5 percent and may allow you to have a total debt load of as much as 56 percent of your income. (Although I'm not advocating you borrow that much!) You must have a decent credit rating. You also must pay a premium (about 1.5 percent) at closing for insuring the loan, and a yearly premium as long as you hold the mortgage. The amount of an FHA loan is limited depending on where you live and will generally be in an amount equivalent to a moderately priced home in the area. The FHA appraiser who will evaluate your potential purchase may be a little tougher on the condition, and it can be harder to get the loan if you're buying a wreck to renovate. It never hurts to try if you're in the right purchase-price marketplace.

Lending Institutions

Credit unions, banks, and mortgage brokers may all be able to offer you a loan. Rates, terms, and what it will take you to qualify literally change from week to week. Banks are probably the toughest place to get a loan. A mortgage broker (you can find one on your own or your real estate agent can refer you to one) may have access to a variety of lenders and sometimes can make a deal happen that a bank would turn down. Credit unions, also, might offer different plans to work with your circumstances.

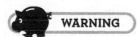 **WARNING**

> Should you refinance your home? Online calculators will tell you whether you'll save enough to cover the closing costs. What they won't tell you is that most of the payment you make goes to interest for the first years. When you restart the clock, you're paying that interest again and extending the period you'll be paying. Refinancing may mean you'll be paying on your home for 40 years instead of 30.

If your down payment is less than 20 percent of the purchase price, you will probably be required to pay private mortgage insurance (PMI) as part of your monthly payment, to insure the lender's ability to collect if you default. Once your equity (or the property's value) rises to 20 percent, you might be able to get this removed, but they may force you to refinance.

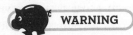

WARNING

Be careful when you hear the words *creative* and *lending* in the same sentence. In every mortgage crisis, people lose their homes because they've borrowed with payments too high to afford, or they have some type of adjustable loan. Adjustable loans have low initial rates but adjust based on current interest rates. These are best used when you know you'll be able to refinance into a fixed-rate loan in a short time (5 years or less), because you'll move, will receive a big income increase, or know an inheritance is coming.

The Bank of Mom and Dad

Sometimes parents think of lending their children money to buy a house (or the kids come up with the idea). This works, but it's fraught with problems for both sides.

Parents lending cash should be certain they can afford to lose it entirely. Your child may have every intention of paying you back, but can become ill or unemployed and unable to pay. If you need the money for retirement, you can't really afford to lend it. If you do decide to go ahead, be certain that you both agree in writing as to what the transaction actually is. In the event that the child goes through a divorce, or one spouse gets sued for any reason, this money can be considered joint assets and divided accordingly. Even if it's a gift, get the agreement specified in writing. Spend a little money on an attorney to make sure you have an agreement.

Adult children who are borrowing should at least pay an interest rate above what the parents could get in a conservative investment. There may be tax consequences to both parties if this isn't done and the IRS catches up with you. Please check with a CPA, attorney, or other knowledgeable party before you do this. If it's a gift above $14,000, a gift tax return may need to be filed.

Oh, and did I say get it in writing?

What Investments Should You Make to Build Funds?

You're probably hoping that buying a home is a fairly near-term goal, as in 2 to 5 years. If so, you probably need to build your down payment in a steady, stable investment, such as a savings or money market account. Sure, some of us would be willing to take a chance that a good investment in a more risky investment will generate a higher down payment. But in general, savings is what will build your down payment, with a little boot from investment returns.

If your time horizon is 2 years out, your investment should be in something that won't lose your principal, like a savings account or money market fund (see Chapter 7 on where to stash your cash short term). If you're a relatively calm investor, and have a time horizon of 5 years or more, you may want to consider a balanced fund, equity income fund, or life strategy fund for the possible extra return you could achieve.

Protecting Your Investment

I've emphasized the need for an emergency fund over and above the amount you've saved for a down payment. Your mortgage company will undoubtedly require homeowner's insurance not to protect you, but to protect their interest in your property if, say, the place burns down or you destroy the kitchen frying donuts. Even if you've gotten the loan from the Bank of Mom and Dad, or paid cash, do not own a home without homeowner's insurance!

The Importance of Regular Maintenance

Now that you've unpacked the boxes, start thinking about planning for the cost of regular maintenance, or your investment will quickly deteriorate. As a rule of thumb, plan on spending at least 1 percent of your home's market value in repairs and maintenance per year.

I'm not talking about the kid who mows the lawn; I'm talking about treating your trees for ash borer, replacing a rusted gutter, fixing a shorted-out electrical outlet, repainting, replacing the water heater (mine is 20 years old and I'm praying). If you've invested in an old home, 1 percent might even be low.

You won't necessarily spend this much every year, but then you'll get on a roll and everything will come down on you at once. If you're not paying out every month on some repair, squirrel a little away in a segregated checking account as part of your monthly expenses—when your dryer lets out a puff of smoke and dies, you'll be glad it's there. Well begun is half done.

Making Improvements That Increase Value

Clean and neat probably beats everything else. Buyers always tell their real estate agent that they can "look beyond" the piled-up magazines, the icky towels, and the stinky cat pan, but in the 7 years I sold real estate I never met one who could. Nor can the other real estate agents—the first thing they ask the listing agent is whether it "shows nice."

It's your place and if you plan to live there a while, go crazy. If you've always wanted a purple dining room, go ahead, but know that when you sell you're going to have to repaint it. Buyers (and agents) like a home that's up to date but doesn't have so much personal stamp on it that they can't picture themselves and their stuff in it.

There are trends that seem to take over the housing market. They become essential for that era, but scream outdated 10 years later. For example, in the 1980s you could hardly sell a condo or midpriced home unless the kitchen cabinets were white laminate with oak edging. Still like that look? Jacuzzi tubs were a hit until people got wise to how often they saw their friendly plumber. If you upgrade to the trend of the moment, and sell 10 years later, just be aware that you'll probably have to change it out to something then on-trend.

> **TIP**
>
> The best time for upgrades, from an investment standpoint, is when you want to sell, not when you move in. Of course, then you won't get to enjoy them, but you also won't have time to beat them up. If you plan to live there forever, let your heirs worry about your creative decorating.

If you plan to live in your house forever, but can imagine a time when you might need serious medical care, keep up with maintenance. As we become older, we might not see the need for freshening paint, or fixing the slight leak in the closet, or repairing the fence that's falling down (that would be my place), or updating the electrical system that's no longer up to code. Remember that your home is a significant investment asset, but it must be maintained to retain its full value. If you have to sell to afford nursing care, that sale can be delayed a long time while your spouse or your kids chase down contractors, come up with the money, and get it done.

> **WARNING**
>
> Although I hope it will never happen to you, people do have strokes and other health crises at any age, and sometimes the need for money can change in an instant. A home isn't the easiest investment asset to convert to cash, so don't make it any harder.

The kitchens, the baths, and the way your place looks from the street are the three main places to improve value visually. Don't improve it more than the neighborhood, but make it look a little better than it does now. You don't have to have a professional landscape designer if every other house just has foundation plantings of evergreens. Ask every Realtor you interview for suggestions, and consider hiring someone to stage the place for sale.

If you've considered leaving the place empty before you sell, try to have at least a little furniture so buyers can get an idea of the real size of the rooms. Empty rooms look smaller because the eye has nothing to provide scale. If, on the other hand, your place is full to the brim, try to remove some pieces and all clutter to make it seem more roomy.

If it's a cookie-cutter kind of property, try to give it something distinctive. Give the buyer something that will make it feel as if this home is better than the rest. At least one sale has been made in this world because someone loved the red front door or the swing beneath the tree (even if it's stuff you're ultimately going to take with you).

Selling with a Real Estate Agent Versus Going It Alone

Should you sell your house through a real estate agent, or do it yourself? It depends on the market. If houses have sold before the truck can come to pound the "For Sale" sign into the ground, you probably can try to sell it yourself. Be aware, however, that you're going to get far more calls from real estate agents than buyers, because many find their listings working FSBOs (for sale by owners). They may even suggest that they have a potential buyer (rarely), and show up with someone (their cousin).

On Your Own

If you have a property where the sign can be seen from the street (and that's permitted in your area), it's a lot easier to sell than if you're trying to sell a condo or a house in a restricted-access community. If that's the case, then you have to place an ad, list it on a website, and sit back to screen all the lookie-loos who call or show up. A real estate agent can do a much better job of screening prospects, pitching the property to other agents, and convincing their clients to go look.

Two things people believe are important to selling their home that actually aren't:

Putting ads in publications   The people who call are almost never right for that property, and the company advertises mostly as teasers to get those calls and convert the prospect into whatever else is in the listing inventory.

Holding open houses   Once in a while is fine, but mostly you will get all the nosey neighbors. This, however, will make your agent quite happy because your neighbors might want to list their home with her, too.

 TIP

Most agents hold open houses when they want to pick up buyers for other properties. After one or two, they won't be so enthusiastic.

I might consider going solo without an agent if I were the buyer, although you'll miss being connected with a lot of properties that you might have overlooked and you won't get help with mortgage brokers, lawyers, and the title company. I would always use an agent if I were the seller.

Using an Agent

Your listing agent is legally required to represent your best interests, unless she is also working with the buyer, with whom she also has a duty. If you're working with an agent, you should be absolutely certain you know who she is legally representing. If she has the listing, she is representing the seller.

> **TIP**
>
> If you're working with an agent to find properties to buy, you should have a signed buyer's agent agreement with her. Some agents will handle both ends, but open up your mouth and ask—it's not an insult.

The only reason not to use an agent when selling your home is that you will have to pay the commission. Selling as a FSBO might tempt you because you think you'll save the commission. Except that's exactly what every buyer is also thinking—I can get this for less because there's no commission being paid. I'm not sure if anyone actually saves the money, especially if the agent is a smart negotiator for you and does everything to facilitate the sale.

How much is that commission going to be? It varies by area, but it's often 5 or 6 percent of sale price. You can probably beat your agent up by negotiating a lower-than-normal commission, but in my view you're shooting yourself in the foot—not only is she going to be angry and cut back on her efforts, but every other agent in town is going to put your house at the bottom of their show list.

You may think you're paying $30,000 in commissions, but it's unlikely that your agent is getting paid that. First of all, she has to split it with her broker. It's also likely that she will not be the one to bring in the buyer. So she's going to split that commission with the selling (buyer's) agent (who also splits it with her broker). So maybe she's made $7,500 from that $30,000.

Deciding When and If to Sell

When should you sell? It's a difficult answer with any investment, and your home is an investment at some point.

Sell if you can afford to upgrade. Most people's first home is not their dream home. If your first property has appreciated enough that you can walk away with more cash on sale than you started with, and you've managed to save and invest in such a way that you have a goal fund account to apply to a new home, it's time to start looking.

Sell if you truly need more space. I've felt that way nearly every day, but the truth is, I would have plenty of space if I'd gotten rid of more junk. Consider investing in assistance from a professional organizer; it'll be cheaper than moving.

> **TIP**
>
> If you've owned your home for a while, you might be stunned to discover that you will have to pay much, much more to buy a better place. You may be better off building an addition or reconfiguring your current property.

Many people feel they need more space once they have a couple of teenagers draped seemingly everywhere, with the clothing, sports equipment, and general junk that seem to follow them. However, buying a much larger house (or building a huge addition) may be one of the worst timing mistakes you can make. The kiddies will go off to college or a trip around the world in a few years and you'll be stuck with huge heating and air conditioning bills, perhaps a property tax reassessment, and a lot of empty rooms they'll use as a giant storage locker. Unless they plan to return home after college (which you may or may not want to encourage!), don't spend a lot of money for space you'll only use for 3 or 4 years.

> **WARNING**
>
> People often consider a HELOC (home equity line of credit) as a way to pull cash out of their appreciated home, for repairs, to buy a new home before the old one is sold, to pay for college, and so on. HELOCs are often interest-only, which makes them seem cheap, until you need to repay the whole amount at the end of the term. I've seen people roll these over four or five times, paying a fortune in interest and never getting out of debt.

Sell if you could live with less space or would like to move to a cheaper property or location, realizing the gain in your investment. I love this reason because your purchase has truly resulted in investment gain. Aside from the obvious reason that it will prevent your jobless relatives from parking in your extra bedroom, many people find they don't need all the space, or the maintenance or utility bills that go with it, once the kids are grown.

Maybe you'd like to move to someplace warmer, or nearer to grandchildren or your own aging parents who live, hopefully, someplace cheaper than Manhattan or where you live now. You can get a lot better property outside the center of major cities.

On the other hand, moving from the big suburban home to a condo downtown may cut living costs in other ways—you won't need the car or a lawn or snow-removal service, and the building may have amenities like a pool or health club that you're paying for now.

A smaller home also may be more accessible as you age. The biggest difficulty that drives people out of their homes against their will is mobility and maintenance issues—they can't handle stairs, gardening and snow removal has become an overwhelming physical effort, or they need assistive devices that won't fit in the space available. If you're moving in your retirement years, be certain that you could negotiate the space if you were less healthy than you are now.

Should You Pay Off Your Home?

This is perhaps the number-one question I'm asked in financial planning. The answer is not clear-cut.

The financial answer, in a low-rate environment, is no. If you have a low-rate mortgage (say, under 5 percent), you would probably be better off over the long term by investing that money instead. If rates were closer to 5 or 6 percent, it's a bit of a toss-up—you could compare it to the rate on bonds, since paying it off is virtually a sure thing. Still, over the course of a few decades, you would probably do better in a diversified portfolio of investments, and you still get the tax deduction of the mortgage interest.

Then, there's the behavioral answer. Most people, particularly those who are near or in retirement, feel much more secure with a paid-off house. It reduces the largest component of your fixed costs (although you will still have repairs, maintenance, and property taxes).

As long as it doesn't deprive you of income-generating investments that you need for retirement, I can support paying off your mortgage—maybe not when you're younger and could grow your money better in other investments, but certainly at retirement.

The Least You Need to Know

- Invest your down payment goal money based on how long it will be before you want to purchase.
- Don't necessarily borrow the most money a lender will lend you, because they may allow you to borrow more than you can afford, given your lifestyle.

- Maintain and update your home in order to maintain the value of your asset.

- Good reasons to sell your home include wanting to use built-up equity for another investment, wanting a different-size or more-accessible space, or wanting to relocate to a different environment or to be nearer family.

- Paying off your mortgage is as much an emotional decision as it is a financial one.

- Working with a real estate agent enables you to sell your home much more easily.

CHAPTER 17

Investing for College

The price of college has far outstripped pay increases and all other types of inflation. The days when someone could work their way through college are about as long-gone as shag carpeting. Although it's still possible for some families to qualify for financial aid, and some few students do land significant scholarships, you should plan as if you're not going to receive such help. Luckily, there are several steps you can take to help your children pay for the college of their choice (or at least, the ones that admit them).

In This Chapter

* How much should you save for your student's college education?
* Will your family qualify for financial aid?
* Types of programs available for tax-favored saving
* Choosing appropriate investments

Investigating the Costs of College

The news media frequently reports the cost of tuition, but tuition isn't the whole story. A truer measure of college cost is the *cost of attendance*, which colleges will provide you (usually on their website). Just know that this estimate is a bit of wishful thinking, because certain costs can vary wildly in real life.

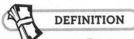

DEFINITION

A college's **cost of attendance** includes all the estimated charges and budget items your student will have to pay each year. This figure includes not only tuition, but also fees, books and supplies, housing, food or meal plan, health services fee, and so on.

For example, depending on what courses my daughter selected in any given semester, her cost of books ranged from $29 (all ebooks) to over $500 (a couple of lab textbooks). If you're looking at a state university but it isn't *your* state, your nonresident costs will be much higher. Certain majors (usually science and health care) may have significant add-on differentials.

TIP

Attending a college within driving distance of your home will save you a significant amount of money. Flying back and forth from home to college can add thousands per year in the form of transportation and moving and storage costs.

While you've probably seen myriad articles discussing average costs for state universities and private colleges, there's a pretty good chance those averages will be lower than any place you're actually considering. Let's look at myth versus reality. The following table compares the cost per year of attending a public university to the cost of attending a private university.

	National Average	University of Illinois (Resident) (2015)	University of Illinois (Nonresident)	Northwestern University (2016)	Lake Forest College, Illinois (2016)
Cost of attending a public university	$24,061	$30,336	$45,496		
Cost of attending a private university	$47,831			$68,060	$53,926

I've used examples of a flagship state university, a top-ranked private university, and a quality (but not Ivy League) small private college. Of course, if you hunt around you can find some less-expensive colleges.

As you can see from the table, if your child were to enter Northwestern University today, the total tuition bill would be $272,240. Except that it would probably be more, because costs go up every year.

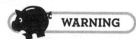

According to FinAid.org, during any 17-year period from 1958 to 2001, the average annual tuition inflation rate was between 6 percent and 9 percent, ranging from 1.2 times general inflation to 2.1 times general inflation. On average, tuition tends to increase about 8 percent per year.

Let's say your child is a newborn and you're already picturing him yelling "Go Wildcats!" How much would you have to save to cover 100 percent of that tuition by the time he's opening his Northwestern acceptance letter? Let's be conservative and figure 6 percent inflation, and optimistic and assume your investments earn 8 percent. The total is $5,972.60 a year.

That's a lot. Is it realistic that you'll be able to save enough (and achieve those investment returns) over the next 18 years? It's possible, but you need to start saving early, because if you wait to start until Junior is 10 years old, here's how much you're going to need to save per year (same inflation and return assumptions): $17,454.69 a year.

As with retirement savings, the later you start the more you must save per year. And the harder it may be to achieve high annualized returns. When you're looking at 18 years of market ups and downs, you have a pretty good chance that they will smooth out; in 8 years, market gyrations are going to have much more of an effect.

FinAid.org has a number of calculators to allow you to try out different savings schemes and cost projections. If you own Quicken software, it also offers a variety of planning calculators.

Many families look at these figures and despair. But let's step back and consider whether you have to plan to save the whole bill, plan to even *pay* the whole bill for your child, and whether you will end up having to pay sticker price.

Setting a Reasonable Savings Goal and Payment Expectations

I'm going to suggest that you don't have to save the whole projected cost, if it's a strain on current finances. If you're maximizing your 401(k), saving into a Roth or IRA (if you're still eligible based on income), and contributing to your other savings goals, go right ahead and contribute to one of the college savings strategies I describe later in this chapter. They will allow you to grow your college savings tax-free.

 TIP

If the projected need seems daunting, saving *something* is better than saving *nothing*. Even if you manage to accumulate only $5,000 by the time your child heads off to college, at least you've got the books covered. You're going to be very happy to have even a small amount to help out.

You might want to consider where you'll be in your own career by the time your child starts college. Many parents find themselves in their peak earning years at that point. In addition, you'll discover some cost savings on the home front with your child out of the house—groceries, transportation, and no more extracurricular activities. Some part of the cost of attendance can be paid from then-current income.

It becomes tougher to pay out of then-current income if you're an older parent who will be near retirement age at that point or if you have more than one child who will be in college at the same time, or others still at home. It can be tough to pay while also saving for retirement or education for other children.

There's nothing wrong with expecting your child to contribute to college costs by working summers, having a part-time job on campus, and taking out reasonable loans. A child who has some skin in the game, especially because they've worked for their education, is more likely not to waste as much time and money, be better organized, and understand the consequences of not finishing in 4 years.

 TIP

According to research by Professor Laura Perna of the University of Pennsylvania, "students who work a modest number of hours per week (10 to 15 hours), on campus, are more likely than other students—even students who do not work at all—to persist and earn degrees."

You can fiddle with the percentages, but I suggest clients consider a goal of saving one-third of the cost, paying one-third from then-current income, and expecting the student to shoulder one-third. That way, if your student does manage to get merit aid, you can reduce your (and maybe their) out-of-pocket spending and drawdown on the savings. To be fair, if the student lands scholarship money through their own hard work, under this method I think it should be credited to their third.

If you have no idea where your child will attend, consider as a target savings goal the cost of attending your in-state university. Using the University of Illinois as an example for your new-born, you would need to save $2,662.13 a year. Start out for a 10-year-old, and you'll need to put away $7,779.53 a year.

Will You Have to Pay Sticker Price?

Let's consider the possibility of scholarship or grant money—money that does not need to be paid back. There are two general categories of financial aid available: merit aid and need-based aid.

TIP

According to *U.S. News and World Report,* only 3 percent of students get a full cost, free-ride scholarship from all sources combined (federal, private, or outside scholarships).

Every school will award federal aid first—if you qualify based on the Free Application For Student Aid (FAFSA). For public universities, that may be the only money available. Some public schools will have small awards available for specific student characteristics, but generally these will be quite small—almost certainly not enough for full cost of attendance. Public schools, however, don't care whether you can pay. Most admit by a formula based on SAT or ACT score, grade point average, and rank in class (and occasionally recommendations). If you score above the cutoff for that year, you're in.

Private schools, on the other hand, may have other funds available, and they can do anything they want with that money, including asking you for far more financial information.

At most highly competitive first-tier schools (think Harvard), the only aid available is need-based. Think about it for a minute and you'll understand why. You probably won't even apply to a Harvard unless you're already outstanding (or your family name is on a building, but that's a whole other topic). You have about a 6 to 10 percent chance of getting in, given the ratio of applications to acceptances. (Or as I once heard one dean of admissions say, "We should just send all our rejections a letter saying 'Kid, you were great. There just wasn't enough room on the bus.'")

There is no reason that super-competitive private schools need to give your child merit aid, and more than 50 percent of students at such schools pay full sticker price. Many schools claim that their admissions are need-blind, but I've heard several college admissions coaches dispute this. If the school uses the Common Application (and most do), they know by a box you check whether you intend to apply for financial aid. As the coaches have put it, if you have two outstandingly qualified students, and one needs aid and one will pay full freight, which one looks like the better admit?

 TIP

The Department of Education requires colleges to post a net price calculator somewhere on their websites. You answer some questions and it gives you an estimate of what you might have to pay (including scholarships and grants, but not loans).

Understand that, with a huge excess of qualified candidates, selective private schools use their aid to balance and diversify their student body. So if your child is a visually impaired harpist from Wyoming who needs aid, you might attract interest. If your child is a Caucasian short-story writer with 8 Advanced Placement scores of 5, or an Asian American math whiz from a top suburban high school, not so much—they have plenty of those already.

In schools where need-based aid is the only aid, they'll still have plenty of qualified candidates, so the needy who will also balance the student population in some way—racially, regionally, or by planned field of interest—will get not only whatever federal aid is available, but also whatever resources the college itself has.

Okay, so that's the reality when we're talking about those colleges that are the focus of the admissions arms race. What about the next tier down?

It depends on two factors—how good the endowment of the school is, and how much they want your child.

How much they want your child really comes into play if your child is one of the most highly qualified applicants to a given school.

 TIP

Check the admissions statistics of the most recent class on the school's website. You'll be able to tell the minimum scores (grade point average and SAT/ACT) of admitted students, and what scores would place an applicant in the top 25 percent. If your student would place in the top 10 to 25 percent, they'd have the best chance of being offered merit aid if the school has any.

A second- (or third-, or fourth-) tier school is more likely to offer enticement to a student who will upgrade the student body. They'll distribute their private aid funds, including school-specific scholarships (and most scholarships are school specific).

Applying for Need-Based Aid

If your child is very young, you're going to need to make a guesstimate of what you might be earning, and what investment portfolio you might have by that time. If your child is near college age, you can make a better estimate of these factors. Let's look at how you're evaluated for need, and the differences between public schools and private.

Public Colleges and Universities

Most public colleges and universities are fairly cash strapped and have limited funds to give. Your qualifications will be evaluated on the Free Application For Student Aid (FAFSA).

The FAFSA asks about the student's and parents' assets, income, and family size. Federal aid considers 5.6 percent of the parents' assets and 20 percent of the student's as being available to pay for college *each* year; 50 percent of the student's income and between 22 and 47 percent of the parents' income is also considered available to pay. And therein lies a world of gamesmanship!

Assets that are *not* included in the asset calculation: your primary home, the value of money in retirement accounts, the value of your business, and money in investment annuities and life insurance. Also, the amount you're expected to pay is reduced by an asset protection allowance that depends on parental age and whether there are two parents or one in the family.

If you just want an estimation of whether and what you might qualify for, FAFSA offers an easy calculator you can use without filling out the full, multiscreen FAFSA. Go to FAFSA.ed.gov and click on FAFSA4caster. Be sure to have your most recent income tax return and an estimate of the value of your *nonretirement* investments in hand.

The FAFSA4caster will give you an amount they determine is your Expected Family Contribution (EFC) as well as some idea of whether you qualify for a Federal Pell Grant, Work Study, or a subsidized Stafford loan. Your school may also offer Perkins subsidized loan funds if they participate in the program.

In reality, unless you qualify for a Pell Grant (currently an EFC under $5,723), a state college or university will offer you work study and loans. Most likely they will not have any other source of funds.

Just because you have a low EFC, schools do not have to make up the remainder. While some schools promise to meet all demonstrated need, or all demonstrated need for those under a certain income level, that need does not necessarily mean free money (grants or scholarships)—it can mean loans (albeit often at subsidized or lower interest rates).

Private Colleges

Most private schools add a layer of information gathering in the form of the CSS/Profile application. Private schools can interpret and award need-based aid (aside from federal funds) in any way they choose. Or as they put it, according to their own proprietary formula.

On the CSS/Profile (and any supplementary questions the school chooses to add), you will indeed be asked about the value of your home, your business, your car, your retirement assets—in fact, just about all the things you won't be asked to reveal on the FAFSA.

Private schools have figured out that at least some of the families who apply for aid are fairly savvy about stashing assets in categories not examined by the FAFSA. While the school may have a formula for how it counts these assets, if you're living in a $3 million dollar home, driving a Mercedes-Benz or better, have a huge 401(k) and no assets outside of those, maybe they're on to you, ya think? Your EFC is no guarantee of what you will actually be asked to pay.

The Importance of Saving

While you may get some money off the sticker price, for most families a failure to save is going to result in the need to borrow often significant sums of money. For families who find themselves in this state, I strongly recommend seeking admission to state schools. A 4-year state school will be more affordable, even if paid for through loans. If the student is not as strong or motivated, the family should consider beginning at a junior college to avoid a great deal of money wasted on a student who might not finish.

If you have a very strong student, I believe it is still worthwhile to secure an admission to your state university and to private institutions. It is sometimes possible to bargain for a better financial aid package if the private school really wants your child and you can show them a better offer from another place. Again, private schools have much more flexibility in awarding aid from their private, nonfederal funds.

You can hardly go wrong with saving. If you're in an income bracket where you are likely to qualify for aid, you probably aren't going to be able to save enough to disqualify you from any aid. If you have saved a significant amount, some of it can be realigned into retirement accounts, purchases, or principal pay-down of your home.

TIP

Two sources for information on college financial aid specifics and techniques are FinAid.org and SavingForCollege.com. Each has many articles explaining rules and regulations and how they apply to a variety of situations.

Places to Save for College

By now I hope you're convinced of the advisability of saving at least something toward college funding. But where should you put your investing efforts?

Workplace Retirement Programs

Your 401(k) may be your largest source of funds, but it's one of the worst places to consider withdrawing for college funds. You'll be forced to pay income tax on it (adding to your income for college financial aid determination) and will also be hit with a 10 percent early withdrawal penalty if you're under 59½. In addition, you should not be reducing your retirement funds at that point in your career.

Your employer may allow you to borrow funds from the account, but be aware that they generally have to be paid back if you quit or are fired, or the loans will be considered income. If you're a young parent who has been contributing the maximum, and have some hope of repaying the loan, this may be a last-ditch strategy. But in general, because it's not easy to get tax-deferred growth on your investments, your 401(k) funds should probably be left alone.

Traditional IRAs

You can withdraw from a traditional IRA for purposes of education without being socked with an early withdrawal penalty, but you will have to pay ordinary income taxes on it.

Roth IRAs

Finally we get to an appealing possibility. You can withdraw from a Roth IRA without penalty for postsecondary education costs. As long as you withdraw money attributable to your contribution (not the earnings) you won't pay any tax on it. If your Roth has been open for at least 5 years and you are older than 59½, you can withdraw any of it (principal plus earnings) tax- and penalty-free.

Contributing to a Roth with the intention of having it available for college is a great choice for parents who have limited funds (particularly while their income is low), who want to leave open the possibility that the funds will be reserved for their own retirement if the child does not need or deserve the contribution, or who do not want to allocate funds specifically for each child.

The drawback of planning to use a Roth for your children's college funding is the amount you can contribute. Even at the maximum contribution ($5,500 a person, $1,000 extra if you're over 50), a Roth may not allow enough investment to pay for college, especially when several children are in the family. And, most people should preserve their retirement funds for their own retirement. Still, if this strategy is planned with an eye to the other family investments, it can work quite well. Also, although withdrawals from a Roth are allowable for college costs, the withdrawals will be considered income for college financial aid purposes for the year they were withdrawn. Some families wait to withdraw from the Roth until the child's senior year.

TIP

If you're still convinced that your student might receive scholarship or merit aid, you might emphasize the Roth, or divide your savings between college accounts and the Roth. That way, you can leave your retirement funds in place if you don't need them.

You can contribute to a Roth as long as you have earned income, and it does not exceed $183,000 (joint, your allowable contributions will be phased out on a sliding scale until income reaches $193,000) or $116,000 to $131,000 (single or head of household).

529 Plans

In a 529 plan, you deposit your savings, and the money grows tax-free. As long as the money is withdrawn to pay for qualified educational expenses (tuition, room and board, books, and other required fees) you can withdraw it tax-free. You don't get any federal tax deduction for your contribution.

If the student or the parent is the owner of the plan (with the student as beneficiary), the plan is considered an asset of the parent, so it is assessed at the 5.6 percent rate as available to pay.

WARNING

If the grandparent is the owner of a 529 plan, with the student as beneficiary, it is not considered by the FAFSA. However, when the grandparent uses it to pay for education expenses, that withdrawal is considered income to the *student* for the next year's financial aid determination. You can avoid financial aid impact if you wait until the student's final year in college to withdraw from a grandparent-owned 529.

There is no specific limit on how much you can invest in a 529 plan. Each parent can gift up to $14,000 per year (as of 2016) without having to file a gift tax return. Or parents can preload an account with 5 years' worth of their gift exclusion allowance and then not contribute for 5 years. Plans must be "reasonable" in size—generally no more than about $350,000 at the outside. If your student does not use the money in the plan, it can be used for graduate school or the beneficiary of the 529 plan can be changed to another close relative. If the student gets a scholarship, the corresponding amount can still be withdrawn from the 529. For withdrawals for noneducation purposes, you will pay a 10 percent penalty and tax on the earnings.

You don't have to invest in the plan offered by your state, especially if it is a weak one or has a poor selection of investments. However, many states give their residents tax deductions for investing in the 529 plan, so check before you give it up. You can also invest in the plan of most other states. Since each state is making some money in fees for these investments, they'll be happy to take your money.

Probably the biggest drawback in investing in a 529 plan is the poor selection of investments available. State plans generally confine your choices to a selection of mutual funds. Depending on what company's funds are offered, you may have a great array of no-load, low-cost funds or a collection of high-cost or proprietary funds. A good plan will offer you an array of packages— risk oriented (aggressive, moderate, conservative); age based (transitioning to increasingly more conservative as your child gets closer to college); actively managed or index; or your own choice from the selections offered.

Some states offer prepaid tuition plans, another type of 529. These may be restricted to use in your state, but usually the amount is pegged to the state school tuition, even if it is used at a private school. You're essentially buying a deferred annuity—making a lump-sum payment now with the guarantee that a larger payment will be repaid later. It's difficult to know if these are a good investment from a purely investment return standpoint. As with annuities and pensions, you give up access to the money, and they rarely pay a return as high as you might expect to get from a well-diversified portfolio. However, they do provide security that the money will be there when needed, so from an emotional standpoint they may give great peace of mind.

If you have a lump sum to put into a prepaid plan, particularly if your child is very young, it may be appealing as a use for inheritance, gift, or bonus money. Be sure to check exactly what guarantees are offered, whether you can get anything back if your child does not attend college, and what the restrictions are on using the account for private college or out-of-state tuition. If your state is in financial trouble and the only backing is appropriations by the state legislature, your payout may be in trouble.

Coverdell Plans

Coverdell plans were originally pitched as "education IRAs" but have never become as popular as 529 plans because you can only contribute a total of $2,000 per year, per child (from all sources). Because of their relatively small balances, they won't accumulate enough to fund an education, and most such accounts have such small balances that many of the big financial institutions don't offer them anymore.

 TIP

In order to contribute to Coverdell plans, your adjusted gross income (from your tax return) must be under $190,000 for joint returns and under $95,000 for all others.

I like them a lot for several reasons. First, their small contribution limits can be a worthy first goal. To a family overwhelmed by the idea of the money needed for college, $2,000 may represent an achievable goal. Second, you can invest in stocks and bonds in addition to mutual funds. Third, Coverdell funds can be used for qualified educational expenses *before* college. If you are certain your child may attend a private high school, you can apply the account's funds.

You can have a 529 plan and a Coverdell. Why would you want to? Well, maybe the Coverdell is the account where you try for bigger gains by investing in more risky investments, or putting a bet on a few stocks you've researched that you believe have good potential. Big capital gains will not be taxed within the account as long as you withdraw funds for qualified educational expenses. And if you have losses, well, it's not your main source of college funds. It's that old risk versus reward tradeoff, again. Or maybe you segregate contributions: the gifts your child receives go into the Coverdell, and your main savings goes into the 529 plan.

U.S. Savings Bonds (Series EE or I)

In recent years the rates on these have been so low that they're hardly worth investing in if you're just starting your college investment program. However, if you've received them as gifts, or have old ones sitting in a drawer, you can use them for college without paying tax on the interest, as long as your modified adjusted gross income is under $115,750 (joint) or $77,200 (all others).

Loans

Many lenders will be happy to loan money for college if your credit is good. Parent PLUS loans, private loans, even HELOCs have all been tapped by desperate parents seeking to come up with college cash. Interest on PLUS loans is only deductible if your income falls below $155,000. Borrowing against your home equity via a HELOC may give you a lower-cost loan, but you're really tapping out your wealth.

I would never borrow or cosign a college loan for my much-beloved child. I've seen too many cases of the child not finishing, or having employment or disability issues. While in rare instances a child may be able to get loans absolved for illness, the parents cannot. A 20-something can recover from poor credit over time in a way that older parents cannot. And in the horrible case that the child dies before a loan is paid off, the parent who has borrowed will still have to pay off the loan. You can always help your child pay off their loans in the future if you find you can afford it.

The Least You Need to Know

- You can't rely on scholarships or financial aid to pay for college.
- The earlier you begin saving, the less you will have to put away year by year.
- Save for college in tax-favored accounts to take advantage of sheltered earnings growth: Roth IRAs, 529 plans, and Coverdell plans.
- When shopping for colleges, be sure to consider what kind of aid the school has available.
- Make sure you're saving for retirement before beginning a college investment program.

CHAPTER 18

Investing for Luxury Purchases

Is there anyone who doesn't yearn for an around-the-world tour, a top-of-the-line possession that speaks to a passionate interest, or a dream car, vacation home, or boat? Purchasing a luxury item doesn't just mean splurging on something you wouldn't ordinarily buy. In many cases, it represents a goal of your working life.

In this chapter we're going to consider how you might go about achieving that purchase or experience while still getting the most bang for your buck—in other words, how to make your luxury purchase a profitable investment.

In This Chapter

- Deciding whether to make that luxury purchase
- Strategic ways to pay for big purchases
- Tips for traveling, getting a car, and buying a vacation home
- Getting the most from your luxury purchase

Planning for Your Luxury Purchase

If you've read through the previous sections of this book, you know that you should choose your investments based first on your timeline. Most luxury purchases are probably ones we hope to achieve in the mid-term, although some (like an around-the-world tour or a vacation home) may also be long-term goals, since accumulating funds may take a while.

As with all investments, you'll have to assess your appetite for risk—if this is a purchase for which there's no specific deadline, you may be willing to invest much more aggressively, in the hope that you'll achieve your goal sooner. Conversely, if an investment takes a downturn, it may not matter quite as much since a luxury purchase is not, by definition, a necessity or critical to your financial survival.

There are two ways to pay outright for a luxury purchase: pay for it out of your own savings or investments, or receive a windfall (lottery winnings, royalty payment, proceeds from selling an idea or company, inheritance) that allows you to think about getting something you've always wanted. (See Chapter 19 for more on managing sudden money.)

Before making that purchase, do you have a solid financial goals plan in place? That means, are you contributing the maximum to your workplace retirement plan? Are you investing enough, if necessary, outside your workplace plan to arrive at retirement with enough portfolio income? Do you have an emergency fund? If you're saving for the kids' college, is that on track? If you're at an appropriate age, do you have a long-term-care plan, and estate documents? No? That's the stuff that needs to be taken care of first. Yes? Congrats, maybe it's time to be nice to yourself!

Deciding If a Luxury Purchase Is Worthwhile

First you should reflect a bit on what your luxury purchase is worth to you. As with purchasing stocks or other investments, there are always multiple options. With investments, you'll probably consider a variety of possibilities as you try to decide which makes the most sense. You should apply some analysis to your prospective luxury purchase, to determine whether it's what you really want, and at what scale.

 TIP

I'm biased in favor of spending the least money possible in order to save, and squeezing out the most value for dollars spent, consistent with what will satisfy your objectives.

Developing a Decision Scale

Let's walk through how to develop a decision scale. First, choose something you really love to do or buy, don't do very often, and know the price of. I'm going to use a 3-day, 2-night weekend at a nice little bed and breakfast within driving distance of my home. I'd do this as often as possible.

What's it going to cost me? Let's call it $200 per night ($400 total) for the B&B. Say the town has a lot of cute little restaurants and I want to eat well, sample a few craft cocktails, and have a decent bottle of wine. I'll chalk up $200 per day for food (breakfast is free at the B&B). I'll probably eat breakfast at home on Friday and get back to my house for dinner on Sunday, so let's make it $500 total for food. Include $50 for a tank of gas. It's a pretty good bet that I'll do some shopping in all the cute little stores, so let's just call it $1,000 for the weekend, although it would be easy to spend more. Let's assume I currently go on four of these weekends a year.

TIP

I'm not big on impulse buys for two reasons: you often pay too much, and the purchase turns out to be unsatisfactory, whereas if you'd put a little time and thought into it, you would have a far better experience. And sometimes, the planning is part of the fun.

Now I have a concrete standard to measure any purchase against. Would I enjoy buying that luxury item more than I would enjoy a weekend at the B&B? Would my purchase have more entertainment value? Would it give me more lasting pleasure?

Let's say I want a nice new bike. The one I have is perfectly functional, although ugly, so buying this new one is purely for fun, not because I truly need new transportation. (Substitute new car if you wish—the numbers for a bike are easier to manage.) The bike I covet costs $4,000. That means I'm going to give up the possibility of four nice weekends away, and also some really great time with my daughter, who usually goes on these weekends (a somewhat intangible benefit) but won't have anything to do with the bike.

Maybe I belong to a bike club, and a new, lightweight bike would allow me to participate in more and better expeditions with the group and, therefore, I wouldn't want to go away from May to October anyway. There's at least a $2,000 contribution redirected to the bike fund because of two weekends I wouldn't be going to the B&B. Also, I have a goal of better fitness and I'll definitely ride more if I have this wonderful bike. The bike will last me at least 2 years, so it's paid for by redirecting money away from one activity and toward another. Certainly a reasonable luxury in these circumstances.

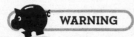

WARNING

The richest people I see in my practice don't necessarily look rich. On the other hand, people who come in with four-figure handbags and flashy cars are often short on investments. This is just as true today as it was when I sold real estate in Chicago's Gold Coast more than 20 years ago. So when you're wondering how a coworker or neighbor pays for all that stuff, I have two answers: family money or credit cards.

Alternatively, let's say I'm lazy and would never go on a 50-mile bike ride (closer to reality, actually). I want the bike because it's a beautiful object, works with a precision I've never before experienced, and will impress people every time I tool down the street. Also, I'm hoping it will encourage me to ride more and get fit.

Here, the choice is less clear. If I gave up only 1 weekend, I could probably replace the old clunker with a nice $500 model and join a health club at $30 a month for a year. Would I like a $500 bike as much as a $4,000 bike? Probably not, but for the use I actually put it to (pedaling to the grocery store and the library), it would be a nice change at a more affordable price. And I'd probably use it more because I'd be less afraid of it getting stolen or scratched, which would make me sick if it cost $4,000. So in this scenario, the real luxury would be not giving up the weekend trips, but getting a moderately better bike.

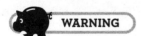

WARNING

I have pretty strong opinions on buying your kid luxury items, which can be summed up in one word: *don't.* My daughter's dorm has a "Free" box where students can discard usable items they no longer want. Dear daughter has acquired a brand-new pair of Ugg boots and a set of Bose noise-cancelling headphones from the box. I'm glad I'm not the parent who paid for those. Respect your kids enough to believe they are capable of earning these things themselves.

The Yardstick-of-Luxury System

One more scenario: I adore sewing and make a lot of garments, with the odd quilt and dog coat thrown in. When my machine went kaput 3 years ago, I wanted something top-of-the-line, because, well, my skills are top-of-the-line. But to my shock, sewing machines have gotten a bit more expensive over the past 20 years, since I paid $3,600 for my old Viking. As in $14,000 expensive for a current top-of-the-line model (which, if I analyze investments as doubling every 10 years, actually makes the current price just about equivalent, but gives us a sewing machine inflation rate of 7 percent).

I went home and analyzed the features I actually use. I made a list, went back, and purchased an embroidery machine with a ton of stitches for about $1,800. Does it give me more pleasure than two weekends away? Absolutely—I use it every week, and I've now had it for 3 years, so the total "pleasure" cost is $600 a year. If you have a hobby that actually saves you money (I'm not sure sewing clothes does), you might figure the savings into your cost analysis.

I have a friend who is an incredible quilt artist. She also teaches classes on weekends, it's just about her only hobby, and the vacation she takes is to the huge quilt show in Paducah, Kentucky. She has a sewing machine the size of an old Volkswagen, and its sticker price is around $14,000. Would it be worth giving up weekends away for, like, forever? Not for me, but she's figured out how to make this luxury work. (See the next section on ideas for strategies to make luxury purchases worthwhile.) And in her case, because she has a side business as a quilting instructor, at least some of the cost of her machine, and supplies for samples and demos, is deductible against the income she earns in the business.

This yardstick-of-luxury system can be applied to almost any purchase you contemplate, and illustrates that all expenditures require at least some choices. Would a vacation home give you more pleasure than a yearly trip to Paris? Would it be more satisfying to drive a BMW or have a sailboat? How much time do you have to actually use your purchase, or will it collect dust? How much will it take to maintain one versus the other?

 **WARNING**

A 2015 study by the Camelot Group found that 44 percent of those who have ever won a large lottery were broke within 5 years. The Certified Financial Planner Board of Standards found that nearly a third went bankrupt.

Even if you win the lottery, you will still have choices to make. Even if money is unlimited, time is not, and at some point you will reach a point where you don't have time to enjoy what you have. Make planned choices and keep control of your wealth.

Strategic Ways to Buy Luxuries

Pay cash or don't buy at all, we often hear. But many sellers of luxury goods have figured out that they'd sell a lot more if there was some other way than cash to peddle their wares.

Enter 0 percent financing. Theoretically, you negotiate your purchase price and then make payments over an agreed upon-period of time—let's say 5 years.

With this type of financing, however (sometimes available for cars, sewing machines, and any variety of durable consumer goods), you must be very careful to puzzle through any hidden costs. Would you have gotten a much better purchase price if you'd have paid cash? There may not be any financing charge, but if you could have gotten 10 percent off the purchase price, that's what you've paid for financing (which may be worth it or not).

Are there other service charges added at the last minute? Can you get out of the financing or return the product if it proves unsatisfactory? If you miss a payment, what happens to your rate?

If the interest charge is truly 0 percent, or if the interest cost is lower than you could reasonably expect to make by keeping your money invested over that time period, go with the financing.

WARNING

For most people, there's no money kept invested—it's simply a way to buy something they couldn't afford up front. At that point, you really can't afford the luxury, because you're not buying out of your surplus.

What about trade-in value? You may decide to upgrade during the term of the financing or at the end. How will your purchase be evaluated? Trade-in value can be particularly important if you're purchasing a product whose technology is rapidly improving and which may be obsolete in 5 years.

In such circumstances, a monthly payment becomes more like a subscription or use fee. Remember my friend the quilt artist? She trades in her computerized sewing machine for an upgrade at the end of the period, and always has the (luxury of) the most current tools for her art.

"If I Had More Money I Would ..."

The number-one thing people tell me they'd do with more money is travel. Buying a better car is second, and third in the running is a vacation home. In this section we'll look at each of these three luxury purchases with an eye toward obtaining them as economically as possible.

Travel More for Less

If you want to travel better and/or more often than you could otherwise afford (at whatever level of luxury), there are ways to work the system. As in all money-stretching schemes, you either need to invest time or money, then make it work for you. Investing time in learning about the travel points game can make your money work far harder.

Before getting into the specifics of using points, please be certain you can pay your credit bill off each month. No amount of points is worth getting over your head in debt.

Over the last 3 years, I've been able to accomplish the following (always with my daughter included, so these figures apply to two people):

- Flew from Chicago to Miami and took a 5-day cruise to the Western Caribbean. Total cost: approximately $400 (for shore excursions).

- Spent a long weekend in St. Louis at a top hotel. Total cost: approximately $300 (for gas, two dinners, one lunch, and museum admissions).

- Flew from Chicago to Key West, with 5 days in Key West. Total cost: approximately $500 (for food and drinks).

- Flew from Chicago to London, 10 days total, including 2 days in Bath and 1 day in Oxford by train. Total cost: approximately $1,000 (mostly food and museum admissions).

- Flew from Chicago to Austin for a professional conference for 2 days. Total cost: approximately $200 (for the hotel because I didn't have enough points on my card to cover the whole cost of 2 days).

- Flew to Philadelphia for my daughter's graduation, stayed for 3 days, took the train to New York City, stayed for 4 days, and flew both of us home from New York. Total cost: approximately $1,000 (museum admissions, Broadway play, restaurants, and subway/cabs).

Right now you're thinking, *I've been amassing flights on Crowded Airlines for about a million years and I still don't have enough points to make a single round trip.* You'll feel worse when I tell you I almost never travel for business. Let me outline how it's done. (See Appendix B for more resources.)

TIP

I've given many talks on traveling with points, and after every one someone will come up to me and say, *It's just too much work.* Really? It's too much work to spend a couple of hours in an evening and, say, 2 hours on the weekend for a month, then browse a couple of blogs over morning coffee, to save $5,000 on your next trip? That's a pretty good return on investment.

Sign up for credit cards with sign-up bonuses. In order to do this you must have a very good credit rating (740 or above for the best cards). These cards will give you anywhere from 10,000 to 100,000 bonus points (rare, but I did get 100,000 from British Airways). There may be a yearly charge (sometimes waived for the first year) and a minimum amount you must spend ($3,000 in 3 months, $6,000 in 3 months, and so on) on the card. Be sure you can meet the spending minimum or you've wasted the application. Also, watch what the yearly fee might be. If it's $85 a year, you need to get more than 8,500 points to break even (depending on the redemption value of the points).

Some cards will give you upgrade perks as well. You might get a few airport lounge passes, an automatic hotel status upgrade, free baggage check, and if you spend enough on some hotel cards (for people who travel for business) you'll get room upgrades and private lounge access. Focus on amassing airline points and you can use points to upgrade from coach to business or first class.

Most people do well with a couple of hotel cards for chains that are located in their destination, an airline card or two, and a couple of points-earning cards that apply to any travel.

Funnel virtually all your spending through the appropriate card. Some cards will give you much higher points for spending in certain categories. For example, I use a business card that normally gives you 1 point per dollar, but on office supplies, internet expenses, and a couple of other categories I get either 5 points or 2 points per dollar. Another card gives me 2 points on any purchase. A hotel card gives me 5 points at grocery stores.

Even if the card doesn't have a "favorites" category, funneling everything you can through the card—anything that won't charge you a service fee for using a credit card—can really build up points over time. As long as you pay the balance off each month, it's easy to rack up a lot of points.

That's it. Your work is going to be to figure out what cards will be most worthwhile to you. Figure out a couple of places you would like to go, know which hotels and airlines are on that route, and concentrate your card applications on those. Since it can be a little confusing which card to use where, I just stick little paper circles on my cards with "Groceries," "Gas," and so on.

Your credit score will take a temporary hit, about 20 to 30 points per card in my experience. This is because a number of credit inquiries will suddenly show up, and because your average length of credit history will shorten. These are minor. Within about 90 days your score will be back to normal, and you might even see an improvement—because credit score also is influenced by your *credit utilization ratio.* If you're planning on applying for any type of loan, do that before beginning credit card applications. But as long as you're not buying a home or car in the next 90 days or so, you should be okay.

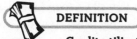

DEFINITION

Credit utilization ratio is the percentage of credit you use compared to the amount of credit you have. If you have a card with a $10,000 credit limit, and you routinely charge $5,000, which you pay off every month, that's a 50 percent credit utilization ratio—not so good. Now let's say you've applied for a bunch of cards, and the total limit on all of them is $50,000. You still charge $5,000 per month, your ratio is only 10 percent—much more creditworthy in the eyes of credit score companies.

As with many plans for profiting from investments, if it were easy, everyone would do it. It does require some research, experience to maximize return, and a bit of risk (applications, turn-downs, and credit score). Just like every other investment.

Getting That Car

In the past, the most economical way to purchase a car was to pay the negotiated price with cash (to wrangle the best deal), keep the car until the wheels fell off, sell it for whatever you could (when it was essentially worthless), and start over. Most of us went the more costly route, providing a down payment, then paying for 3, 4, or 5 years. The car could then be kept or traded in.

However, leasing has become a viable option, especially if it includes maintenance for the life of the lease. Lease payments are significantly cheaper than car payments for purchase. Depending on the brand and the deal you negotiate, you may get free maintenance for 5 years, or none at all beyond the warranty. It's the difference between cost to carry (the payments including financing, or lost investment income from paying cash), which goes down the longer you keep the car, and the cost to operate (the maintenance, service, and repair costs). In general, the more expensive the car, the more expensive the operating costs.

Consumer Reports can give you a good idea of total ownership costs for the car you're contemplating. A car with a poor repair record is no luxury, because you'll pay plenty in time and aggravation.

TIP

Check out the true cost of ownership via the calculator at Edmonds.com (a great source of information on car values). Marketwatch.com has a lease versus buy calculator. Every April, *Consumer Reports* puts out a car issue discussing both new and used cars. Many libraries offer access to *Consumer Reports* online via your library card.

Leasing can put you in a better car than you might otherwise afford and allow you to upgrade more frequently, but it's important to remember that when the lease is over, your car is gone. Don't allow a desire for luxury to lock you into an agreement that you really can't afford. Having a car repossessed is a disaster for your credit and probably your self-esteem. If you're considering leasing, it should be used as a way to lower your costs, not as a way to upgrade to more than you can really afford.

Vacation Home Strategies

Maybe hauling suitcases down cobblestone streets isn't your idea of a relaxing vacation. Maybe a nice drive (or familiar flight) to an ocean-view condo or log cabin in the woods sounds way more relaxing.

The most successful strategy I've seen for purchasing a vacation home is to keep your primary home's cost on the low side of what you can afford. As I discussed in Chapter 16, upgrading your home every time your income rises tends to be a risky strategy that can be wealth diminishing. But if you do the opposite (keep your housing costs under what your income qualifies you for), you're likely to have more money to make loan payments, qualify for better rates, and have more ability to save for a down payment or even pay cash for that dream retreat.

 TIP

It's usually harder to finance a vacation home than a primary residence. Lenders often charge higher interest rates or may have more stringent standards for qualifying. Slightly under half of all buyers pay cash. Depending on the financing you can secure, you should expect to pay about 25 to 35 percent of purchase price as a down payment.

Before you plunge in, however, I'm going to suggest you think carefully about how often you will use the property. Is it within easy driving distance of your primary residence, or will you have to fly every time you visit? Do you have the sort of job where you can easily take 3-day weekends or work remotely? Have you visited the area frequently? Falling in love with Key West when you live in Chicago is probably not the best idea for a stress-free, frequent retreat.

Next, think about maintenance, cleanup, and security. Will you be spending spring and fall weekends housecleaning and doing yard work at a second place, or does the property (or the area) have a service that handles that? Will you have to make a 4-hour drive if someone breaks in?

If your planned vacation home is part of a complex with management services in place, know what the nonowner rental rules are. If the place is primarily rented to nonowner occupants, there's going to be far more wear and tear, resulting in higher assessments for all owners, and a shorter lifespan for the property because of more wear and tear. On the other hand, if you can't rent it or are restricted in the number of days you can rent it, you'll have no way to ease the costs of a property you aren't using.

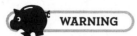

WARNING

> Don't buy a timeshare. You will never be able to sell the place. It will deteriorate. The taxes will go up. The maintenance fees will skyrocket. You won't be able to trade your 2 weeks for time at another property when you really want it. Your friends will laugh at you. The current management will quit. Please, look at the For Sale sites for these turkeys. Owners give them away if someone will just take over the costs.

Compare the costs of what an equivalent hotel space or renting someone else's vacation property would cost you, especially if it's just for a month or two in season. Add it up for, say, 10 years. Would you really go back there that often?

What are the property taxes? Since you may not be considered an owner-occupant by the local taxing authority, your property taxes may be higher than year-around residents.

You're going to need insurance on the property. Also, over time, you're going to have to think about updating décor, replacing appliances and furnishings, and paying minimum heating and air conditioning to keep the place from freezing, becoming mildewed, and getting infested with creepy crawlies.

Will you use the property only in season, or are there activities that appeal to you for at least three seasons? What about the rest of the family? If multiple generations of the family will gather at the vacation home, or someone will use it just about every weekend, it can be a terrific family experience.

Finally, have an exit plan. I can pretty well guarantee you're not going to be making a 4-hour drive or flying to Key West 6 times a year when you're 95. And if you're buying a vacation home for future retirement, check out the health care and available transportation (especially off-season). Being out in the woods with 3 feet of snow on the ground and chest pains is not a happy prospect.

However, not everybody uses a vacation home in the same way. For some people, it's used a month or so in the summer, with the property rented out for the other months. This can give you some help with the cost of purchase (perhaps with a plan that you'll stop the rental in the future). I've already mentioned that you should know rental rules and figure out the cost of wear and tear, maintenance, and cleanup before you do this (and if you're the cleanup squad, figure in whether you have time to do so). In your plan, you should also consider tax consequences.

Rental income must be reported to the IRS. You can deduct rental expenses up to the amount of income, if you use the home more than 14 days per year, or more than 10 percent of the time it's rented to other people (whichever is greater). You are then considered a resident. You must divide the expenses between the number of days you use it, and the amount it is rented.

However, if you rent it for fewer than 15 days, you don't have to report the income, although you can still deduct mortgage interest, property taxes, and casualty losses.

 TIP

IRS publication 527, "Residential Rental Property (including Rental of Vacation Homes)" is available online. We all know the IRS has a bad rep for confusing people, but their publications can be quite helpful. Take some time to read this one if you're thinking of buying and renting your second (or third, or fourth) home.

Some other things to think about: How popular are rentals in the area? Have you talked with other property owners in the area? What if the weather is bad, or the economy takes a dive, or gas prices or airfares skyrocket, or somebody will only rent from you if they can have it for the whole summer? These aren't necessarily reasons you should discard the idea of purchasing, just issues to think over if the financial viability of your plan depends on some rental income.

Sometimes family vacation homes are left in equal shares to the children. You need a better estate plan than that, including how shares can be bought or inherited. It's fine when you have three children who get along and enjoy using the property. But what happens in the event of divorce? Death? What if all your children are gone, but they each had three children, some of whom live far, far away? By the third generation it's easy for a family property to be owned by dozens of people, many of whom will not want to pay the taxes or upkeep. Be sure your estate plan considers these eventualities and provides a mechanism for transferring ownership.

No matter what luxury you have your eye on, you should consider all the costs of ownership: not only purchase price, but cost of financing, insurance, maintenance, depreciation, residual value, and passing it on when the time comes. Investing sensibly in luxury is a lot of work!

The Least You Need to Know

- Whatever you purchase or invest in requires sensible choices so be sure to weigh the tradeoffs between owning, leasing, financing, and forgoing other possible uses for the money.
- Consider how much you will actually use and enjoy the luxury purchase after the first thrill.

- Consider not only the purchase costs, but the costs of ownership.

- A credit card points-accumulation strategy for travel can help you travel more for less, but you should only do it if you can manage your credit card spending.

- Calculate carefully to see if buying or leasing a car makes better financial sense in your situation.

- Think through repairs, maintenance, insurance, taxes, and financing costs before purchasing a vacation home. Also consider whether you will use it enough to make owning worthwhile.

Managing Windfalls and Sudden Life Changes

Experiencing a sudden life event, whether thrilling or devastating, that significantly alters your expectations for the future can be extremely destabilizing. You may feel confused and unequal to the task of managing your new financial state, and everyone you've ever known will have advice for you.

In this chapter we look at how to evaluate the financial challenges, get trustworthy advice, and sort through the possibilities of how to manage your money.

In This Chapter

- Evaluating your new spending power
- Taking steps to protect yourself
- Sorting out spending priorities
- Considering long-term needs

Understanding Your Spending Power

A million ain't what it used to be. As we discussed in Chapter 15 on retirement, a $1 million portfolio will give you a safe, sustainable income of about $40,000 per year. Many people who come into sudden money go on a spending spree that's not sustainable and deplete their portfolio at too rapid a rate. Particularly if that's more money than you've ever seen before, or if you grew up in a lower-middle-class household where investments were never discussed (my hand's up here), you may overestimate what you can spend.

 TIP

> Chobani Yogurt has announced that it will give a 10 percent share in the company to employees when the company goes public. That is estimated to be around $150,000 per employee. The headlines accompanying this news suggested that the employees would be rich. They won't. After they pay taxes, they'll have enough to make a decent contribution to their retirement savings. It's a very nice bonus, but it won't make anyone wealthy.

It's important to manage sudden money for growth, not to go on a spending spree. It's very hard, especially if you're new to the game, to avoid feeling like *Now I can buy anything.* Any level of wealth still requires choices and plans. You want to view this sudden lump sum as seed money to sustain and grow your wealth. You do not want to blow it and end up back where you were, or worse.

Protecting Yourself

Whether your windfall comes from an inheritance, a book contract, an invention, the lottery, a publicized divorce settlement, or other means, one of the biggest problems with sudden money is the worry that everyone is out to profit from your good fortune and inexperience.

Do not rush into anything. Don't pay off anyone's loans, put a down payment on a house for a relative, rush out to buy a car, or take the whole clan to a four-star resort. You must establish an overall plan and understand just how all the parts will interlock, before you—well, there's no better word for it—squander your money.

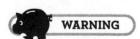 **WARNING**

> If there's anything you can do to protect your identity or the amount of your windfall from being broadcast by the press, do so. People always wonder why a lottery winner doesn't come forward immediately. I hope it's because they're seeking legal help to preserve their privacy. The fewer people who know about your windfall, the fewer who will be trying to scam you.

Assembling Your Team

Begin by assembling a team of professionals with whom you can consult. You're going to need the following:

A financial adviser   See Chapter 9 for a discussion of choosing an adviser. A fee-only fiduciary adviser can help you walk through issues of spending, debt repayment, planning for the future, and charitable giving. A financial adviser can act for you the same way an internist takes care of your health: looking at the big picture, working on specific issues, and referring you to reputable specialists for help in specific areas.

A Certified Public Accountant (CPA) and/or tax attorney   You need to understand what taxes you must pay, what your actual net will be, and whether there are any strategies you can use to lower the bill. There's not necessarily any magic wand they can wave to eliminate taxes, but they can help you pay as little as possible. This person should work in conjunction with:

An attorney who focuses on estate planning   Hardly a month goes by without a news story about a famous person who either died without a will, or failed to update it when family circumstances or their own wealth changed dramatically. While I'm sure the IRS does a happy dance every time this occurs, you should take more control over your money. An estate attorney can prevent your private details (and those of your heirs) from being splashed all over the internet, as well as structuring some prudent control of your heirs. They can plan trusts that minimize estate taxes, and structure charitable bequests.

A psychologist   If you've experienced a significant psychological loss through death or divorce, or even a positive event that changed your life, it helps to talk to an experienced third party who can help you work through your feelings. Even if the event was anticipated or welcomed, you're going to have emotional fallout. Also, a psychologist is probably going to be way less expensive than getting "counseling" from your lawyer or financial planner, who aren't qualified to help you in this area anyway.

A business attorney (possibly)   You may want to consider the possibilities of establishing a corporation or foundation, both for tax and for privacy reasons (if the windfall is large).

Lest you think I'm only offering advice for lottery winners, let me point out that, with the exception of the business attorney, a divorced or widowed person is going to need this team as well. You want to make your money last (whatever its size), be sure you understand your tax picture, and be certain you have an updated estate plan.

Give yourself time to think, recover, and look forward. A divorce or death can fell us with grief and indecision. Nothing seems certain in a world that is not as we knew it. You may feel as if you don't have a life anymore. You do have a life, just not the one you expected. Your plans must change, but with those changes come possibilities.

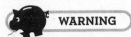

WARNING

There have been countless legal cases where the now-divorced spouse failed to change beneficiaries and left retirement plans and other investments to the ex-spouse, or all the heirs predeceased the individual and the inheritance reverted to the state. I'm guessing neither of these scenarios is what you intend.

Choosing Between a Lump Sum or Structured Settlement

In some cases of windfalls, you'll be offered the choice between a lump sum payout or a structured settlement that pays a portion each year. These offers are common in cases of personal injury awards or lottery winnings. If you're offered these choices, you should consult a financial adviser to work through your individual needs and options.

Here are some considerations you should address:

- If you were to choose the structured settlement, how guaranteed is it? Is it guaranteed by a highly rated insurance company (equivalent to a first-class annuity) or is it dependent on appropriations by the legislature (as for Illinois lottery winners)?

- Will your money grow with inflation in the payout, or would you be better off growing a lump sum in a diversified investment portfolio?

- If you took a lump sum, do you have a plan for preserving the money and fending off the temptation to overspend?

- Do you have the experience and expertise to manage a large sum of money (with expert, reliable advice)? Have you ever managed a large sum before?

- Have you investigated the tax consequences of the possible choices?

Please see the discussion in Chapter 15 on pensions and annuities. You're facing most of the same issues—finding ways to ensure that your money lasts a long time, keeps up with inflation, and doesn't incur too much risk.

TIP

No matter what your friends and family say, there's nothing wrong with putting your money into a low-paying bank account while you decide what to do. It's better to keep it secure than to lose it by making a hasty, inappropriate decision or purchase.

Thinking Through Your Spending Priorities

Whenever we plan investing, we must also consider spending needs. Whenever there's a sudden influx of money, most people consider debt repayment, helping out friends and relatives, and paying off or buying a house as high priorities.

Should You Pay Off Debt?

There are two answers to this question: the financial one and the psychological or behavioral one.

The financial answer hinges on the interest rate you're paying, and how high the debt is in relationship to your income. If you have a low interest rate and have been paying on time, there's no real reason to rush to pay off the debt; you're probably going to be able to earn more by investing.

Let's say you have student loan debt of $50,000 at 3.5 percent interest. You earn $60,000 a year in salary. Should you pay off your loan? Probably not. It's a low enough amount at a low enough interest rate that you would be better off (by the numbers) investing your money in a diversified portfolio.

But what if you owe $200,000 at 6 percent and you still earn the same $60,000? Here, the monthly payments have probably been a struggle, and the interest rate is high enough that a conservative investment portfolio probably won't exceed it by a lot. Here, it begins to make sense to pay off the debt.

In the preceding example, if $200,000 represents the entirety of your windfall or inheritance, you're going to need to consider your overall financial picture. Are you young, with the possibility of earning more and building savings? Are you near retirement with not enough to live on? If the debt were paid off, have you changed any spending habits so that new debt won't be acquired? These are all behavioral and psychological issues as well as financial ones.

If paying off debt would only open the door to new spending, then you're probably better off creating a disciplined plan to accelerate repayment but moderate your spending. If the debt is keeping you up nights, destroying family relationships, or making you feel hopeless, then these issues trump any number crunching. Once you get expert advice, the best use of the money might be debt repayment.

Should You Pay Off Someone Else's Debt?

What if it's someone else's debt you're thinking of paying off? Here, you should evaluate the idea much like any other investment: what's the risk, what's the reward, and does the investment have a reasonable chance of being profitable?

If someone in your life has dug themselves into a financial hole by unwise spending, poor finan- cial choices, or a peripatetic employment history, think carefully. The idea that we can solve someone's problems with one action is very romantic and appealing. However, I urge you to consider the other person's behavior. Saving someone without any participation by them often produces the opposite result the giver intended: the recipient can feel demeaned, powerless, or free to repeat the behavior that brought the trouble in the first place.

I recommend that you make your recipient responsible in some way for the gift. For example, you might give the gift once they have paid off a certain level of debt themselves, or performed specific services for you, or agreed to repay you over a structured period of time (with conse- quences if they don't).

Maybe you're thinking about buying your kids a house or paying off their school loans. Here, you have to know your kids, and make some judgment about the effect such a gift might have on their motivation in life and their own relationships. One person with money can really drive a wedge into a marriage. Of course you love your child, but you don't want to take away their pride in standing on their own two feet. On the other hand, helping a hard-working child, investing in their business, or starting a college fund for the grandchildren may be exactly what you'd like to do with a windfall.

 TIP

Whether you lend or give money to another person, you should have a written agree- ment. If your recipient gets a divorce or is sued for some type of damages, it's very important to have evidence of how the money is transmitted, and to whom it belongs.

The most common scenario is a parent giving their adult child some money for a house, with a handshake agreement that "you'll pay me back when you can." The adult child then gets a divorce and in court the other spouse will almost certainly claim that the money was a gift to the couple (marital property) rather than a loan (marital debt obligation). Not only will the money be gone, but the ex-spouse will benefit by it. It's ugly, and happens routinely.

If you're contemplating paying off your partner's debts, see a family law attorney for advice on how to document the terms of that repayment, and what would happen to the money in the event of death, disability, or divorce. It may never happen, but if it does it will save you a lot of legal fees wrangling over it in the future.

What to Do About the House

The comments above about paying off debt also apply to the decision to pay off your mortgage. However, it's even more important to consider your other circumstances. You don't want all your money invested in your house, especially if you're close to retirement and need income.

A house generates no income and in fact costs you in maintenance and taxes, even if you pay off the mortgage.

For this reason, divorced people should think very carefully about the house. In a divorce, people will fight to keep the house, especially if there are children involved. The reasoning goes something like this: "The kids already have enough disruption in their lives. I don't want them to have to change schools. They're afraid of losing their friends."

If your children are young, they'll adjust (and you should invest in psychological help if possible to assist in the process). If they're older, they'll probably be in college in a few years, and then you'll be stuck with a big, expensive-to-maintain house. Life will go far better if you're not stressed out by the cost of the house and the burdens of maintenance. I often tell people going through a divorce that if they really hate their spouse, they should give him or her the house, and take the investable cash for themselves.

For widows and widowers, you probably have a house filled with memories, but you must consider whether you can really keep up with maintenance. Do you have children or family who can help? Can you pay for any services you might need? Would you be more secure and less stressed in a different living arrangement? The most tragic scenario is the spouse who can't let go of the memories of the happy years in the house, but who becomes increasingly feeble, with little cash flow. When they need care, they can't afford to pay for it without selling the house.

 TIP

Cleaning out 50 years' worth of memories and making needed repairs in order to get the house on the market is an overwhelming task that can't be accomplished rapidly. Plan ahead and you have a chance of controlling your own destiny and making your own choices.

Let's look at the flip side: you suddenly have enough money to buy the house of your dreams. Should you? Maybe, but not until you've scoped out your entire situation with your team of advisers. Moving, even when it's to something better, is still a stressful activity. You don't want to change your life radically without some thought and investigation. Would you like the new neighborhood or location? Maybe you should consider renting in the locale first. You might find you actually don't like Paris, or Key West, or Maui as much as you originally thought. If you do, you'll have a much better sense of the market and the right neighborhood after you live there a while.

I was once a Realtor, so I'm going to give you another piece of advice: don't upsell yourself. In all my years selling real estate, people always bought the maximum they could afford. Any little flaws in the cheaper properties could always be overcome by just spending more. If you don't have more, you won't be able to spend more and will content yourself with what's available to you.

In almost any price band, what would be a palace to me might be a cottage to you. Set yourself a maximum purchase price based on your overall financial plan, and tell the Realtor your top price is 10 to 20 percent less than that. You'll have some room to upgrade, but you won't be tempted beyond your prudent initial decisions.

Changes to Other Plans

Any change in financial circumstances is going to require a new look or reevaluation of any goals you had before the change.

Saving for College

If you receive a large windfall, you're going to have to face the fact that you can't qualify for financial aid. If your children are still years away from college, consider sheltering the earnings on some of your savings by prefunding 529 plans for college (see Chapter 17). You can contribute up to 5 years' worth of your gift allowance (5 × $14,000) per parent for each child. The money then grows tax-free (and you can do it again after 5 years).

Depending on the exact nature of the money (if it's an inheritance, for example, instead of royalties, which are income), you might be able to systematically transfer money into a Roth and/or maximize your 401(k) contribution if you're not already doing so. These plans require you to have earned income (below a specific level for the Roth), but you don't necessarily have to write the check from that income—you can use funds in a taxable account to transfer to the Roth (or increase your deductions at work but withdraw a little more money to live on from your windfall investments). It may not make you qualified for financial aid, but at least you'll be sheltering earnings and can use the Roth for college costs if needed.

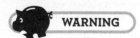 **WARNING**

> Just because you can afford the best advice doesn't mean you'll take it. Actors, musicians, writers, and sports stars have all made the head-down stroll into tax court, and mostly, they lose. Before you buy that monster truck, you need to settle your taxes. What's left is what you can invest (or, sigh, spend).

But what if you were on track for college savings, but now, because of divorce, aren't able to continue to save?

Although everything is negotiable in a divorce, courts generally agree that the money in 529 and Coverdell plans belongs to the child and is not joint marital property. The difficulty can come when one spouse is the owner for the child beneficiary (as is usual in these plans). Unless there is an agreement in the divorce decree, there is nothing to prevent the spouse-owner from cleaning out the plan, paying the tax and penalties. Try to secure an agreement that this cannot be done.

No one should jeopardize their retirement in order to pay for college. If you would have to withdraw from retirement funds or emergency savings in order to cover college costs, you need to retool college plans. Either the children will need to go to a less expensive college, or borrow more money, or work for a time to accumulate money, or some combination of the above. Yes, a parent is going to feel terrible delivering this news, but it's not a cataclysm. Much of life requires making a choice, not among the optima but among the least bad choices. And then making them work.

TIP

Widows and widowers with young children should review Chapter 15, and be certain to collect dependent benefits.

Depending on state law, a parent paying child support may have no legal obligation after the child graduates from high school or turns 18. This is negotiable in a divorce settlement. However, even if the parent is not compelled to pay for college, the income will still be considered as part of the financial aid determination by many private schools (using the CSS/Profile financial aid evaluation). Let's say the mother has an income of $50,000 per year and no assets except the house (probably qualifying for financial aid). The father has an income of $200,000. Because his income is probably too high to qualify for aid, the child may not get any financial aid even if the father refuses to contribute a dime.

TIP

For financial aid based solely on the FAFSA (most public schools), only the custodial parent's income is included in the expected family contribution.

It is very difficult to get an exemption from having both parents' income evaluated for financial aid by private schools. It will generally require documentation of serious reasons (history of physical or sexual abuse) why the child has no contact with the parent, and why the parent will not or cannot pay. Be prepared with evidence from attorneys, psychologists, and law enforcement. It's going to require a big investment of time to accomplish this.

(Early) Retirement

Can you take that job and shove it? Depends on the size of the windfall, your age, your current portfolio, and your spending needs. You're going to need those advisers to calculate what's left after taxes, how many years you can expect to live in retirement, and how to invest the money so it beats inflation. You can really start to consider handing in your resignation if your windfall is in the seven figures.

> **TIP**
>
> Don't feel you have to keep the same investments your spouse or parent selected. They may have been good choices when selected, or selected as appropriate for someone with a different risk profile or time horizon than yours. A portfolio is a dynamic thing; the original investor would almost certainly have made changes to it. Do what's right for you.

On the other hand, a publicized windfall (like the lottery) may make it very uncomfortable for you to continue in your present job. Even a smaller inheritance may have you dreaming of making tracks out of there. This is a terrific time to consider retraining, upgrading your education, or taking a time- and money-limited sabbatical to explore a new career, a new location, or a new workplace. Get a referral to a professional career counselor and use some of your money to get the best advice to help you make a plan.

Death of a Spouse

Losing your spouse may mean that you have to reenter the workforce. A career counselor, particularly one who focuses on second careers and job changers, can be a real help in repackaging your résumé in more current terms, coaching you to present yourself in the best possible manner, and suggesting retraining opportunities that you may not have considered.

Be sure to collect all the Social Security benefits to which you're entitled. If your deceased spouse had a higher benefit than you, you can switch to that full amount as a survivor's benefit. If you are divorced, have been married at least 10 years, and have not remarried, you are entitled to spousal benefits as if you were still married, and survivor's benefits if you did not remarry before age 60.

You may find yourself in a situation where your inheritance or settlement comes to you already invested in a complex portfolio that you neither understand nor feel capable to manage. You're going to need study and advice for this one. Be sure to read the basic information in this book to get you started on asking the right questions, either for further reading or for a fiduciary adviser.

Special Concerns in a Divorce

Dividing everything in half may not be an equitable settlement, because some current investments have more potential future worth than others. At least in the current market, a house is far less likely to appreciate as much as retirement or other securities investments. As I've hammered on before, a house also costs you something to hold (securities don't require repairs) and it's very difficult to convert a home into instant cash. In addition, if you have low current income, you may not even qualify to borrow against the equity in the home.

Too often, the custodial parent will say, *I'll keep the house and you can keep your retirement account.* This is usually not an equitable division. A Certified Divorce Financial Analyst (CDFA) can help you understand why by showing you projections for the relative growth of any proposed settlement. You may find out that while the house owner and the investment account owner start off in relatively the same place, the investment account owner will end up in a far better financial condition in 10 or 20 years due to the difference in investment growth.

TIP

The best time to get a CDFA involved in advising on financial arrangements in a divorce is before the final settlement is inked. Even in an amicable divorce where both parties want to be fair, the results of different alternatives can be dramatically different. Invest the time and attention in understanding what the agreement actually says.

If money is to be transferred, be sure you have a solid agreement as to not only the amount to be transferred but also the timetable by which the transfer is accomplished. Plenty of people sign divorce settlements without understanding how a 401(k) will be divided, how the transfer will be accomplished, by when, and what paperwork is needed. In the case of retirement plans and pensions, a Qualified Domestic Relations Order (QDRO) will be required to move funds. You should also be certain that the order makes provisions for how the settlement will be handled if one person dies before the order is completed.

Remember that just about anything in a divorce ends up being negotiable, particularly if one person is determined to bleed the other person by continuous legal fees. Most courts will not even consider the financial division until a plan for care and custody of the children is agreed upon. The less wrangling you do, the less time and money will be spent on attorney's fees.

As with all situations involving financial transactions, you need to make every effort to keep in calm control. You need to understand your attorney's plan for accomplishing a settlement, and the strategy for doing so. A reputable attorney can work with you on a realistic timetable and what the alternatives are likely to be. More than one person has felt that their attorney has accomplished very little for the hours billed; if this is the case, you need to demand accountability.

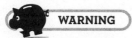

WARNING

Attorneys can and do fire clients, often when the client is noncooperative and frequently when the client fails to pay. Clients switch attorneys, also, for failure to pursue the case. If you have concrete reasons you believe the attorney is not handling your case properly, by all means get another one. But be sure you're grounded in reality—attorneys can't get everything your way.

On the other hand, attorneys' biggest complaints are that the client has failed to produce the necessary expense reports and other data, has not listened to reasonable advice on settlement, and though things have been explained multiple times, the client hasn't paid attention.

If you don't understand, keep asking (and requesting meetings) with your attorney until you do. The money spent to understand and team up to pursue a strategy should ultimately save billing hours. Recognize that you may be rattled, and bring your financial adviser or perhaps even a trusted friend along if you cannot understand on your own.

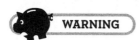

WARNING

Many people are quite angry during a divorce and decide to hire an attorney with a reputation as a bare-fanged junkyard dog. Don't do it! The usual result is the settlement is much more prolonged and you pay soaring attorney's fees for what might have been settled equitably far earlier. In addition, judges hate unruly attorneys and will be much more severe in rulings.

While divorce proceedings are going on, you must get a grip on yourself and think through the issues that will confront you after the divorce. Now is a great time to read some books or take some classes on investing. If you must return to work, don't wait until the divorce is settled—begin as soon as possible. Too often people who have been out of the workforce wait until the divorce is final to begin looking for a job or retraining, in the belief that this will make them look more pitiful and more deserving of support to a judge. Not so. In modern times, the courts expect that each party will do what they can to make themselves independent and self-supporting.

No one comes out of a divorce as wealthy as when they were a couple. At a minimum, two households must now be supported instead of one. But neither is a divorce necessarily a hopeless condemnation to eternal poverty. With a solid financial plan, steps taken for emotional recovery, and judicious management of investments, people can and do recover.

The Least You Need to Know

- Take your time to learn to cope with the initial shock and stress of finding yourself in changed financial circumstances.

- Assemble a team of reliable fiduciary advisers to help you make a plan to manage your money wisely.

- Think carefully about paying off debt with your windfall. Be sure it makes financial and psychological sense in your circumstances, and get the agreement in writing if you're paying off debt for another person.

- Divorce has an impact on all your plans: housing, income, retirement, college financing. Manage your emotions, and get expert advice.

- Realize that your life has changed and your now-different financial possibilities and challenges may affect the goals and plans you had previously formulated.

- Balance some prudent spending to achieve goals with preserving the bulk of your windfall to continue to serve you long term.

When to Buy and Sell Investments

Even though I advocate (mostly) long-term investments, nothing is forever. In this part, we'll look at the reasons to buy and sell. No matter how carefully you've researched and evaluated an investment, not every investment performs as you expected.

You'll learn to recover from disasters, decide whether you should take action or sit tight, and distinguish temporary fluctuations from true changes in circumstances. You may choose to sell high and move some of your gains to investments that seem to offer a market bargain. If your investments have achieved the goal you set for them, you'll be able to let the profits ride, or sell and use the money.

The final chapter in this part will point you toward resources to help you continue your education, augment your experience with the benefit of others' years of investing, and gain opportunities to refine your analysis. And then, you will no longer be a beginning investor.

Good Reasons to Buy and Sell

All of us love to buy. Nobody likes to sell. While I encourage staying invested for the long term, not making snap or emotional decisions, that doesn't mean you should hold on forever. There are good reasons to sell, but even for those reasons, there are good ways and bad ways to do so. In this chapter we explore good reasons and good ways to sell your investments.

In This Chapter

- Overcoming the reluctance to sell
- Deciding which investments to sell
- Selling for the right reasons
- Overhauling your portfolio for better performance
- Continuing to look for opportunity

Bad Reasons to Hold on to an Investment

Before we get to good reasons to sell, let's look at the most popular reasons people are reluctant to sell an investment. As you might guess, these reasons fall purely into the realm of emotional decisions, and are not based on any analytical judgement of the investments.

Waiting Until It Gets Back to the Price You Paid

It's true that if you sell when something has lost a lot of money, you've locked in your losses. However, if you continue to hold a deteriorating investment, there's no guarantee it will ever improve, and it may plunge even further. I'm not talking about the small glitches—say, less than a 10 percent change in share price—which may be normal variations in any stock's price (and volatile stocks may have an even greater range). I'm talking about abrupt plunges or slow but continual declines.

When you purchase an investment, you should have a planned floor for the price, beyond which you will evaluate a possible sale. It's possible to enter a *stop-loss order,* which will automatically sell your investment if it falls below a specific price. Some people view them as protection (especially if an investor will be unable to observe their portfolio for a significant period of time), but I personally don't like them because I prefer to monitor and analyze an investment based on the underlying fundamentals, not just temporary changes in share price. Also, in a situation such as a *flash crash,* a price can rapidly drop and revive in a matter of minutes, and you can take a large loss only to be locked out of a big gain.

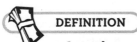

> **DEFINITION**
>
> A **stop-loss order** sells a security once it reaches or drops below a specific price.
> A **flash crash** is a market event where a price drops precipitously and then returns quickly to the original price.

You need to go back and reevaluate the investment to see if there is genuine hope of recovery in a reasonable time horizon by reviewing the reasons you purchased it and deciding whether factors have changed. Otherwise, you may be better off taking what money remains, and finding a better investment. In any portfolio, some investments will underperform your expectations. But if you hold on to all the losers, soon your portfolio will be overwhelmed by them.

Under current tax law, if you do have a significant loss, you can deduct the loss first against *short-term gains,* then *long-term gains,* and then up to $3,000 per year against your ordinary income. It doesn't remove the pain entirely, but it does help a bit.

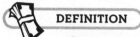

> **DEFINITION**
>
> **Short-term gains** (or losses) are gains (or losses) on investments held less than 1 year.
> **Long-term gains** (or losses) are gains (or losses) on investments owned for more than 1 year.

It's Gone Up; Maybe It Will Go Up More

It might, but sooner or later there will be a glitch in the price, or the company (or industry) will become out of fashion or stabilize and go from growth to stagnation.

This comment arises more often with individual stocks than with a portfolio of mutual funds. There's no automatic answer to when to sell. You have to evaluate whether it continues to be a good investment. Would you still buy this stock at the current price with the current financial fundamentals? You'll need to review the reasons you bought it, and ask yourself whether the expectations you had for it are still true. You should work through the rest of this chapter to see if the reasons to sell apply to this investment.

What about the idea to sell enough to get back your original investment? I don't think that's a terrible idea, but as with selling bonds, you now have reinvestment risk.

Let's say you put $5,000 into a stock that's now worth $10,000. You sell half (getting your original investment back) and invest it in a new stock that goes bust. You're not out any money, but you haven't made anything either. And if the original stock has continued to go up, you're going to wish you'd stayed put.

So I'll repeat that I don't think you should sell purely by following a formula, but rather reevaluate the investment periodically. And to be clear, you're reevaluating the fundamental condition of the company (earnings, sales, and so on), not just temporary changes in the share price.

"I Can't Sell Because I'll Have to Pay Taxes"

If you have a big gain in an investment, you will most likely have to pay taxes on that gain (not the original investment) if the investment is held in a nonretirement account. If you've held the stock or mutual fund for less than a year, you'll be taxed on the gain at the same rate as your ordinary income. If you've held the security for more than a year, you'll be taxed at the capital gains rate.

TIP

Whether or not you pay taxes on long-term capital gains depends on your tax bracket. Current tax law states that the 10 and 15 percent tax brackets owe 0 percent capital gains tax, income at or above the 25 percent bracket but below the 39.6 percent tax bracket owes 15 percent capital gains tax, and the 39.6 percent tax bracket owes 20 percent capital gains tax.

However, investment decisions should not be made solely on the basis of taxation. Sure, if you have a gain so large that it will push you into another tax bracket, you might consider getting advice about spacing out the sale over multiple years. But what if the investment takes a major drop in price? You might have been better off selling, taking your gain, and paying taxes rather than taking a loss. This is particularly worrisome when you have a large amount of company stock—say, more than 10 percent of your investable wealth.

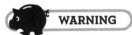

WARNING

Keeping too much of your wealth in company stock has a double risk. If the price of the stock drops significantly, you can lose a huge percentage of your wealth. But if the company stock is plunging, the company may be in enough trouble that you also might lose your job (and your income) while also losing your assets.

Remember, however, that in order to be able to enjoy the benefits of having the money, at some point you're probably going to need to pay taxes on it. Right now, capital gains taxes are fairly low, but they can change in a political heartbeat. Tax consequences should certainly be considered, but if you have good reasons to sell the investment, tax consequences should not totally drive the decision. It's always good to make a profit, even if some part of it will always go to taxes.

Good Reasons to Sell an Investment

While I've been encouraging you to invest and hold on, at some point, it will be necessary, or wise, to consider selling or changing investments. Let's look at good reasons to do so.

You Need the Money

If you've followed my advice, you have an emergency fund and won't need to tap your other investments except in the case of a long-lasting emergency (such as long-term disability) or unexpected but worthwhile expenses or opportunities (you saved enough money to send your child to the state university but she gets into Harvard).

You may also have planned to run the risk of better returns by keeping more money invested and less in cash. However, the tuition bill has now come due, or you decide to retire a little earlier than planned, or you're offered the deal of the century on your dream home. What to cash in?

Once you become a dedicated investor, it can be hard to cash in anything! You'll just hate to see all that potential gain stopped in its tracks by the actual need to spend money. At this point it's time to remember that you're investing for goals, and now you're going to use those investments to achieve those goals.

Before you cash out, you might think through whether there are better options. Could you pay for your expense by some belt tightening on current income? Would it make sense to take a home equity line of credit for a short-term expense you could then pay off in a reasonable amount of time from income? Do you have anything you could sell (like a second car) to raise needed cash? Could you put off a purchase or upgrade and use those funds for the expense? It depends on the expense, the return on your current investments, and the amount and duration of the need.

Next, look to your emergency fund. Could you reduce this temporarily with a plan to build it back up in a reasonable time?

Finally, let's survey your investments. Look first to your taxable investments (as in, brokerage accounts or savings), next to your Roth (no problem if you're over 59½, or need the money for serious medical expenses or college), and only as a last resort, your 401(k) or traditional IRA.

In these accounts, consider investments with the most gains. Can you skim the cream off a mutual fund with big gains? Is there a particular stock that has outperformed such that you might sell some portion of the shares? You might want to take some portion of your profit on one of these.

Do you need to rebalance your portfolio anyway? Maybe it will be less painful to rebalance from your gainers (taking out the money you need), and not only withdrawing but also reinvesting some in other investments. It's a psychological trick that might ease your sale.

Finally, are there some stinkers you really should get rid of anyway? Now's the time! Use the opportunity for some housecleaning and take the loss on your tax return.

The Investment Isn't Working Out

If your expectations for an investment have not performed as you'd realistically projected, it may be time to decide to move on. Has it crashed and burned, underperformed your expectations, or simply stopped growing?

In the case of a specific stock that's crashed and burned, you have to go back and review what's happening with the company. Has there been bad news about a product or some scandal attached to management? Is the news temporary and likely to blow over, or is the company so tainted that its image is permanently tarnished? Is it a large company, able to absorb the problem, or a small company whose fortunes depended on a product or public image? Depending on how you assess the damage, this could be a point to cut your losses and get out, or an opportunity to take advantage of temporarily depressed prices and buy more.

With mutual funds, your evaluation process is a bit different. If your investment is in an index fund, it just may be a sector or asset class that is temporarily out of favor in the marketplace. There may be specific economic or political conditions that have caused the specific sector to go kaput. Or you just made a poor choice to invest in that asset class.

Let's look at a few examples. After acts of terrorism, funds that focus on that particular geographic area may take a plunge. A dip in commodities or basic materials of which a country is a major producer may cause emerging market mutual funds to crater. If you've chosen funds to provide diversification, well, that's what diversification means—some will be going down while others go up. You can probably sit tight and let the markets balance volatility over time.

But what if it turns out that the sector just doesn't perform well over time? I've included commodities funds in my portfolio design for years, believing they do well when everything else does poorly—a good negative correlation. However, I (and other advisers) have moved off that position for several reasons: commodities funds have been extremely volatile, with such huge percentage losses year after year that they have been more risky than even some volatile stocks; they pay no dividends so there's nothing to cushion the blows; and there's no real recovery in sight. So far I haven't sold out of the investment, but I'm not rebalancing into more.

Another danger that may indicate a sell signal is, having invested in a hot sector, you conclude that sector is hot no longer. Maybe you chose biotechnology, or oil and gas, or something that looked like it had huge potential. Since these are specialized sectors, not broad market segments, you hopefully had a sell point in mind when you purchased. I don't think a large investment in a specialty is a prudent choice, but if you watch it carefully (or perhaps are even in the industry), you may be able to evaluate whether your sell point has been reached.

If you invest in actively managed mutual funds (which I don't generally recommend), you should be particularly vigilant if the manager changes. If you've bought a fund because of the performance of a manager, when he's gone, the management style may be gone. Subsequent managers generally have a tough time replicating performance.

What about when the company you selected is the subject of a *takeover* or *spinoff?* The first thing you should look at is whether you would want to own stock in the takeover or spinoff. Generally, smaller, hard-charging companies are taken over by bigger, richer, but slower-growing companies. If you bought the small company for its possibility to outperform, the takeover bid may be the reward you were waiting for, so take your profit. During the time between announcement and actual completion of the sale for the specified price, the share price may gyrate on investors' hopes that maybe an even better offer (or a bidding war) may come along. You'll have to make a judgment on the situation, but try to keep down the greed for a few cents' difference. As I said before, be satisfied with a profit.

> **DEFINITION**
>
> A **takeover** is an attempt by one company to purchase another. The takeover may be friendly (the target company wants to be sold) or hostile. A **spinoff** occurs when a larger company decides to create a new, independent company from one of its divisions or business segments.

Spinoffs are a similar but complicated situation. With no real track record for the new company, you'll have to decide what the reconstituted business might be. Companies rarely spin off their most profitable divisions. It's not a hard-and-fast rule, however—sometimes the spinoffs are the spunky, volatile, and ultimately more profitable sectors.

Decide if you would buy the spinoff if it were a company you were considering afresh. There's some research that spinoffs do outperform the parent company: suddenly they've become a smaller and more nimble entity with newly motivated management staff. If you do decide to keep the spinoff, recognize that you now probably own a different kind of company: smaller, more volatile, with less experience. There may well be more upside potential, but there is usually more risk. See how that fits into your overall portfolio design.

Are the fundamentals deteriorating? Many good companies can have a bad quarter (when earnings or profits drop significantly), but if the trend continues overs several quarters, it may be time to sell. Be certain there's not a seasonal pattern to these drop-offs by comparing quarters from the previous years. Some companies do all their business around Christmas, or in the summer, with significantly less earnings the other three quarters.

Maybe the investment hasn't lost money, but hasn't gained share price, either. Here you have to review the fundamentals. For an individual stock, are earnings and sales still going up at least at the rate you expected? What about *pretax profit* and *return on equity*? These should all be either stable or up. If they're negative, it may be why the price has stalled: the company just doesn't look like that good a value.

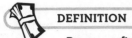

DEFINITION

Pretax profit is a measure of how much of a company's earnings are actually in excess of expenses. **Return on equity** is a measure of how much return shareholders are getting for their investment. These figures are available at Morningstar and through BetterInvesting software.

You might also check out whether the percent of long-term debt to equity is rising or dropping. A company that is spending more on long-term improvements may be confident of expanding, or it may be overborrowing in an attempt to shore up the business or keep paying the dividend. A company that is not increasing long-term debt may be solvent enough without additional borrowing, or may have no further opportunities to create new business. You have to understand what the trend means, and may be able to get some clues through news coverage or the annual report.

What's the current price-to-earnings ratio? If you bought it at a high P/E, the expectations of the market may have already factored in any current business improvement—because everyone expected good news, nobody got excited when the news *was* good. On the other hand, these high-flying P/Es can cause a dramatic drop if the company misses predictions, or earnings are just not quite as spectacular as expected. High P/E companies can be very volatile. You may want to look for a better value.

Some companies are simply heartbreakers. For several years I owned a company where everything looked good. It had great earnings, was well managed, was a leader in its industry, and the stock price went nowhere. Warren Buffet eventually bought it out (at a small premium to what I'd paid)—because, I assume, he recognized a profitable company at a bargain price.

It's Time to Overhaul the Portfolio

Even though I strongly advocate choosing an asset allocation and sticking with it, nothing is forever. Your thinking may change, the market may change, and even new research may reveal a better idea. Also, as you get older or circumstances change, you may want more conservative or easier-to-manage investments.

Once upon a time, 80 percent of my investments were in individual stocks. I was young, interested in keeping close track of individual companies, and could not understand why anyone would invest in mutual funds (mine were making around 6 to 8 percent collectively) when I was averaging 12 to 14 percent in my individual stocks. Then, 2008 happened. My stocks plunged about 45 percent, and I learned about the importance of balancing a portfolio with safer investments.

My hubris was due to not having been investing significant, important sums for very long, and once I was older and very, very busy, I didn't have time to pay all that close attention to each individual company. I wanted a more balanced, less risky, and less time-consuming portfolio.

I overhauled my investments to be about 20 to 25 percent individual stocks, with the remainder diversified among mutual funds. I'm still invested far higher in equities than I think most people my age should be, but because I'm pretty risk tolerant and plan to retire late, I'm comfortable with my balance. However, what's right for me may not be right for you—it's very individual.

Recently, many people have had the desire to overhaul their portfolios to more socially responsible investments in a desire have their money align with their beliefs. They may be searching for proactive investments that support social initiatives or simply companies whose business does less harm. I don't think this is primarily an investment stance, but rather a behavioral and political one.

Nevertheless, it's possible to overhaul at least some of your portfolio by choosing socially responsible stock funds (which will usually emphasize large caps) and/or socially responsible bond funds to replace those asset classes in your investment mix. However, these investment changes should still be evaluated for management fees, performance, investment philosophy (value, growth, etc.), and what's actually in the portfolio. See Chapter 10 for more discussion of choosing these types of funds.

The research I encountered while studying for the CFP® also convinced me that a portfolio based mainly (and in many cases, exclusively) on no-load mutual funds was in fact a better idea. I continue to read and listen to a variety of opinions, and learn from my own and client experiences, and lately I've seen research (mainly from Dimensional Fund Advisors) that has influenced me to believe that there may be certain research-based factors that have the potential to improve upon the performance of passively invested funds. So I'm always looking to upgrade my thinking.

 TIP

Dimensional Fund Advisors (DFA) walks a different path—a third way between active and passive management—called research-driven. DFA believes you cannot beat the market (its board member, Eugene Fama, won a Nobel Prize for his economic theories on efficient markets), but it believes its research has shown certain factors that, if portfolios are chosen to tilt to those qualities, will help investors outperform market segments over long periods. DFA funds are only available to clients working with investment advisers, because DFA believes the method requires ongoing education and low turnover to control costs.

What I don't do is try out every investment scheme that sounds good but whose results are only based on backward-looking statistics. It's usually a good bet that the books explaining these purportedly successful schemes hit the bestseller list for a time, then crash to join their companions that predict sensational market collapse or spectacular gain. Take a look at the financial bestsellers from 20 years ago to see how their schemes have performed, and whether their predictions occurred. While there are a few classic works that have stood the test of time, most are in the trash bin of history.

Besides adjusting your investments and your thinking based on solid research, or shifting your asset mix based on a different risk tolerance or need for security or simplicity, you may need to change your investments simply because you've moved from the accumulation phase of your life to your distribution phase.

This means that you're no longer in a mode to be working and saving, but instead have met your goals (like college or house purchase) or are at the stage when you can in fact retire and live off portfolio and any other retirement income.

In the case of a segregated investment destined for a specific goal, you will cash out that investment but may not need to overhaul the entire mix of the remainder of the portfolio. If, on the other hand, you were managing your money as one cohesive portfolio, withdrawing a significant sum may require you to rebalance the entire portfolio in order to get your mix back to the correct percentages. This can be accomplished by selling and buying shares in your funds until the percentages are back to your plan. Or, if you're still working, you might accomplish the rebalance by directing future contributions to the asset categories that are depleted, evening things up again.

For people who have focused on saving and accumulating, moving to a point where you're actually withdrawing from the portfolio can be difficult. I've had more than one client ask me how much they should save from their retirement income. Outside of maintaining an emergency fund and enough cash to meet income needs for whatever you've planned in retirement, you won't be continuing to save.

However, being in the distribution phase doesn't mean you can now ignore your investments. You still need to monitor how well they're doing (in order to adjust your spending if needed), but you should also sell anything that becomes too large a percentage of your portfolio. Yes, that's success, but it can also move your portfolio, over time, to generally become too stock-heavy, since over the long term stocks will generally outperform your more conservative investments. Not always, though. If bond (mutual fund) investments have outperformed your equity portfolio, this is your opportunity to buy stocks or stock mutual funds at "bargain" prices.

While you don't need to rebalance too frequently, and may indeed do worse if you do, at some point your investments will deviate so far from your target percentages that you'll need to trim some holdings and increase others if you want to stick with the same risk profile (or move it in a different direction).

Of course, if you hold individual stocks, you can never stop monitoring them. In fact, often older people predominate at investor events, perhaps because they have the time to spend on study, and some money available for investing that's now under their control, not in their old 401(k) restricted to the company's choices of available investments.

However, I do suggest that as you get older you have someone else in the wings who can manage your individual stocks and make buy and sell decisions. You can't park stocks in quite the same way as a portfolio of mutual funds, because you have to keep evaluating the performance and prospects of the individual company. At some point, if we're lucky enough to live a long life, we're going to get sick, or tired, or concerned with other things, and someone else—your adviser, the person with your power of attorney, your child—should understand what's going on with your stocks. It's a great opportunity to transmit your experience and knowledge to your children or grandchildren.

A Better Opportunity Has Arisen

We've already considered that a good reason to sell some investments is that the goal for which they were directed has been accomplished. Or a better investment has presented itself: maybe your parents are selling the family manse and will give you a good deal, or you've decided to buy yourself a job by selling your REITs and investing directly in real estate, or you can buy a partnership share in the business or practice you work in.

But with individual stocks and mutual funds, you should challenge the investments at times. With mutual funds, you may decide to move from active to passive; or to funds that are in the same asset class, but socially responsible; or choose ones with lower management expenses; or consistently adhere more closely (or even exceed) an index. Or you may decide that some of the asset classes you originally picked aren't working the way you expected or are correlating more closely with your other picks (and thus not providing the diversity you wanted). Sometimes you've housed all your investments with the funds of one company, but service deteriorates or sales pressure mounts. Maybe you've been in a target date fund, but either don't want to move to the balance it's now shifted to, or want to design your own targeted diversification rather than trusting their selections. It's time to look for another fund that more closely matches your objectives.

With individual stocks, you want to regularly challenge your current holdings with potentially better investments. You're aiming to have excellent stocks in good industries, purchased at a good price and sold (eventually) at a higher price.

Let's say you own several health care stocks. First of all, is this a growing or stultifying industry? If the stocks have done well, have any of them taken over too big a portion of your portfolio? What about the sector—do you have investments in other sectors as well? Let's say you have three to five stocks in the sector. Is there a better company than the worst one you own? Should you sell it and buy the potentially better company? Or perhaps invest more money in the top performers you already own (particularly if you still believe they're undervalued)?

Maybe you have stocks in an industry that was formerly going great guns but has had a reversal of fortune. Is it coming back in the foreseeable future, or have conditions changed? As I write this, the oil industry has less demand and is glutted with product at a time when it appears there's a worldwide shift to cleaner energy. Many oil producers appear to be bargains right now compared to their past prices, but will prices return? The need for oil is not going to disappear, but would it be better to invest in a good company in a downtrodden industry, or shift funds to an entirely different and growing industry, and the excellent companies within that industry?

If you've focused primarily on growth companies in the past, your circumstances may have changed enough that dividend payments are more important to you in evaluating a stock. So you may want to begin to shift your stock investments to prefer stocks that pay at least some dividend over ones that are a pure play on capital gains expectations.

You may have a portfolio of primarily mutual funds, but have segregated a portion of your portfolio to focus on much more speculative investments, or an asset class that's of particular interest to you. You might concentrate on an industry you know well, or a kind of stock (e.g., small-caps) where you want to focus extra effort in hopes of outsize returns. This might be a small opportunity to get better returns by taking a big risk, but confining it to only a small amount—the amount you can afford to lose.

On the other hand, you might decide that a certain asset class—for example, large-caps—offers enough opportunity to select quality companies that you'll take the opportunity to put together your own "mutual fund" of 15 or 20 large-cap individual stocks, with the rest of your portfolio diversified among mutual funds, excluding that class.

Effort usually contributes to opportunity. Don't trade the investments you've carefully evaluated and selected for any new kid on the block, but don't hold on forever when a better opportunity can be found. Don't get sentimentally attached to a stock just because you like the product, or a celebrity promotes it, or you like or dislike the political stance of the CEO. Look to the fundamentals of the investments, whether it meets your needs and portfolio design, and whether you can improve upon it with another investment.

The Least You Need to Know

- If you need the money, find a better investment, get rid of investments that didn't perform as planned, or want to rebalance to keep your asset plan on track, you might consider buying or selling.
- Have target sell prices in mind when you buy an investment.
- Reevaluate the strength and original objectives of the investment to decide whether and when to sell.
- Update and revise your investments as you gain more knowledge and experience.
- Strive to continually upgrade your portfolio as better investment opportunities arise.

Recovering from Mistakes and Bad Markets

It's impossible to invest for long without losing money on something. Even if you have a beautifully diversified portfolio, its value will fluctuate. You will most likely need to tap your emergency fund or your insurance coverage at some point in your life. Or maybe you weren't adequately covered before the divorce, or the illness, or retirement arrived. This chapter is about steps you can take to improve your situation.

In This Chapter

- Disaster, or temporary setback?
- Recognizing a buying opportunity
- Taking advantage of government and legal benefits
- Strategies to get back on track

Stock Market Disasters

Many people tell me, sometimes proudly, that they got out before the worst of the crash of 2008 and 2009. Not a single one has told me they got back in fast enough to take advantage of the huge upswing the next year. In fact, many of them are still sitting on their cash 7 years later, having missed one of the biggest increases in the market ever.

Don't do that.

If, and only if, you have a nicely diversified portfolio, you have two choices during a market crash—stay put and do nothing, or buy more. If you're primarily invested in individual stocks, you'll need to determine whether your stocks are being affected by the market-wide drop, or whether there is something specific to the company that merits selling, or even increasing your holdings.

I'll permit you to feel a little panic if you're a new investor and you haven't seen one of these market crashes before. Sure, you've probably read about the Great Depression, or Black Friday (it sure feels different when it's your own money, no?), but let's remember our fundamental principle: buy low and sell high. If you decide to bail *out* of the market, you're doing the exact opposite.

In the situation we're considering, there's nothing wrong with your actual (diversified) investments, so you can't determine if any of them should be weeded out. It's too late, when a crash happens, to "fly to safety"—that's something you've already done by diversifying your portfolio. You may discover that you actually have less tolerance for risk than you thought, but you shouldn't make any radical overhaul in a panicked situation.

Start Buying

Even better than standing fast and just waiting for the upturn (which always happens) is to start buying, prudently. That means that you should consider purchasing the broad categories of what's dropped—usually stock funds. It takes a strong stomach to do this because you will find yourself worried that, no matter when you buy, the market could go even lower. Remind yourself that it is highly unlikely, and only quite by chance, that you will *ever* purchase any investment at its lowest price, or sell it at its peak. But slanting toward buying low and selling high is always your goal.

While it's true that it's tough to beat an index over the long term, your individual performance can be positively affected by taking an opportunity to buy that mutual fund or increase your holdings during a downturn. By using such opportunities, you may be able to improve your return compared to the average return of the fund.

TIP

It's ironic that most people flee to cash when the market's bad. In fact, we should do the opposite: keep some cash in reserve in very good markets so that we have cash to invest in bargains during downturns.

Similarly, this may be the time to revisit your stock watch list. (See Chapter 11 for a discussion of developing a list through paper trading.) Are some of these good companies still showing excellent fundamentals? Sure, they're going to be likely to have some downturn in earnings or sales in a really terrible market, but do they have fundamental strength that will make it likely they'll bounce back? Check out how they did in previous bad markets—not only the huge crashes but the little downticks that happen much more frequently. Unless there's been some bad news specific to the company, this may be your chance to buy into a great company at a bargain price.

I want to encourage you to steady your nerves. As I write this, the market is booming, but I know with absolute certainty that I'll see more crashes in my lifetime. If you're young, forget about it. Or buy a couple of cases of tuna, some bottled water, cans of chili—whatever will allow you to feel calm and survive the zombie apocalypse. And realize that time is on your side, keep saving, and try to pick up the bargains. It ain't over 'til it's over.

If You're Retired or Close to Retirement

But what if you're retired, or nearly retired, and the dip is endangering your current income? It's time to take a hard look at how much your portfolio has really dropped. If it's diversified with stocks or stock mutual funds, bond or bond mutual funds, and some cash as I recommend, you can probably wait it out. Don't necessarily do a major rebalance (although, again, some rebalancing at the appropriate time can allow you to pick up bargains); instead, draw from your cash, and sit it out. Do whatever you can to reduce your spending—some research indicates that if you can simply reduce your spending by 10 percent in years with terrible markets, your portfolio will still recover and survive.

TIP

Some software shows gains and losses, but reinvested dividends and mutual fund capital gains count in cost basis. It's proper accounting procedure, but it's not what you pulled out of your pocket. Let's say I invested $28,693.95 in ABC fund. It paid $1,232.20 in dividends, capital gains, and so on, but the share price dropped, and the value is now $29,018.63 so the program shows a loss of $907.85, or approximately 3 percent. I've lost money from the payouts, but I still have more money than I started with.

Ask yourself, or your adviser, how much your *overall* portfolio is down. Is it down 20 percent, 30 percent? Then do your best to ignore the news stories blaring that the market is down 46 percent. Your personal market isn't down that much, and some belt-tightening will go a long way toward riding it all out. Save your mind by *not* looking at your investments every day—it's just short-term crazy making. (Review Chapter 15 for steps you can take in retirement if things are really desperate.)

At times, the world has seemed to be going to hell in a handbasket. It certainly felt like that after the World Trade Center attacks (when the stock market crashed as well), and I'm sure it did to people who lived through the Great Depression. But the world, so far, hasn't ended, people still make money, and there's still no real alternative to investing if you want to keep pace or exceed inflation. In the end, it's buying power, not rate of return, that determines whether you can afford a decent life.

TIP

The Great Depression was more long lasting than recent crashes, but people who stayed with their investments, and collected and reinvested dividends (if they had investments at all), saw their buying power even out in about 5 years. This was partly the result of price deflation, so that buying power was increased for less absolute dollars. It took until 1954 for the market to return to previous levels.

Personal Disasters

Maybe it's not the market's gyrations, it's your own personal life events that have dragged down your financial security. Sooner or later, most of us have some personal crash—some of us more than one!

How do you recover from a personal disaster? Not all of these suggestions will work in your individual situation. But even if you can't get back to where you were, you can always improve where you are. So let's look at some major changes you can try to remedy your situation.

Take Advantage of the Safety Net

Everyone hates the idea of government "handouts." But we also hate the idea of people starving in the streets, old people unable to pay for heat, and children missing school because they have no winter coat. Government programs provide that net to catch you when you're in free fall. They're designed to get you back on your feet, so use them to do so. I can assure you that you won't be the first formerly middle-class divorced person to apply for SNAP (Supplemental Nutrition Assistance Program; a.k.a. food stamps). Google "Famous people who were homeless," and you'll come up with plenty of people who know how to sleep in a car.

Illness

Many financial reverses come from illness. If you have become disabled and have no disability insurance, you should most definitely apply for Social Security Disability if you have enough work credits to qualify. The same is true if you have a disabled child or a child who is an adult and has become disabled. If your adult child's disability began before age 22, he or she may qualify for disability based on a parent's work record. The complex rules for qualifying are beyond the scope of this book, but *Nolo's Guide to Social Security Disability* is a good reference. Spend an afternoon in the library reading this book and then head for the local Social Security office (or online, in some cases).

> **TIP**
>
> Most pharmaceutical companies have appeal programs for people who need medications but who can't pay. Payment with doctors and hospitals can also be negotiated. These things can be time consuming and depressing, but the payoff per hour spent can be worthwhile. Pull out all the stops you can.

Be prepared to fill out a lot of paperwork. You'll need statements from your doctors and medical records that are approximately as thick as an old phone book. Also be prepared that your application for disability will likely be declined. There has been such a surge in disability claims in recent years that unless you have a slam-dunk case (you're blind or dying), you're probably going to have to appeal, as is your right. At that point you probably want to engage a lawyer, who will take a percentage of the settlement. Interview two or three to get their assessment.

Veterans

If you're a veteran, you should also investigate whether you might qualify for Veterans Affairs disability benefits. If you have certain medical conditions, you are presumed to be disabled due to service-related disability.

> **TIP**
>
> If you're a veteran, be sure to browse va.gov to understand your benefits. You will be able to see a list of medical conditions for presumptive disability. While some benefits are reserved for people who have made a career or retired from the military, others are available to all veterans.

VA and Social Security disability benefits can take quite a long time to be approved and issued—6 months or more. However, once you're approved, the benefits are retroactive to the date you applied, so you might get a lump-sum check. Stay on top of your claim (it can be checked online) and don't hesitate to call.

It seems there's hardly a financial issue that doesn't lend itself to a scam. Be very careful of people who claim to guarantee they'll help make your claim successful, or charge you for "consulting" on VA benefits. While some nonprofits do provide legitimate advice, you can probably garner any assistance you need by reading a few publications (including from the VA) and filing your own application.

Seniors

If you're a senior citizen (which may be age 55, 60, or 65, depending on the program), you should check out the services of your local senior center or Area Agency (or Office) on Aging. These programs can give you free or low-cost assistance with household chores, repairs, and maintenance, companion services, meal assistance, and assistance in preparing taxes. You're entitled to them thanks to the federal Older Americans Act. Many local chapters of the AARP can help with tax preparation as well, often for free, which can easily save hundreds of dollars.

I urge you to work the system. At some point in your life you've paid tax dollars to support these programs, so think of it as a cost of insurance you've invested in, for which you are now claiming the returns. The main difficulty with these services is identifying and accessing them in the first place. Begin your research online or with the assistance of a librarian, and apply for everything you can.

Bankruptcy

Bankruptcy is a last resort, but it's also the ultimate assistance. Bankruptcy is designed to get people back on a productive life path when there's no other way out. Be aware that there are a few types of debt that can't be jettisoned by bankruptcy: school loans, child support obligations, and income taxes. However, it's possible to go back to court to revise child support, and income taxes can be negotiated (if in good faith).

There are two types of personal bankruptcy. Chapter 7 is the most severe; assets will be sold to pay off all debts. Some types of assets are protected, and some debts cannot be wiped out, but in general this gives you a clean slate. Chapter 13 allows you to work out a 3- to 5-year payment plan based on your salary. For more information, check out *Solve Your Money Troubles: Strategies to Get Out of Debt and Stay That Way*.

You might consider bankruptcy when your debts become too large to pay even the minimum payments or when you could not pay them off in 3 to 5 years (including finance charges). When they reach 100 percent of your yearly income or more, you should definitely consult a bankruptcy attorney. Whether you should declare bankruptcy depends on your age, future prospects, and what kind of debt it is. As long as you continue paying your mortgage, you won't necessarily lose your house, and retirement funds are not generally available to creditors. Be sure to consult a bankruptcy attorney before you sell your home or clean out retirement funds. Neither may be necessary.

Make sure you understand how your bankruptcy attorney will be paid—believe me, they've figured this out. It sometimes involves stopping payments to your creditors in order to find money for a retainer. Yes, your credit will be ruined, but it doesn't last forever and you can begin to slowly reestablish it. Have a heart-to-heart with a reputable attorney to understand the different types of bankruptcy and what will work best for your situation.

WARNING

Be careful of credit counselors and credit consolidation schemes. Some are legit (usually offered through reputable nonprofits), but some simply prey upon the unfortunate. Ask for references, and call those references—people often reveal surprising things.

Changing What You Can

The answer to almost all financial problems is to spend less, save more, and invest the difference. Simple, but not easy. Once you've explored outside resources, you next need to look to your own efforts to recoup losses and build back your investments. Let's work through the possibilities, from mild to drastic changes. It all depends on the severity of your loss, and how profound the impact.

Discretionary Spending

It's called discretionary spending because you have some choice in the matter. We all have givens we believe we can't live without, but recovering from your setback means you should examine these expenses very carefully. It's often derided as the latté factor, but over time a lot of little wins can add up to a big win. It's easier to shave off a little than completely change your life.

If you can't completely eliminate something, downshift it. Choose a cheaper restaurant, less often, for lunch rather than dinner or coffee and dessert rather than lunch. Examine whether you need online streaming, anything but basic cable. Could you get the kids off your cell plan, shift them to a prepaid arrangement, or make them responsible for paying their own?

The biggest budget leaks I see are in the areas of eating out (people spend amazing amounts on this), clothing, hair upkeep, gym memberships and personal trainers (seldom actually used), and car expenses. I've discussed this in previous chapters, but we're looking at strategies this time with more urgency.

If you have a family, everyone should be called on to contribute resources. Parents hate to tell the kids they're having trouble, but, as a psychologist once told me, the kids always know. They may be keeping a family code of silence, but they know. How empowering is it to recognize their competency and acknowledge their importance to the family's success?

Of course, it's all how you present it. "We're broke, so we need to get tough around here and cut everything to the bone" is probably not going to be met with a positive reaction. Rather, kids need an honest picture of what the challenges are, and brainstorm ways to meet them in order to go forward.

A huge expense for many families is the cost of kids' activities. The amount of involvement in these has increased at a startling rate, with a cascade of expenses attached: the minivan or SUV, because kids and equipment have to be driven everywhere; and the equipment, musical instruments, fees, competition travel, and lessons. Yet parents and kids complain of constant exhaustion. It's my observation that almost all these activities are dropped once the kid goes to college and can decide for themselves how they're going to spend their time. It's why I have three harps acting as clothes hangers in my own home.

Screen these activities as a family. Establish how much (if anything) you can afford to pay for all activities. Work out a choice, and if possible, have the kids earn part of the cost of the activity. It may break your heart to see them quit something you cherish, but it should be at least partially their choice. (I realized eventually that it was *me* who loved playing piano, not my daughter.)

Transportation is not entirely discretionary, but what you spend on it is somewhat in your control. Reevaluate how you get around, and use anything but a car as often as possible. Walking, biking, and public transportation are probably viable in most suburban areas and all cities. The kids will almost certainly howl about this, until they realize the independence it gives them. Most adults can use the exercise.

If you can change your auto usage, you may be able to downsize to one car instead of two, and a smaller car if possible. If you or your partner travel a lot for business, or could commute by public transit (a great time to read investment books!), you should investigate the possibility of owning only one car and perhaps a supplementary day or weekend rental when you really need it. Renting a car for a day or two a month, every month, is way cheaper than owning a car for a year. Before you rush out and sell the second car, experiment with disciplining yourself to leave it parked for a couple of weeks and see how it goes. If you can do without it, and sell it, you've just nailed an infusion of cash. Reserve some for rentals as needed, and funnel the rest back into rebuilding your investments.

Cutting Fixed Expenses

Fixed expenses are the hardest to alter, but the place where you might be able to make the most impact. Housing is the area to analyze first.

Is there any way you can generate a little income from your home? In some areas, renting out a garage for parking, storage, or use as a workshop is a viable alternative. If you can get $50 or $100 per month (and much more in some urban areas) you can build up a new investment fund with very little change in lifestyle (except for parking your own car on the street).

 **WARNING**

Check with your homeowner's insurance to make sure renting part of your home or garage does not affect your coverage. Also make sure that if your renter's possessions are lost or destroyed, you're covered for any liability.

What about renting out a bedroom? If you're near a college or professional school, a large corporation with young employees, or any place where people come in to stay for a few months, renting a bedroom can be quite lucrative. I have a good friend who, after a messy divorce, moved her young daughter into her bedroom and rented the spare for $500 per month. She had much-needed income for several years, and she and her boarder became long-time friends.

Many people discard this idea as too much trouble, or because of fear of getting a crazy renter. However, if you're careful about where you advertise, and selective about the candidates, it can work.

Would renting your space through one of the online B&B arrangements generate more money? Probably, but it depends on the space you have and the extra work you're willing to put in (and your community's regulations). Your renters are much more transient, you're going to be washing sheets and cleaning, and more and more of these renters are looking for condos or guest houses rather than a bedroom in a family home. As with all ways to generate money, it depends on your individual situation, how much time and effort you can devote, and how badly you need the money.

Could you move out of your home for a time and rent it out? In order for this to make sense, you have to find a place to live that's cheaper than what you can get in rent for the old place. This is probably most viable for a single person or a couple without kids. Some people have managed to move out of their place and house-sit for someone else for a time, move in with their parents (gasp), or relocate to another, cheaper, country for a period of time.

Improving Your Earnings

I've already discussed the idea of managing your career like any other investment (in this case, the investment of your human capital). Avail yourself of any free career improvement and counseling services you can—senior centers, libraries, and maybe even your company's human resources department. No matter how much you love your job, you can find one that pays more that you love, also.

TIP

In the mid-1990s, Amy Dacyczyn published a newsletter called *The Tightwad Gazette.* They were masterpieces of tips on frugal living, and are still available today collected into books. In 1996, she and her husband were able to retire. I suspect this was made possible by two factors: her frugal lifestyle and consequently low expenses, and the money she made from her self-created gig and the book sales that grew out of that—an ideal combination.

If you have a family, you need to approach this from a standpoint of what all members of the family can contribute. It's as if a corporation has a large cash reserve—you have human capital. You, your kids, and your spouse probably all have unrealized earning power. If any members of the family are unable or not old enough to work for pay, they can certainly take over household tasks that would allow other members to have the time and energy for a part-time job.

I'll be a bit snarky here and say that I see no reason why any household with able-bodied children over 10 years old needs a landscaping or snow-removal service or a cleaning person. If money is tight, or you're trying to rebuild finances, these are tasks that require very little expertise. Children in other generations and from other countries have always been expected to contribute to family income. It's also a great opportunity to introduce a child to the idea of investing and making money grow—once they've put some time and effort into real work, the idea of money growing without that effort will be very powerful.

Finally, in really dire circumstances, parents should consider a second job. The biggest obstacles for most people are the supposed shame attached to dumb jobs, and the fear of being seen by someone you know. I don't think there's any shame in taking a job for a specific goal that's beneath your education or earning capacity—you're making a smart decision to get back on your feet fast. If you're concerned about "the neighbors," find something where you won't be seen. Because they'll certainly see you if your home is foreclosed.

These measures don't need to be forever, unless your spending rises to the level of the new income. As with all efforts at generating and increasing wealth, make sure you hold on to some of the money. Get right back on the horse and start riding those investments again.

Delaying Social Security Benefits

In Chapter 15, I discussed the benefits of delaying Social Security, but there are additional benefits to working longer if you need to rebuild an investment portfolio. As long as you keep working and contributing to a 401(k), you'll still be getting the employer match. Although 401(k)s require you to take a minimum distribution after 70½, if you are still working for the company, you don't need to take an required minimum distribution from a 401(k) at your current employer.

If your employer offers a Roth 401(k) option, or you're eligible for an individual Roth and have at least as much earned income as your contribution, you can continue to build up retirement funds without having to take any distribution, technically forever. You are also shortening the time your portfolio has to last; shaving 4 or 5 years off the term of withdrawal can allow higher withdrawals when you begin.

What about the flip side? What if you're faced with forced early retirement? This happens more frequently than we might wish—workers in their 50s and early 60s are informed they are being laid off, or their position is being eliminated. Then they discover that a new position is created, and filled with younger, cheaper workers. If you are retired early and against your plans, I urge you to consult an employment attorney who may be able to negotiate a better deal for you on severance, health insurance, and any retirement benefits or salary payments.

Don't give up hope on getting a new job. I've spoken to a number of people who are forced into involuntary early retirement, but who have been able to find new jobs. It can take a while (up to a year in my experience) and it may not be at your former salary, but if it allows you to let your investments ride for a longer period, or ride out withdrawing from them in a bad market, it's usually worth it to continue working.

The Least You Need to Know

- Try not to panic during market downturns. The long-term trend is positive.
- If possible, use a market drop to benefit by buying at bargain prices.
- Take full advantage of safety net programs for which you're eligible; they exist to get you back on your feet.
- Cut your spending in every way you can. Involve the whole family.
- Delay retirement if you need to rebuild your portfolio; working longer can make a portfolio last far longer, with a potentially higher rate of safe withdrawal.

CHAPTER 22

Becoming a More Advanced Investor

As I've said before, if investing were easy, everyone would do it. Actually, most people do invest, but they're often completely uncomprehending of their choices, as in their 401(k) plan, or they've made a few bad choices and given up. You've made it through this book, but someday soon you're going to have more complicated questions. How can you improve as an investor?

Do you want to increase your understanding of how markets might affect you? Do you want to learn to scrutinize companies in more depth? Could you benefit from a place to ask questions, get feedback, or hear other investors' ideas and analysis? In this chapter we look at how to become a more advanced investor.

In This Chapter

- How to judge the integrity of financial advice
- Finding free information and education
- Benefiting from the experience of others
- Worthwhile organizations you can join
- Developing your own system

Knowing Whether the Source Is Reliable

One of the best ways to judge the reliability of financial advice is to understand how the author is getting paid, or what the financial interest of the business is. For example, if you're getting free information from an insurance company, that education, while perhaps valuable, is going to emphasize strongly the importance of insurance. A mutual fund company's brochures and webinars are going to highlight the company's products and the advantage of their particular investing philosophy. That's not to say that there's no good information to be had—you just have to dial down the sales-y portion of the materials.

When it comes to popular media—television programs, cable channels, newsstand magazines, even venerable newspapers like *The Wall Street Journal* or *The New York Times*—you have to realize that part of their reason to be is entertainment, and the other part is finding something new to say. If they offered the same old sensible advice every day, subscribers would be bored into cancelling.

Bias

Advice and coverage of the marketplace also generally carries a strong political bias. I suppose there might be a socialist or left-wing Democrat who works for *The Wall Street Journal*, but in more than 20 years of reading it daily, I haven't identified who that might be. This conservative, capitalist leaning of much of the financial press means that corporate governance and behavior may not be scrutinized as closely as the individual investor might like, and tax policy that consists of anything but lowering taxes will be roundly criticized. In the 8 years of his presidency, I don't think *The Wall Street Journal* ever published a flattering picture of President Obama.

 TIP

The Wall Street Journal isn't all business. The weekend edition has extensive features in two sections: "Review," which covers many arts and culture topics, and "Off Duty," for food, fashion, travel, and other consumer articles. If you're afraid you might not understand more technical parts of the paper, start there.

While coverage of business and government policy tends to be moderately to extremely conservative, consumer issues and advice can be a bit more evenhanded, although the advice will emphasize personal action and responsibility rather than any kind of structural or societal change. I suppose that's no surprise. Nevertheless, you don't have to be conservative to make money. Just know that the coverage you're reading in every publication has its own biases.

Magazines

The stock-in-trade of every financial magazine used to be screaming cover articles such as "Our Top 10 Picks for Mutual Funds in the Next Year" or "Three Stocks to Buy Now" or "The Sky Is Falling!" or "Next Year Will Be the Best Ever!" I recently saw a hilarious presentation that selected a dozen or more covers or lead articles, and in every single case what happened was the exact opposite of what was predicted in the magazine.

The magazines have finally figured out that they haven't done all that well with their predictions, and it's become questionable legally how much liability they might have if anyone relied on these recommendations. So whenever you read any financial publication, tap your ruby slippers and remind yourself that there's no one who knows the future.

Now these magazines focus on what you can do to recover from the latest disaster or poor choices you may have made. I find the articles that focus on a family's finances particularly heartbreaking. They ask advisers to comment, but the problem is always similar—not enough money saved, no insurance, too much debt, no will or estate plan—and the answers are always the same: save more, pay off debt, protect yourself. I hope it helps readers to see themselves and take the same advice.

I do think these magazines are valuable in one respect: they cover changes in laws and tax policy that might affect you. Have the rules changed for Social Security? Is there any change to taxation of capital gains or dividends? What's different about retirement accounts? Regularly reading a financial magazine or two will keep you updated.

Gurus and Other Personalities

Before you become enamored of any book author or broadcasting guru, please think through their background. Be especially suspicious of anyone who promises to help you get rich quick, recommends hot stock picks, tells you the sky is falling, or (maybe) has a brokerage background. You know how well all those diet gurus have worked out, right? Same with financial advice.

I think there should be a special hell reserved for financial media personalities and people who counsel people mired in debt, but then refer them to high-commissioned salespeople via their website. Often these referrals are, or should be, in direct contradiction to the advice given to be frugal, to be aware of costs, and to seek a fiduciary adviser. Sometimes the main qualification of these referred advisers is that they've paid a big chunk of change to be listed on the website.

Just because you've heard about a program or an adviser at your church, or because the adviser purports to be an upstanding member of your religion, don't necessarily trust. Many marginally scrupulous people and programs seek to cloak themselves in credibility by claiming kinship through religion.

Just because it's published doesn't mean that it's been carefully vetted by an editor or expert in financial issues. Or that the journalist writing the article really understands the field. And the experts quoted may have some agenda of their own, or the letters after their name may be a professional designation that takes 2 weeks and a nonproctored exam to obtain.

> **TIP**
>
> If you read, consistently, a variety of publications, you'll develop the sense to smell a rat. Read enough to garner several different opinions until you begin to feel there's a consensus, and also that you understand the contrarian viewpoint.

Try to avoid overly pessimistic, world-ending scenarios. The world marketplace isn't going to collapse, and if it does, we'll all go with it except for those who have stashed cases of tuna and canned milk in their basements.

Choose Your Preferred Method of Learning

Try to combine a few different ways to broaden your perspective.

For beginning to intermediate investors, *The Wall Street Journal* and the business section of *The New York Times* are near-required reading. You will not understand everything you read, especially at first, but over time and with regularity you will build your store of knowledge. Concepts are repeated so often that eventually you come to understand them by exposure.

Much as I love actual newsprint, I've switched my subscriptions to electronic format. I find it much easier to browse, skim, shut out the noise, and get to the content I want. Look especially for news on any company you own or are contemplating, note management changes or regulatory sanctions against any of the investment or mutual fund companies you're connected to, and do try to read through the special reports or focused reporting on taxes, investments, and so on. Both newspapers also regularly run articles on college financial planning issues, home buying, divorce, and retirement. Spend 20 or 30 minutes on one of these papers every day and you'll build your knowledge significantly in a few months.

Even though I'm somewhat skeptical of magazines, I do recommend you pick one up from time to time—monthly if possible, quarterly if you're pressed for time. Alternate your selection among a few publications until you find one that's easy for you to understand and that actually runs articles that interest you.

Next, browse a few financial blogs. You have to be very careful here because most bloggers make money by running ads, and some of the commentary may push people toward the products. If there are reviews, try to figure out whether the writer has a financial interest in the product or service recommended (that doesn't mean there isn't worthwhile information there). Blogs can be especially valuable because they often have the latest news long before it reaches print publications.

Webinars and podcasts are available from nearly every big mutual fund company. These will generally be goal-based, giving you information about retirement, college, planning, asset allocation in their (in-house) mutual funds, and so on. Many of these are recorded and on-demand, but you might seek out the few that are live-cast, because you may be allowed to ask questions.

In addition, most of these companies put out consumer-oriented brochures, and additional material that any adviser can get for you. The companies do everything they can to make these user-friendly (lots of white space and lovely photographs). While they're often a good free introduction or reinforcement of the basics, they can come to seem pretty simple, pretty quickly.

Advisers also usually have access to white papers oriented to professionals, giving more in-depth background research. Ask your adviser to give you research on any topic you want to study in depth. Once you feel ready, and feel the need, you can ask questions like whether intermediate-term TIPS or short-term TIPS are better, and in what market environments? Can the benefit of using an adviser be quantified? Questions about making strategic portfolio decisions, ETFs as tax strategies … you get the idea. Maybe it sounds deadly dull now, but eventually you'll want to know more.

I've dissed bestsellers, but there are some classic works that continue to offer sensible advice. After a time, the prices quoted and the companies mentioned may become out of date, but the principles endure. Plus, it's fun to see how right they were, if some time has passed since the book was published. I've included a list from my own bookshelf in Appendix B.

It's hard to discuss financial gurus without mentioning Warren Buffett. No matter how much you read, you're never going to invest like he does. He has every possible resource at his fingertips, a support staff available 24/7, and more than 60 years of experience. You don't and I don't. But what you can access, for free, is his annual letter to shareholders of Berkshire Hathaway. The letters are all available on Berkshire Hathaway's website going as far back as the 1990s. Reading through a few recent ones will give you a pretty succinct education in the Great One's thinking. Reading through all of them, particularly when he analyzes his mistakes, is worth at least one college course in investing. And they're witty. The new one comes out in May of each year, so put it on your calendar.

Speaking of college courses, junior colleges and adult education centers (as well as senior centers and libraries) frequently offer seminars, talks, and courses in investing, retirement planning, and other areas. These offerings have a veneer of respectability, but don't necessarily believe everything you hear. All it takes is a proposal and convincing the venue that you have a good topic (or, in the case of community colleges, that you can scare up enough paying students). Some speakers are very good, some are shills for the brokerage industry.

I speak frequently at libraries. In the Chicago area, one week in April is designated Money Smart Week, and the Federal Reserve Bank sponsors and promotes activities about consumer financial issues. While some excellent events are offered all around the area, the program is sponsored by banks and brokerage houses as well as others with less of a financial interest in the advice. Most speakers (myself included) offer the programs as a way to let people know they exist and what services they can offer. Check with a librarian to find out what programs might be offered for consumers. You can get information on specific topics, and a chance to ask questions when you have a live presenter.

Find a Group

You can't get all the experience you might wish for in a few months, or even a few years of investing on your own. But you can benefit by the experience of other individual investors by joining an investment club or finding a group that offers programs on investing. I recommend you check out at least two: BetterInvesting and the American Association of Individual Investors (AAII).

BetterInvesting

BetterInvesting used to be known as the National Association of Investors Corp. (NAIC). It's weathered a few storms since its founding in 1951.

In the 1990s the organization was made famous, then infamous, when one investment club (the Beardstown Ladies) published a number of books claiming outsized returns. Eventually, an independent audit showed that they had miscalculated by including their own contributions in returns. Their popularity, and the fad for investment clubs, took a downturn. However, the Ladies are still investing.

There were also some gyrations in management during the 2000s, which appear to have settled down since the hiring of the new CEO.

As I mentioned in Chapter 11, BetterInvesting promotes a method of analyzing individual stocks using their Stock Selection Guide, which analyzes many factors derived from a company's data to consider whether the company has good growth potential and currently appears to be a good value. The basic form of this software is available online to members, and a more extensive software package, including portfolio management tools, trend analysis, and a whole raft of other tools that can take you a significant amount of time to learn, are available as purchased software.

BetterInvesting's magazine (published 10 times per year) focuses on analyzing a Stock to Study, an Undervalued Stock, revisiting previous stock picks (even some that did not do well), and various articles on financial topics. There's a specific section for beginners. Although BetterInvesting and its members are primarily focused on stocks, beginning in the 1990s, BI began coverage of mutual fund investing as well, because so many members expressed a need for help in selecting investments for their 401(k)s.

> **TIP**
>
> BetterInvesting's principles are worth following for almost any beginning investor: invest a set amount regularly; reinvest earnings, dividends, and profits; invest in quality growth stocks and equity mutual funds; and diversify your investments.

Local investment clubs under the BI umbrella focus almost exclusively on individual stock analysis and purchase—you won't hear much about mutual fund investing at the meetings.

What you will hear in a good club, however, is a lively give-and-take about how other members view current trends, analyze a company, and have different takes on the same data analysis. Some members may have worked in a specific industry and have insight into what makes a good company in that industry. If the club has been around a while, you'll hear about previous portfolio successes and disasters. Even if you join or form a fairly new club, the process of working through the Stock Selection Guide will teach you a lot about the workings of a company.

Most clubs meet once a month and require a monthly contribution to the stock purchase fund—usually $20 or $30. I view this as the price of tuition—you probably won't get rich or retire on your share of a club's portfolio, but you will probably make *some* money. What you learn, however, along with the opportunity to interact with other members, will be priceless for your own long-term investing success. Generally a club will require members to prepare and present a stock analysis on a regular basis, and monitor some part of the club's current portfolio. Members will vote on what to buy and sell.

> **TIP**
>
> Sometimes members in a club will be hurt or annoyed when the other members do not approve the current stock pick. Remind yourself that education is the reason you're there. You can always go home and buy a stock for yourself that you believe in.

The one difficulty you may have is actually finding a club to join. It does require an investment of time to participate in a club, and because good clubs want dedicated members who will stick to analysis and not be enamored of wild bets on crazy investment schemes, most clubs do not publicize.

The best way to find a club is to seek out and attend local or regional events. Most regions will put on an annual investor's fair (with many educational sessions) as well as workshops and training events. You'll be able to network to find a club or two to visit.

Make every effort to participate live in a good club. But if you're rarin' to get started, or can't find or attend a club in your area, you can still enjoy many of the benefits of an investment club by joining BI as an individual, at-large member. Membership will give you access to many website tools and articles, a subscription to the magazine, and the opportunity to participate in webinars. The webinars offered might include information on basic stock selection, when to sell, a magnifying-glass examination of a specific data point and what it means, or a panel of experienced investors discussing their favorite current stock picks, and why. Many webinars are free or low-cost, and most are archived on the website.

You can sign up for a myriad of free email newsletters. Several people involved in BetterInvesting also offer paid subscription newsletters using Stock Selection Guide principles. These can give you some good stock ideas, and walk you through how the recommendations were selected and analyzed. I've found their *SmallCap Informer* to be a worthwhile subscription for a type of stock that's harder for me to identify. Before you plunge in to any of the specialized products, give yourself some time to learn the analysis methods, watch some webinars, and (hopefully) join a live club.

Because I think behavioral and psychological considerations profoundly influence investment decisions, I think one of the most valuable benefits from participating in an investment club is the stabilizing influence it can have on our attitudes. In a roiling market, it really helps to hear the concerns and accumulated wisdom of other investors, and it can prevent panic selling, over-optimistic buying, and tunnel vision on one hot industry or company. It's crowdsourcing at its best.

I've been a member of BetterInvesting for about 20 years now, and have belonged to two investment clubs over time. The more I've used the methods, the better understanding I have of analyzing investments. The instruction and analysis far exceeds anything taught to CFP®s, and I'm betting the broker on the street doesn't know the half of it.

American Association of Individual Investors (AAII)

AAII has been around since 1978. Its offerings and orientation are different enough from BI that you should consider joining both.

AAII doesn't offer investment clubs, or promote one specific methodology for analyzing stocks. There are, however, a number of local chapters that meet to hear presentations and offer seminars and discussions. In addition, the organization invests and tracks two model portfolios, the Shadow Stock Small-Cap portfolio, and a portfolio of the choice of mutual funds.

The AAII website offers the ability to select and monitor portfolios using a number of stock screens. So if you're curious just how well the Dogs of the Dow, or the Motley Fool, or dozens of other investment schemes are doing, you can monitor your choices on the website. It's a great way to follow a potential scheme over time, before you put real money into it.

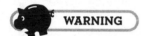 **WARNING**

Remember, your personal results will not perfectly mirror any model portfolio. You will purchase at a different time, on a different day, than the model. Also, performance reporting by some models has sometimes turned out to be less than reliable when investigated independently by journalists. Take stellar results with a dose of skepticism.

Take some time to explore the website. AAII offers some model asset allocation strategies (which I can't, due to regulatory constraints on registered investment advisers offering specific investment advice to nonclients). There are plenty of basic courses, often with a little test to see if you really got it, and advice on investing in specific areas: stocks, bonds, and mutual funds.

Some of the material will be familiar to readers of this book, but it's always an excellent idea to see content presented in several different ways in order to reinforce your learning.

AAII's 10-times-a-year *AAII Journal* has a very different tone than BetterInvesting. AAII doesn't focus very much on specific investments, but rather runs articles discussing various strategies for buying and selling, but also on consumer topics such as Social Security updates, retirement, and withdrawal strategies.

I find that sometimes the articles are quite technical and can present more math equations than the average investor will be comfortable with. It's not a newsstand magazine; on the other hand, *AAII Journal* often presents research that is otherwise only available in magazines and journals aimed at financial professionals. If you find the material challenging as a beginner, save a few of your issues and take a few of their online courses. When you return to the *Journal*, the articles will really sing with relevance.

Just like BI, AAII offers a bunch of supplementary materials you can purchase in addition to your membership. Both organizations also offer software (at extra cost) that allows you to search on specific criteria for stocks that match. I've had very little problem finding more investment ideas than I had money for, but for some people, or clubs, these might be useful. Try using Morningstar's stock-screening tools (free through your library, remember?) to see if they will generate enough ideas for you, first.

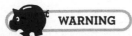

WARNING

Avoid the tendency to think that purchasing is doing. That's how I ended up with an enormous yarn collection. Work through what you've already purchased in your membership and you'll know whether you should purchase additional resources. We're all about conserving money for investing, right?

Exploit Online Resources of Media and Websites

There are tons of websites and online magazine content, and because I can't possibly vet every one (and they change frequently), I've included a few I like in Appendix B. Two, however, deserve special mention.

Morningstar

Morningstar will drive you crazy with pop-up promos each and every time you visit the home page, until you sign up for basic membership, then a free trial membership, then their rather pricey full 1-year membership (currently $189). If you have the patience to click through, there's lots of free information on the site. We've already examined Morningstar's usefulness for giving you extensive data. But they're also a professional source for other information.

The tab for personal finance will give you plenty of articles, discussion, and interviews with prominent financial commentators (some of whom are pretty out there in my opinion, but you may judge differently). You have to be on your guard, as is usual with media, against gloom-sayers and overly optimistic prognosticators, but it's worth a listen from time to time.

While I discourage you from daily worrying about the market and even your individual investments, if you suddenly find yourself asking some variation of the question *What the heck is going on with* _____? you can probably find some information about the issue on Morningstar. They provide a daily market watch on a number of indices, and usually commentary on the issues and events du jour. You can set up a portfolio (or several, if you wish) and track performance and news alerts.

I'll confess that I check the site just about every day, and while it's probably worth the bucks they charge, I'm even happier to go through my library and get it all for free. See how much you actually use the site—in fact, you may have to limit your time on it in order not to disappear down the rabbit hole.

Seeking Alpha

I have some reservations about bringing this website to your attention because some of the content can be dubious. It's a crowdsourced information site about any specific investment you want to track and read about. Much of the content is written by financial professionals, but there's no guarantee that it's free of self-interest or sellers flogging their own products or investments.

My other caution is to be careful what you sign up for. When I first became aware of the site I input about half a dozen stocks in which I was interested, and in very short order had 892 emails. You may want to limit the onslaught by restricting yourself to searching the site online for any investment you're interested in, and prevent your email from overload.

That said, if you're thinking about buying or selling a particular investment, it's quite interesting to read the commentary of several authors, which may come to very different conclusions. Part of the task of any individual investor is sifting through different interpretations in order to arrive at what works in your particular situation, with your particular investment orientation and needs.

Codify Your Own Path to Investment Selection

As you advance or seek to improve your investment knowledge, you'll begin to find a path that you feel works for you. For mutual funds, I pretty much set my asset allocation, choose low-cost funds that meet or exceed their index, and rebalance regularly.

Investing in individual stocks requires much more attention and participation than investing in mutual funds. I urge you to keep good records of your thinking by doing the following:

Keep a list of stocks that interest you. Even if you don't have the money at a specific time, you should keep a "watch" list and monitor the performance of stocks that interest you.

Have a target buy price and a target sell price, from the moment you purchase the stock. When these triggers are hit, you should reevaluate. You might not necessarily buy or sell, but you should use these indicators to jumpstart your reevaluation.

Write down your reasons for buying the stock, so that you will know whether or not the stock has really met your expectations.

Use several different sources to gather analysis. Before I buy a stock I read the analyst report on Morningstar and check out a few commentaries on Seeking Alpha. If I'm still interested, I do a Stock Selection Guide (SSG) on my BI Toolkit software, and look on the BI website to see if anyone else has done an SSG and how close their judgment is to mine. I also look at BI to see whether there have been any feature articles covering the proposed investment. While many of my ideas actually come from the BI magazine, I love to find old articles to give perspective on what the company and the stock looked like 2 or 5 years ago. If I like what I see on the SSG, I'll trek to the library to check the stock (and the industry, if I'm not familiar with it) on Value Line reports.

Set regular dates to review your current investments. I recommend you check out your stock investments quarterly, when earnings are announced, in order to see if the stock is performing as you predicted. While I look quarterly, I'll rarely sell an investment unless I've held it at least 18 months. BI reevaluates investments at 18 months and 5 years, and pretty much that's a schedule I follow. Unless the stock has dropped like a stone (and by that time it's probably too late anyway), I'm generally willing to give it at least an 18-month chance.

Quarterly, I also monitor whether any of my investments have done well enough to overwhelm the others (at which point I'll consider selling some to bring back a little balance and diversification), and whether I should chuck the worst performers for my next better idea (or more investment in stocks currently in the portfolio).

Develop and write down your sell policy. Both BI and AAII have numerous ideas and checklists suggesting criteria for deciding to sell. These are going to have to be adapted (and changed, when appropriate) for your own personal risk tolerance and belief in what's important in a stock. For example, some people will sell if a stock drops 5 percent; personally, I'll tolerate a 20 to 30 percent drop if I can figure out the reason and believe it's temporary. Because we all have a natural bias against selling and losing money, you should exercise the discipline to write down some questions to review when evaluating your current investments.

I double-check my diversification. Some picks will inevitably lose money, but I can limit the damage by not concentrating on one company, one cap size, one geographic location, or one industry. Even if the industry is currently in favor and doing well, I don't want all my stocks to be concentrated in it.

You need to think for yourself in making investing decisions, but you don't need to reinvent the wheel. Hook in to the experience and knowledge of others to improve your own thinking and develop your judgments. Many sources of information and organizations can keep you current and expand your investing education.

The Least You Need to Know

- Protect yourself from the crazies and promoters by using multiple sources of information to form your own opinions and enhance your education.
- Keep abreast of current news, changes in investments, and changes in tax and government policy by regularly reading several press sources such as newspapers, magazines, websites, and blogs.
- Benefit from others' experience by participating in an investor group.
- Morningstar.com and Seeking Alpha are sources for information about specific investments. Morningstar also offers personal finance articles, news, and extensive data.
- Use your improving knowledge to write and revise your investment policy and criteria for buy and sell decisions.
- Keep track of what and how you're doing, and revise your methods based on experience.

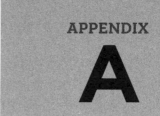
Glossary

401(k)　A retirement program offered by private industry involving contributions from the employee and (frequently) matching funds contributed by the employer.

403(b)　A retirement program offered by schools, universities, and (often) other nonprofits.

529 plan　A state-sponsored savings plans designed specifically for college savings. The earnings grow tax-free, and withdrawals are tax-free if used for qualified educational expenses. There is no minimum investment, and anyone can contribute, regardless of income.

active management　When the manager of a mutual fund uses personal judgment to select investments.

annualized return　The average return of an investment over a period of years, averaged per year.

annuity　An insurance investment that can provide a lifetime income.

asset allocation　A plan to invest your assets according to a specific distribution of types.

assets　Your money or other possessions or investments of value.

assets under management (AUM)　The method for charging for financial planning or investment management where fees are based on a percentage of your total assets being managed by the adviser. An adviser may charge fees based on the value of AUM.

avalanche method　A method of debt repayment in which you pay the minimum on all debts, then concentrate extra payments on the debt with the highest interest rate.

balanced fund　A mutual fund designed to maintain a specific balance between stocks and bonds—for example, 60 percent stocks and 40 percent bonds.

bear　A pessimist who believes the market or the investment is deteriorating.

beta   A measure of how much the stock swings compared to the overall market.

bond   An IOU for a loan you've given a company or government. This may guarantee you an interest payment or a specific amount returned to you after a specific period.

brokerage   A firm that handles buy or sell orders for investments, charging a commission or fee for the service.

bull   An individual or analyst who is optimistic about an investment or the market as a whole.

call   A feature of investments where the investment can be terminated and money reimbursed earlier than the original term.

capital gain   The difference between your purchase price and your selling price (minus any dividends or interest).

CERTIFIED FINANCIAL PLANNER™ (CFP®)   A financial planner who has passed a recognized set of courses, experience requirements, and a certifying exam administered by the Certified Financial Planner Board of Standards.

Certified Public Accountant (CPA)   An accountant who has passed the CPA exam as well as meeting state certification and experience requirements.

closed-end fund   A mutual fund that issues a specific number of shares when originated; the shares are subsequently traded based on market value.

COLA (cost of living adjustment)   An increase or decrease in a payment based on the rate of inflation.

commodity   A raw material or product that's traded, such as oil or pork bellies.

consignment   An arrangement whereby a dealer or shop owner agrees to attempt to sell your item, paying you a portion in return only if it sells.

Consumer Price Index (CPI)   A measure of the typical price paid by consumers of a market basket of goods and services.

copay   The share of a bill you must pay, either as part of the payment (with the remainder applied to your deductible) or your share of medical bills after you have met your deductible.

correlation   A measure of how much different investments move in the same way (positive correlation) or opposite to each other (negative correlation).

cost of attendance   All the estimated charges and budget items your student will have to pay to complete each year at college.

Coverdell savings plan   An individual account in which earnings grow tax-free and withdrawals for qualified educational expenses are tax-free. You can contribute a maximum of $2,000 per child, and must have an income under certain limits to contribute.

current yield   The yield on a bond based on the price the bond is currently selling for.

deductible   The amount you must pay before insurance will pay anything on a claim or medical charges.

deferred annuity   Similar to a SPIA in that you invest a lump sum (or a series of payments) with the promise that at some future date you can turn it into an annuity payout. Rather than beginning immediately, theoretically the investment continues to grow and provide larger future payments.

discretionary   Those expenses for which you have some choice as to how much you spend.

diversification   Distributing your assets among different types of investments.

dividend   Money paid by a company to its investors based on the company's profits or from reserves.

Dow Jones Industrial Average   An index of the price-weighted average of 30 stocks used as an indicator of the rise or fall of the market.

duration   A calculation using present value, yield, maturity, and call features.

efficient market hypothesis (EMH)   A theory that the market reflects all known information about a security in its pricing.

emerging market   A country that shows developing economic activity but does not meet standards for a developed market.

equity   When used to describe real estate investments means the amount of investment or ownership you have in the property above the liability (loan).

equity fund   A mutual fund entirely or primarily composed of stocks.

exchange-traded fund (ETF)   A mutual fund that trades like a stock.

face value   The printed value of a bond, note, coin, or other investment.

fallen angel   An investment that has fallen substantially from its usual price, worth, or quality rating.

fee-based   Financial adviser charges you a fee based on assets and can also charge commissions or management fees on the investments you purchase.

fee-only   Financial adviser charges you only for the time spent on your project, or by retainer or fee based on the amount of assets managed. No commissions or referral fees are paid or accepted.

fiduciary   A financial professional who is legally required to act in your best interests.

fixed expense   An expense you must pay every month and cannot eliminate, such as mortgage, health insurance, and utilities.

flash crash   A market event during which prices change suddenly then return rapidly to former prices.

fund of funds   A mutual fund whose investment holdings are made up of other funds.

futures contract   An agreement to buy or sell a particular product or commodity in the future at a predefined price.

general obligation   Bonds backed by the general revenues (taxes) of a state or municipality.

gross income   The total you earn before any federal, state, local, or Social Security taxes are deducted.

growth company   A company that aims to increase in value by growing its business rather than paying dividends.

hedged   The foreign bond fund has invested in currency instruments to protect against the blow if the dollar varies significantly, so that returns are only dependent on changes in the actual bond.

index   A model collection of investments designed to represent a specific segment of the market.

index fund   A mutual fund that seeks to replicate a specific index.

individual retirement account (IRA)   A type of investment account individual investors can establish that offers tax benefits.

industry   A subdivision of a sector.

life strategy fund   A mutual fund that contains investments designed to produce a specific level of risk or safety.

load fund   A mutual fund that charges a sales commission in addition to management fees.

long-term care-insurance (LTCI)   Insurance designed to pay the cost of nursing care, either at home or in a nursing facility.

long-term disability   Income insurance coverage for when your illness or injury is expected to be permanent or result in death.

long-term gain or loss   A gain (or loss) on an investment owned for more than 1 year.

management fee   A charge imposed by an investment company to cover staff salaries, advertising, and the costs of doing business.

market capitalization (cap)   The dollar amount value of all the outstanding shares of a publicly traded company; a measure of the size of the company.

match (employer's match)   An employer's contribution to a workplace retirement fund, often based on the employee's salary or contributions to the fund.

maturity   The amount of time by which an investment will end.

money market fund   A fund that invests in short-term bonds and other debt securities. Each share usually has a value of $1.

Moody's   An investment rating and research service.

mutual fund   An investment in which people pool their money to buy a collection of investments.

NASDAQ (National Association of Securities Dealers)   A computerized exchange that enables investors to trade securities.

necessary expense   A bill you'd have to pay even if you were unemployed or disabled. You can estimate what the rock-bottom figure is by looking at your fixed expenses, then adding a minimum of discretionary expenses.

Net Asset Value (NAV)   The total value of the investments contained in a mutual fund, minus any fund liabilities, divided by the amount of shares outstanding.

net income   Your income after federal, state, local, and Social Security taxes are deducted.

no-load fund   A mutual fund that's sold without a sales commission.

NYSE (New York Stock Exchange)   The largest stock exchange in the United States.

open-ended mutual fund   A mutual fund the price of which is determined at the end of each trading day by its net asset value.

option   The right to purchase or sell an investment at a future time.

out-of-pocket limit   How much money you must pay before your insurance will pay 100 percent of the remaining charges.

over the counter (OTC)   Stocks not listed on any exchange but may be bought and sold through a brokerage or dealer network.

paper trading   The process of choosing a stock or even a whole portfolio and tracking performance on a regular basis, without actually purchasing the investment.

passive management   When the manager of a mutual fund selects investments to replicate a specific index.

penny stock   Stocks sold over the counter for a very low price, often only a few cents.

PLUS   A loan for education taken out by parents.

present value   The value of an investment today, as opposed to some point in the future.

price-to-earnings (P/E) ratio   A ratio calculated by dividing the current price of the stock by the current earnings per share.

principal, interest, taxes, and insurance (PITI)   The amount that represents the payment for the required costs of purchasing a home with a mortgage.

Ponzi scheme   A type of investment fraud wherein the promoter continually sells shares, using the money from newer investors to pay illusory returns to previous investors.

pretax profit   A measure of how much of a company's earnings is actually in excess of expenses.

principal   The money you originally invested.

real estate agent   A salesperson who sells real estate.

real estate broker   A real estate agent with additional education who can supervise agents.

real estate investment trust (REIT)   A share in a partnership that owns a property or collection of properties.

Realtor   A real estate agent or broker who is a member of the National Association of Realtors.

return   The money you make from your investments. It can take the form of interest, dividends, or capital gains (from selling your investment).

return on equity   A measure of how much return shareholders are getting for their investment.

revenue bond   A bond used to raise money for a specific project, such as a toll road, which will then produce its own income.

Roth IRA   An individually owned and managed retirement account. While there is no tax deduction for contributing, earnings grow tax-free, and withdrawals are tax-free if you're over 59½ and have owned the account for 5 years.

secondary market   A place or service where an original investment can be resold.

sector   The general area of a company's business—e.g., health care, technology, industrials, energy.

securities   Any financial instrument that gives you ownership in a publicly traded corporation (stocks), shows that you are a creditor of a government or a corporation (bonds), or have a future right (options).

segment   A specific characteristic by which investments are grouped.

SEP-IRA   An IRA for self-employed people and small businesses; it allows higher contribution limits than other types of IRAs.

short-term disability   Insurance coverage for when you can't work for up to 6 months.

short-term gain or loss   A gain (or loss) on an investment held less than 1 year.

signature guarantee   A guarantee by a bank that they know you are who you claim to be.

single premium fixed income annuity (SPIA)   An insurance investment product designed to provide lifetime income. You purchase the annuity in a single lump-sum payment. The insurance annuity provider guarantees you will receive a specific monthly check as long as you live.

snowball method   A method of debt repayment in which you pay the minimum on all debts, then concentrate extra payments on the smallest debt until it is paid off.

speculate   To gamble on future profits.

spinoff   Occurs when a larger company decides to create a new, independent company from one of its divisions or business segments.

S&P 500   An index developed by Standard & Poor's of 500 large companies, considered a measure of the market.

Standard & Poor's   An investment rating and research service.

stock   A share in a company.

stop-limit order   Sells a security at a specific price.

stop-loss order   Sells a security once it reaches or drops below a specific price.

stop-market order   Sells a security at a specific price *or below*.

street name   Used when securities are held electronically at a stock brokerage, custodian, or bank.

takeover   An attempt by one company to purchase another.

target fund   A retirement-oriented fund that rebalances investments to be increasingly conservative as the year of retirement nears.

term   The length of time for which a bond is issued.

term insurance   Life insurance for a specific amount for a specific number of years.

ticker symbol   An abbreviation for stocks or mutual funds that represents the investment on an exchange.

traditional IRA   An individual retirement account contributions to which are deductible if you meet income limits.

Treasury bill   A debt maturing in 3 to 12 months.

Treasury bond   A bond that matures in more than 10 years.

Treasury Inflation Protected Securities (TIPS)   A type of Treasury security pegged to the inflation rate.

Treasury note   An intermediate-term debt (1- to 10-year term).

unhedged   The foreign bond fund has no protection in place against currency fluctuation risks.

unit investment trust (UIT)   An investment comprised of a specific set of securities issued for a specific period of time.

value company   A company that might be undervalued by the market. Value companies often pay a dividend to attract investors.

year to date (YTD) return   The return an investment has produced as of today.

yield   The interest or dividends paid on a security.

yield to call   The yield if the bond were to be called on the earliest possible date.

yield to maturity   A combination of the current income generated by the bond, plus any change in its value when it's held until maturity.

Resources

Here are a number of books, websites, and organizations to help you further improve your investing knowledge.

Books

These titles on frugal living might help you increase your savings:

Solve Your Money Troubles: Debt, Credit and Bankruptcy by Robin Leonard, JD, and Margaret Reiter

The Tightwad Gazette by Amy Dacyczyn

Your Money or Your Life by Joe Dominguez and Vicki Robin

These books help with goal-setting and basic financial planning.

I Will Teach You to Be Rich by Ramit Sethi

The Little Book of Main Street Money by Jonathan Clements

For more information on investing and asset allocation, check out the following:

Commonsense on Mutual Funds by John Bogle

The Investor's Manifesto by William Bernstein (and anything else by him)

The Little Book of Commonsense Investing by John Bogle

The Power of Passive Investing and *All About Asset Allocation* by Richard Ferri

A Random Walk Down Wall Street by Burton Malkiel

If you have, or plan on having, children, you might find these books on college planning useful:

Debt-Free U by Zac Bissonnette

What High Schools Don't Tell You and *What Colleges Don't Tell You* by Elizabeth Wissner-Gross

The following are excellent resources on retirement and disability:

Nolo's Guide to Social Security, Medicare, and Government Pensions by Joseph Matthews

Nolo's Guide to Social Security Disability by David A. Morton III, MD

Websites

American Association of Individual Investors (AAII)
aaii.com

Bankrate
Bankrate.com

BetterInvesting
betterinvesting.org

FinAid
finaid.org

Garrett Planning Network
garrettplanningnetwork.com

GetRichSlowly
getrichslowly.org

Haven Financial Solutions
havenfinancialsolutions.com

I Will Teach You to Be Rich
iwillteachyoutoberich.com

Morningstar
morningstar.com

National Association of Personal Financial Advisors (NAPFA)
napfa.org

Index

J–K

L

T

W

Wall Street Journal, The, 282, 284
wealth levels, 21-22
wealth managers, 103-105
    accountants, 114
    attorneys, 114
    fee-based, 106-108
    fee-only, 106-112
    insurance agents, 114
    real estate, 174
    robo-advisers, 112-113
webinars, 80, 285
welfare, receiving, 272
white papers, mutual fund companies, 80
windfalls
    beneficiaries, 242
    business attorneys, 241
    certified public accountants (CPAs), 241
    divorce, 248-250
    early retirement, 247-248
    estate planning attorneys, 241
    financial advisers, 241
    investing, 71
    low-paying bank accounts, 242
    lump sums, 242
    paying off debt, 243
    paying off your mortgage, 244-246
    paying off others' debt, 243-244
    protecting, 240
    psychologists, 241
    retirement planning, 32
    saving for college, 246-247
    spending power, 240
    spending priorities, 243-246
    spousal death, 248
    structured settlements, 242
    tax attorneys, 241
workplace retirement plans, 60-61, 187
    college savings, 219
    contributions, 61-62
    drawbacks, 62-63

    past employer, 68-69
    supplementing with individual retirement
        accounts (IRAs), 63-68
Work Study, 217

X-Y-Z

yard sales, selling items to make money, 70
yardstick-of-luxury system, luxury purchases,
    228-229
yield, 81
youth, investing, 26-29, 33

zero-coupon bonds, 150